WHITHER CIVILIZATION?

WHITHER CIVILIZATION?

by

Frank A. Parker

VANTAGE PRESS
New York / Washington / Atlanta
Los Angeles / Chicago

FIRST EDITION

*All rights reserved, including the right of
reproduction in whole or in part or in any form.*

Copyright © 1982 by Frank A. Parker

Published by Vantage Press, Inc.
516 West 34th Street, New York, New York 10001

Manufactured in the United States of America
ISBN: 533-04882-6

Library of Congress Catalog Card No.: 80-53782

CONTENTS

Acknowledgments		ix
1.	**Introduction: The Problem Stated**	1
2.	**What Is Civilization?**	6
	Man as a Mental Being	10
3.	**Objective Factors Confronting Civilization**	12
	Food and Population	15
	Pollution	20
4.	**Rome and Modern Morality**	23
5.	**Modern Problems and Opportunity**	33
	The Mind of Man	33
	Youth and Dissent	36
	Thought Control	47
	The Role of the Gifted Mind	50
	Education	55
	Dissent and Disobedience	66
6.	**Formation of the Modern Mind**	73
	Problems of Socialism	73

	Evolution of Democratic Representation	77
	Outcome of the Age of Enlightenment	80
7.	**Socialism**	85
8.	**Theories of Communism**	96
	Errors in Principles of Communist Theories	101
	Scientific Certainty	103
	Errors of Economic Man	104
	Lenin	107
9.	**Marxist-Leninist Theory in Practice in Russia**	110
	Society's Development	112
	Decline of Capitalism	115
	Sociopolitical System of Socialism	118
	Education of the New Man	122
	The Party, Our Helmsman	126
	Peace or Peaceful Coexistence	128
	The New Man	128
	Religion	133
	Communist Morality	135
	Communist View of the West	137
	Convergence: Peaceful Coexistence	138
	Political Future: Spread of Communism	141
10.	**World International Organizations**	149

11.	**Disparity of Wealth: Nationally and Internationally**	152
	Money in the Economy	156

12.	**The Welfare State**	165
	The New World Order	172
	Fundamentals of International Economic Relations	173

13.	**Man's Psychological Limitations**	178
	Problems of Democracy	180
	Family	190
	Violence, Dishonesty, and Corruption	192

14.	**Democracy in Industry?**	195
	Changes in Industrial Relations	195
	Yugoslavia	197
	West Germany	198
	United States of America	199
	Scandinavia	200
	France and Australia	201
	Japan	204
	Conclusion: Democracy in Industry	205

15.	**Hope for the Future**	209

16.	**The Ringwood Peace Plan**	214
	A Plan for International Disarmament and Peace	214

17.	**Principles of Associative Living**	218
	Introduction	218
	I. Principles of Social Benefits	221
	II. Moral Quality and the Quality of Life	222
	III. Implications of the Concept of Equality	224
	IV. The Concept of Freedom	226
	V. Society and Individual Rights	228
	VI. Centralization of Power	230
	VII. Violence Is Destructive of Social Values	232
	VIII. Rights to Private Property and Rights of the Family	234
	IX. Obedience to the Law	237
18.	**Conclusion**	239

ACKNOWLEDGMENTS

Grateful acknowledgments to the following: Richard Allen, author of *Peace or Peaceful Coexistence* published by The American Bar Association; Robert Kaiser, author of *Russia. The People and the Power,* published by Random House; and to the American Bar Association for their publication *Social Science Textbook*, an English translation of a Russian social studies textbook.

WHITHER CIVILIZATION?

1

INTRODUCTION: THE PROBLEM STATED

A society is born, it grows and flourishes under the influence of solidarity and of work for the common good. It reaches its heyday as a state. Its decline begins through inefficiency, pomp, luxury, corruption, and extravagance on the part of the rulers, and indolence and addiction on the part of the people. It becomes an easy prey for an enemy from outside.

The above words are a translation of those written by the Arabic philosopher-historian, Ib'n Kaldun, near the end of the fifteenth century. Of him, Arnold Toynbee wrote: "He has conceived and formulated a philosophy of history which is undoubtedly the greatest work of its kind that has ever yet been created by any mind in any time or place." For our purposes the ideas expressed are somewhat limited. The deterioration on the part of the rulers could with equal relevance be applied to many people today. Violence and moral decay are regrettably widespread in our civilization. The threat of falling an easy prey for an enemy from outside is the theme to be elaborated upon in the following pages. If the failure of our civilization were inevitable, it would be a fruitless task to endeavor to divert the disaster. It is accepted with Arnold Toynbee that while the pattern referred to above is there, it is neither rigid nor inescapable.

Can an examination of circumstances and possible remedies do something to avert the calamity? It is optimistically hoped so.

What is the evidence that we are at the end of a civilization; of a cycle of birth, growth, decay, and death? From many sources we are warned of an increasing population encroaching on diminishing resources, accompanied by increasing damage to land, air, and water. Methods of financial operation have imposed on us a colossal debt, a debt owed mainly to a limited number of private citizens. This has resulted in chronic unemployment and inflation, now endemic in the economy. As both contributory cause and consequence, the conflicts between monopoly-labor and employer-owners are coming under greater strain. Warfare, almost continuous on a small scale, threatens to break out into a global holocaust in which civilization itself might well be the major victim. The use of violence and corruption to attain one's ends has become so commonplace as to be taken as a normal part of life—undesirable but unavoidable. Armed attacks against the state are in places continuous, designated as by terrorists or by patriotic freedom fighters, according to the bias of the speaker. Warring groups within the state set themselves up as the true government, carrying on an undeclared war against the "oppressor." Even organized and legally recognized groups refuse to obey the law when it conflicts with their own "laws," punishing by fines, ostracism, mayhem, or even death those who refuse to obey.

Morality is becoming less and less concerned with earlier survival values of honesty, industry, and respect for the person and rights of others. Gang organizations have all too frequently rendered our streets and roads unsafe, especially for women. In education, complaints are heard from parents and businessmen that standards of attainment and attitude to work have declined alarmingly. Teachers, under the thin pretext of objecting to the testing of pupils' standards, are in fact refusing to allow their own work to be measured. Education to an increasing degree has neglected basic needs to include uninformed criticism of existing society; with resultant disillusion and apathy devoid of those skills and knowledge necessary to maintain the standards that are condemned.

As an experiment in social philosophy it is safe to say that democracy, after a century or so of trial, has not fulfilled its promise. The average citizen in his civic responsibilities has shown himself to be uninterested, partisan orientated, unwilling, and, on numerous occasions, incapable of giving the time and intelligence necessary to acquire an informed understanding of the processes that govern his life.

In the following pages it is argued that unless the problems can be subjected to far-reaching and fundamental change, the impending disaster will result. The emphasis is on the word fundamental: not fundamental concepts of morality but of institutions. Science has "liberated" greed, ambition, and power. Unless society can devise institutions to check these, disaster, not too far distant, threatens.

Modern civilization has armed not only Genghis Khan and Tamerlane, but ourselves. We are armed with atomic bombs and radioactive waste, television and financial domination; all the power to control not only the bodies but the minds. The power to destroy civilization itself. We have provided ourselves with previously unimagined luxury and extravagance, alongside poverty and deprivation; the idle rich and the idle poor. Violence, hate, suspicion, and intolerance exist on all sides, side by side with apathy and abandonment to pleasure. Tolerance, goodwill, and friendship have increasingly declined. The world has seen the slaughter of perhaps forty or fifty million people in the last few decades, as a result of the ambitions of ruthless men, a slaughter continuing with little or no abatement. Art and literature now portray the degeneracies of mankind in elaborate detail as a form of mass entertainment. Our writers picture what they themselves see and think, and claim to be reflecting society; and the public, made callous or degenerated in consequence, are part of the decline of civilized living. Religion, ethics, and morality are too often words of ridicule as much as an adult belief in Santa Claus. The machine of production and control has sacrificed true liberation to manipulation. Progress is the slogan of more and more. Bigger is better. Emotion has overwhelmed reason. The optimism of the eighteenth and nineteenth centuries has yielded to apathy and abandonment. Has Adler, aided by the teachings of Marx and Freud and their successors, been proven right? Freud would release the impulses of man's animal inheritance, using a euphemistic jargon. Marx would tell us that the only means to acquire what is ours by right is by violent overthrow of what is in our way. The skeletons, millions of them, are already at the feast. Unless men of goodwill and understanding, committed to no dogma of solution, can combine and show the way, the feast is almost over. The need is not for more theory but reasoned action.

Whether we accept the conclusion of men who have studied history and evolved a political philosophy to explain it, or read superficially for ourselves, certain patterns and phenomena appear. Mankind has continually engaged in warfare, in orgies of destruction and slaughter. Inherent in all this has been the leader who rouses others to action. Acting alone he would be helpless; but his evil genius lies in his ambition and his ability to enthuse others to support him. His followers and his opponents both are the instruments and the victims of his ambitions. This is equally true of the conquerors of the past or their recent and current imitators. As has been said, science has "liberated" greed, ambition, and power, and placed at their service new techniques for rousing mass emotion and imposing mass control. The old method of control was by force and fear, by the release of the impulse to kill and destroy. Today with propaganda and planning, a more subtle method has evolved alongside the old one. Perhaps more by taking advantage of consequences unforeseen by the originators, the financial power is competing with warfare for supremacy. By building a huge edifice of debt, with legal obligation to repay, society is subjected to toil, to obey, and to pay taxes to those who control the financial system.

The facts are well known. Whether from ignorance, apathy or helplessness, men and women have the feeling that a net closing round them cannot be reversed in its action. It is of the nature of all organizations to grow. Or perhaps it is of the nature of all organizers to extend the reach and details of their systems. The supreme example of this is of course the state. As a system, it brings to positions of power those men who desire power. They seek more and more to regulate and control; like an ill-constructed building which will collapse by its own weight. Experience of the past has shown this repeatedly. But no previous age has the wealth of examples and awareness possessed by society today. The trend is not inevitable.

A word and a concept that is increasingly the subject of men's minds today is ecumenism. The process is in evidence on all sides. The position is becoming more and more urgent. The world, separated into a bewildering assortment of ancient, outdated beliefs and customs, and into competing, if not warring forces, is becoming smaller and smaller in terms of speed of communication, interchange of ideas, frequency of personal and political contacts, and the need for each other's goods and services. The need is generally accepted. Various scientific and religious bodies hope by cooperation to bring contending minds closer together. But alongside these movements for ecumenism of minds and thought is the more active ecumenism of control and power. Communism is spreading, compelling acceptance by slaughter and repression, and the obedience or cessation of opposition to its leaders' dogma and authority. Alongside this is the growing world power of finance, spinning its web of control through debt. What is needed for any worthwhile ecumenism is the work of free minds.

Problems confronting civilization today are the outcome, perhaps inevitable, of principles and policies stated two centuries ago. Politically, democracy was an untested theory. Since its enunciation, it has not produced in application the benefits its protagonists predicted for it. The time is long overdue for an appraisal of its application with possible improvements.

Economically, progress based on industrialization from the use of coal, iron, and later, petroleum, and "fired" by loan-debt finance has made enormous development. The theories involved were designed for an age of scarcity and as such are ill-adapted for an age of real or possible plenty. So far, cures applied are an attempt to remedy the evils of the present and the future by applying the practices which caused the disease. The situation at present is one of conflict between conformity and innovation.

Truth has one apex, but it may be reached by many paths. Cooperation and tolerance is one of the paths, control and antagonistic competition is not. The choice of the path is urgent. It is the purpose of the following pages to review results and trends and to show where possible improvements are needed and may be implemented.

2

WHAT IS CIVILIZATION?

In giving a name to any concept it is of course impossible to state clearly all implications involved. It would therefore appear necessary to define the word civilization somewhat precisely before discussing in what way and to what extent it is being threatened or rejected.

Attempts at a complete expression of what civilization is are not new. Many attempts with varying degrees of success have been made. Why then is it necessary to do so again? It can be argued first, that with changing values and objectives of today, the bases of present values can be overlooked in the implications of those new ideas. Again it is desirable that all of us should ponder again and again those bases on which society can endure. Surely no one would claim to grasp fully all the implications of the principles of ordered social association and progress. To anyone who ponders the problems of this or any age, new aspects and new implications are continually discovered. In a new age, new problems and new theories with new applications arise. Furthermore, it is contended that much of the effort to define civilization is logically unsound. It is a common approach to designate certain people at certain periods in history as being civilized, and from their attributes, to arrive at a conclusion as to what are the characteristics of civilization. It is usual to list among these peoples Greeks of the age of Pericles and later, medieval Italy, and France around the eighteenth century. That there were men of outstanding intellect during these periods is not denied. Greek myths of a pantheon of anthropomorphic gods is a unique blend of imagination and a knowledge of human nature; of love, hate, hope, and tragedy. Where else can we read such a beautiful myth to explain the change of the seasons, as does the story of Persephone; or of the beauty and pathos of Echo; or of the dignity and sacrifice of Prometheus. Greek poets and dramatists, covering all they did, still evoke admiration. The works of Plato and Aristotle must be studied by anyone who would acquire wisdom in philosophy or politics. Greek art and architecture has perhaps never been surpassed. Greek mathematics and scientific speculation made great strides from that laid down by older civilizations. In all this, the Greeks laid down the foundations on which later people have built. It was a magnificent achievement for any age.

But there were aspects of Athenian life which can lay no claim to being civilized by modern standards. The life of the intellect was not shared by all. There is little evidence that certain sections were participants in the charmed circle. Barbarians, helots, and married women were only second-rate people, and with the exception of married women, not citizens at all. Further, the Athenian had his life and thinking restricted by concepts which today would be regarded as irrational. He accepted a pantheon of anthropomorphic gods and he believed in soothsayers and omens, a state which modern scientific knowledge can in no way support. Medieval Italy could witness the assassination of one of its leading citizens, while in church, without much disturbance. The papacy was at one of its lowest ebbs in history. The Age of Enlightenment in France witnessed the horrors and destruction of the French Revolution. How far the civilized man would be concerned with the position of his fellow man will be developed later on. It is concerned at the present merely to make the point that he would be so concerned. It would appear necessary then to approach the concept of our definition from a different direction.

A strictly logical definition of primary principles is impossible; but it is possible perhaps to see what civilization is by seeing what it is not. A tribal chief with his spears or his bow and his natural means of locomotion would not normally be regarded as civilized. He is not uncivilized because he does not wear more elaborate clothes, transport himself in a petrol-driven carriage, or have all the advantages of a modern city. He may control his tribe with wisdom and justice on principles having survival value for his society. But the defect lies in his mental limitation. He has not enough knowledge. His decision is based on tradition and tabu. What the lore of his society has laid down, must be done. Sacrifices must be made to propitiate powers which may help or hinder his efforts. His decision is based on limited knowledge and a minimum of logic. In the light of this then a civilized man must be an educated man, and a civilized society must be one where the general level of education must be at least relatively high. Education here is to be distinguished from mere information. Without at present entering into the question of what education is, it may be briefly stated that the information which is designed to assist in the earning of an income is best regarded as merely training; whether it be as an engineer, a doctor, a mechanic, or a shearer. Education here is regarded as such information which is conducive to the understanding of life, of one's position in society, and of the nature and destiny of man, and conducive of a character in conformity with that understanding. It can be seen that this allows a wide divergence of attitudes and appreciation. Here a difference between training and education exists. Training has a specific identifiable and preconceived objective; education truly directed can aim only to provide such relevant information which enables the learner to arrive at his own conclusions. This is not to assume that any attitude based on access to approved information is that of a civilized person. On the contrary, certain attitudes may be considered as civilized, or not. Man is a gregarious creature from which it follows that association with one's fellows is best. If we can assume that some attitudes are better than others, this assumption can be supported by evidence. It is possible, in theory at least, that man could live in isolation as a hermit and ponder the nature and destiny of man. But without access to the thought and discoveries of others, little understanding is likely to follow. And as has been argued, understanding is a fundamental of civilization. Moreover it is probable that in such circumstances a man would have little understanding of himself without contact with others.

Man has certain attributes in common with other creatures that share the earth. In common with all living creatures we experience the pleasures of the senses, the feeling of warmth, the satisfaction of appetite, and so forth. But as man is something more than an animal, he has other satisfactions, satisfactions of the mind. Somewhere in the mind of man is that which responds to music, to goodness, to truth, and to beauty. Whether viewed from the standpoint of religion or of evolution, we can assume that in enjoying these pleasures man is more truly in accord with his nature and destiny. Civilization is not an original part of nature, it is a creation of man's mind, and it is this mind which has enabled him to rise from primitive living. Civilization has undoubtedly encumbered itself with much impedimenta which has contributed little or nothing to man's progress. But this is merely to say that we are not fully civilized, and that some members of a society place more value in the pleasures of the senses than of the mind. A civilized man must perforce come to a compromise between the pleasures of the senses and those of the mind. Warmth, food, and movement are necessary for existence; but desire for these can be destructive of other pleasures, other goods, and of life itself. Resulting from this compromise, man has acquired a conscience, a knowledge of right and wrong, a sense of justice, a sense of guilt, and a sense of regret. And it is this capacity which must, in a gregarious relationship, replace the instincts of the animal.

Turning from man as an individual to man as a member of society, we can assume that despite the absence of clear lines of demarcation between the claims of the unit and of the group, it can safely be said that man derives benefit from association with his fellows. To try to live in a group without consideration of the needs of other members would of course result in complete disruption, with benefit to none. It must not be overlooked that nature confers no rights; but merely the power to strive for desired objectives. Rights exist only in a context of human association, based on the assumption that such association imposes restrictions on freedom of action; but confers benefits which far outweigh the desire for freedom. Life in isolation would impose greater natural restrictions than those imposed by society. But, if rights belong to all in a society, certain obligations follow. This implies that one's rights to freedom and so forth are limited by the possible encroachment on the equal rights of others. This limitation is expressed by custom and by law. The civilized person has learned to regard reason as superior to emotion, as best conducive to those ends regarded as desirable. Emotion seeks an immediate outlet, often selfish and often regardless of the feelings of others. Anger, greed, etc. . . . , are emotions which, given little or no restraint, are disruptive of society. Laws exist to restrain those who cannot or will not exercise self-restraint. The civilized person in this respect is the one who, by an understanding of the issues involved, has learned to place emotion under the control of reason. An action results then from a response which is both emotional and rational to the needs of others. Reason and emotion combine for the benefit of all. In this support of emotion by understanding lies the greatest degree of freedom possible to man. This is not to say that even the emotion of kindness is always wise, but an act of cruelty, as a principle insofar as cruelty is an act deliberately designed to injure, can have no support from reason. The conclusion inherent in this is that a civilized person is one who puts his emotions to the service not only of himself but to that of others as well. Briefly stated we may here define the civilized person as one who by the realization of the consequences of his acts seeks the good of others as part of the good of all.

MAN AS A MENTAL BEING

Man may be considered as a body-mind, each part as being closely integrated in the whole. Previously we have considered man as a being with instincts and emotions common to the animal kingdom; but with the unique possession of a mind which in the interests of the individual should control the animal impulses. At the next level man was considered as a member of a society with both social and anti-social impulses. But there is a third aspect of man to be assessed. In this man is to be regarded as having a brain with the faculty of reason and with an impulse to understand and to make rational as far as is possible the whole of existence as far as it may be ascertained. Here we may learn much from our predecessors, the Greeks, in their efforts to understand. It is in this that man is considered to be at his highest development. The reasoning man must ponder the how and the why of existence. Is there ultimate reality, and if so what is it? To aid in this search man must be receptive to the best of the ages in art, literature, religion, and philosophy not only of his own culture but of all mankind. And whether seen from the theistic, deistic, atheist, or evolutionary position, certain common ideas must result. Man on any viewpoint is to be seen as part of a great sequence reaching in time and space so remote, that a limited human mentality cannot fully understand it. But failure to grasp the full meaning is no reason for not striving for such understanding as may be possible. The best anyone can strive for is to improve one's questions, eliminating the irrelevant, or those answers which appear to lead to a mental cul-de-sac. In this regard the one who claims to know may be the one who has ceased to think. Arising from this are the conclusions that man has a status perhaps not unique in the universe and that elsewhere there may be rational beings either inferior or superior to ourselves. But that man has a status is clear, and that status is consistent with a certain dignity. A civilized man then is one who recognizes the dignity of man. This is not in any sense to be confused with pomposity. The truly dignified man has a sense of humility arising from a realization of his limitations. And the civilized man will have a lively awareness and a critical attitude toward his own behavior in that he would strive to do nothing that would lower his sense of pride in himself as a civilized man. Man is somewhere between the ape and the angel, between the primitive realm of impulsive behavior of the senses and the emotions, and the realm where exists an ideal of something beyond yielding to the pleasures of the moment, a realm where one can hope for an existence better than what we are experiencing. A civilized society is one that gives maximum opportunity and respect for this attitude of mind. The animal impulses are of where we came from. The satisfactions of the mind are of where we may go. Man alone can consciously create the conditions which assist this relationship of mental, emotional, moral, and social development.

3

OBJECTIVE FACTORS CONFRONTING CIVILIZATION

As a beginning it is stated that obviously the danger threatening civilization is of man's own making. The resources and climate of the earth are adequate, or at least were adequate, to sustain human life. If this adequacy has been disrupted it is due to mankind's own actions. The problem confronting us may be reduced to two types: man's relationship to his fellow man; and his relationship to the environment. The first is the problem of sociology or of political science. The second is the question of physical resources and their use.

In this relationship five factors must be considered: population; food resources; technology; pollution; and nonrenewable resources. The problem is compounded in all cases by the exponential population increases which have an impact on the other four. It would seem that in sheer self-defense those countries with lower or stable birth rates must in spite of all the criticism that would be roused, begin an all-out campaign to check population increases in more backward countries. In spite of lack of success in some countries, success in others shows it is not impossible .

Very directly most of our serious problems are for the present and for the immediate future predominantly the result of efforts to obtain mastery over nature. Prior to, perhaps, the last century or so, mankind was plagued by periodic famine; among some endemic poverty, epidemics of disease, and so forth. While these hazards have been minimized in the more advanced countries it should be noted that man's progress has never fully resolved his difficulties. The difficulty of providing adequate and continuous supplies of food, clothing, shelter, disease control, and so forth, is still with us. All that civilization has done, while reducing the impact of the evils, has been to raise the efforts of control to a higher and more involved level. The solution is not one for the individual but for the whole of society. Many, with a Luddite mentality, rage against the machine whereas it is this very machine that gives their fulminations some validity. It is technology that has given to man the luxuries now regarded as necessities. Technology has made possible the improved standard of living now regarded as our right. But it must also be conceded that technology is in some way exacting its Faustian penalty. Among writers on these subjects there are both Cassandras and Micawbers, pessimists and optimists. While readily recognizing the existence of the problems, the attitude taken will be generally optimistic, in the hope that some residual sanity and wisdom remains in mankind, sufficient to cope with problems which everyone now recognizes. Arising from our increased scientific and technological know-how what are our difficulties? To assess fully the extent of the problem is beyond the scope of a consideration of the future of civilization. All that is proposed is to draw attention to it. For any detailed analysis it is necessary to go to the enquiries and estimates of recognized authorities. It must be accepted, however, that they disagree widely, especially as apart from any pessimistic or optimistic attitude. They readily admit that there are fluctuating and unpredictable factors, such as the rate of population increase, advances in backward countries, new techniques, resources, and other factors.

The first problem is the consumption and reserves of unrenewable resources, such as minerals, topsoil, and sources of energy. Modern civilization has developed on a base of three factors: democracy; loan-debt finance and industrialization; round coal, iron, and ultimately, the considerable contribution of petroleum. For energy, modern industry depends in great measure on oil fuel and natural gas obtained either directly from the earth—and refined into petrol or producing electricity—or derived from coal. Estimates of the known and expected supplies of oil range from around fifteen to fifty years. If production from coal, tar, sands, and so forth, is considered, the estimates may range as high as two hundred years at present rates of consumption. This is however extremely improbable. At best, our authorities can only make informed guesses at future consumption rates. It is interesting to note the estimates given by Herman Khan and his associates, and those given by Dennis Gabor. The latter writing in 1963 is much less optimistic than Herman Khan writing in 1976. Both men are of sufficient eminence to justify serious consideration. Coal reserves are, so far as is known, greater than oil. It may be possible if coal is used for the production of oil this source of energy may last up to two hundred years. While this estimate does not produce immediate panic, what must be considered is that as supplies diminish so will access to them decline. How far this could lead to fierce competition, deprivation, and dislocation can only be conjectured. As difficulty in obtaining supplies increases the easily obtainable fuels are exhausted, so of course in spite of improved technology costs will also rise. The impact of the increasing use of oil on the diminishing supply is already affecting industry and international relationships. It is not expected that this will go away. On the contrary increased tension is expected. How far this will develop is unknown, but the problem is there. Could it be that in agriculture, especially, there will be a return to the use of the horse as a source of power? The supply is renewable.

However, other sources of energy are being used or considered. Among these are wind and water power, available in limited amounts but capable of some increase. Others are solar power in various forms, geothermal heat from the earth's center caused by gravitational pressure, photosynthesis, chemical processes, hydrogen power, and the much debated nuclear fission and nuclear fusion. These sources, at present in the laboratory stage or in increasing use, generally leave our authorities in a state of cautious optimism. If authorities take this attitude, surely our man and woman in the street can do likewise. While it is true that fools rush in where angels fear to tread, it can also be said that one can speak with all the confidence of ignorance. Thus, any informed discussion on the various minerals used in industry can result only as the result of considerable scientific and technological knowledge, both of uses and resources, and consideration of possible future uses. Most authorities stress the need for, and the gain from, improved and improving methods of procuring and using minerals. Various minerals, when combined are producing far more effective qualities than are inherent in the original state. With confidence this can be expected to continue. A new source of supply that is receiving attention is the mining of the sea bed. Associated with mining the sea bed for certain ores, however, is a question not receiving much attention so far. This activity will disturb the sea bed. How far it will disturb the ecology of that relatively unknown region cannot be ascertained. It is more than probable that this disturbance will be reflected right to the surface, with an unfortunate impact on sea bed life and fish. We have witnessed the destruction of ecology on the land. Must we repeat this blindness on the as yet untouched sea floor? In some measure synthetic substitutes for non-renewable minerals are in increasing use. While the attitude of certain informed scientists is optimistic, it is yet obvious that increased use of existing sources of supply of both energy and minerals cannot be ignored. While improvements in skill, as have been referred to, and more careful use may postpone the difficulty, the future of civilization in this circumstance is still not clear.

FOOD AND POPULATION

Men as early as Malthus, born in 1776, were aware of the possibility that the population growth might outstrip the food supply. Unless population increase was checked by intelligent means, it was argued, poverty and war would do so. In fairness to Malthus it is admitted that this is a pessimistic summary of his views. It is no doubt true also that he did not foresee the great increase in population in England and elsewhere and the fact that people are now in general far better fed than in his day. Were it not for the discoveries of science and the increased use of machinery, the population of England could not have increased from about fourteen million, in the age of Napoleon, to about forty million today. Pessimistic forecasts have been made based on the exponential rate of population growth over the centuries. It is clear that if this increase were to continue, in time there would barely be standing room on earth. The question to be considered is. "Must this rate continue?" Surely the race of mankind can evolve means of checking growth rate without famine, mass malnutrition, disruption, and war. The idea of zero population is being widely advanced, approved, and disapproved with equal emotion. It is argued that emotion is no substitute for reason. Certain people seriously or facetiously suggest that each girl at birth be given a permit to have 2.5 children during her life. The point five which at first appears to be plain nonsense is not necessarily so. Some women have at all times for various reasons not had any children. This right could be sold to anyone desiring more children. Again, if two fractional rights were sold, two parties could be satisfied. However, the obvious difficulties rule the idea out of serious consideration. More worthy of respect is the example of countries like India and China, where the pressure of population is felt. China has adopted the policy of later marriages with rewards and penalties in accordance with the number of children, two being considered the desirable maximum. Travelers in India, even some years ago, could see public posters directing people to methods of birth control. The fact that this policy reached the stage of enforceble treatment does not discredit the idea. Several other countries in the overpopulated and underfed areas have attacked the problem of population pressure. Results show mixed success. It is generally assumed that the desire for a high birthrate is a device used as an insurance for old age, as it is expressed that most of the children will die. This is doubtless in large measure a rationalization to justify the birthrate. It is more probable that the high birthrate is due to absence of sexual restraint. This has been shown by the spectacular success in Indonesia. As government policies, taking their ideas from advertisers, all sorts of persuasions were used. The government sent lecturers to all parts of the country, giving talks, showing films, and giving illustrations of the benefits of low birthrates. There is no reason why this technique cannot be more widely used.

If one looks at the example of those countries that have become industrialized, a birthrate pattern appears. With increased wealth, the birthrate has generally increased, followed later by a decline. It is not irrational to hope that this pattern may be repeated in the present backward countries. It is ironic that the population increase is largely due to disease control by scientific means. Yet science may still help to save the world from overpopulation by more efficient use of birth control means. Is it too much to hope that self-control is not beyond reasonable expectation? It is regrettable that reduction in family size has a correlation with intelligence and income levels. Thus, it can be argued that increase would be greatest among those who are not our best elements. Various ideas for discouraging large families occur. Apart from long tradition, if the fear of destitution in old age were removed, much of the claim for large families would fade. It must be borne in mind that large families were formerly common in the Western world without any association with wealth or poverty.

Closely associated with the problem of population is that of food supply. In 1950, Lord Boyd Orr, working for the F.A.O. of the United Nations, made the statement that two-thirds of the world's population went to bed hungry every night. It has been stated that his successors in the F.A.O. knew that this was an overstatement. Indeed it has been said that the F.A.O. is "a permanent institution devoted to proving there is not enough food to go round." True or false, it is clear to travelers in backward countries that while there is considerable poverty and malnutrition, it is hard to accept two-thirds being hungry as a correct estimate of world malnutrition. As in other matters, the problem is how to overcome the disparity between the two ends of the cale. On the one hand we have "weight watchers" organizations, and on the other hand there are some people other than those affected by drought and so forth who are underfed. It is not that the world cannot at present produce the food. Countries such as the U.S.A., Australia, and Canada complain that they cannot dispose of the grain, meat, or vegetables, they produce. In some cases, farmers receive government advice and aid to reduce production and, in other instances, to destroy even what has been produced.

It would seem a simple solution to transport the surplus to where the shortage exists. But the solution is not simple. Should a farmer whose livelihood depends on the sale of his produce be expected to forego the sale of some part of it? Of course not. Should the government be expected to purchase the surplus and export it? This could be done to any appreciable extent only by increased taxes; taxes which are already bearing heavily on everyone. Moreover, apart from disaster areas where need is urgent, what effect would this have on the recipients? In some degree, dependence would weaken effort of those in need. It is not irrelevant to ask who aided the affluent countries of today to become affluent? They raised themselves by their own energy and effort. It is obvious also that many of the countries where poverty is widespread were either wealthy in the past or have potentialities of wealth today. Part of the problem is that the population is greater than the country can comfortably support with current methods. Thus, when the French and English arrived in India around the middle of the eighteenth century, the population of some two hundred million was poverty stricken and in confusion. When the English authority departed in mid-twentieth century, the population of some four hundred million, still poor, wasetter off. Improved processes had been operating. If people prefer to invest in children rather than in food production, they must be prepared to take some part of the criticism.

Yet in spite of this, it would be both mentally and economically for the good of all to take steps to improve conditions in backward countries. The earth's possibilities for food production are not limitless. It is calculated that one-quarter of the land surface is suitable for tillage, the remainder being deserts, suitable at best only for light grazing, or mountains. It is obvious that timbered areas cannot be significantly reduced. Timber is essential both for its industrial value and for its ecological value. Fortunately it is a renewable resource, and can be readily increased to some degree. Again it is argued that using land for grazing where crops could be grown, and that growing grain to feed animals, are inefficient uses of land. It might be further argued that despite loud agonized howls of protest, the use of land to produce either grapes for wine or for tobacco, could be a matter of consideration in the future. The case must rest most strongly however on a more efficient use of what is available. It has been said that U.S.A. grain production has been at the expense of much sweat and some inches of topsoil. It is a well-known condemnation of certain farmers by their neighbors, that they mine rather than farm the land. The need is for some guidance to improve farm management and practice, especially in backward countries. Improved methods could do much to raise the production in much of Africa and elsewhere. The soil is not the absolute property of the owner to mine and misuse as he sees fit. This is not, however, to say that governments should assume control of farm management. The cure could easily be worse than the disease. Reason and example are far better than force. That advice, example, and assistance are effective is seen in the case of India. After a too hasty effort to develop industry with resultant food shortage, India has managed to produce a grain surplus in some years. Here, as elsewhere, agriculture is under a burden of debt and ignorance, both of which can be lifted. The practice of subsistence farming, as in Africa and elsewhere, is contrary to improved food production. The farmer merely sows such crops as he hopes will see him through till the next harvest. This can and does result in miscalculation, and halts progress. The primitive, primary production in much of Africa goes far to hold down the living standard. However, the growing practice of growing cash crops from which former nonexistent amenities may be had is of benefit. Governments in all these lands can do much to encourage the use of better machinery, more fertilizers, and other farming aids. The so-called green revolution, with the use of scientifically improved strains of grain and so forth has raised production. This, however, has not benefited to the extent it might have. The benefit too often has not gone to the tiller of the soil himself, but to others already better off than he. Moreover, this requires a greater use of water, which unless carefully controlled can exhaust the soil. Greater and better use of water is being developed, but supplies are not limitless. Large areas such as in the Amazon Valley are still under dense vegetation. Before they can be fully used, methods must be devised to prevent the heavy rains from leaching out the mineral content of the soil. With a combination of a reduced population growth rate and improved agricultural methods, fears of a world shortage of food are not serious. The ocean as a source of food has not yet been fully exploited. It is said that in regards to the use of the ocean as a source of food, mankind is still in the hunter stage of progress and not yet advanced to the farmer stage. The use of the ocean as a source of food supply could be over optimistic. Those areas of the ocean contiguous to England and Western Europe have been seriously depleted of fish, and fisherman have been driven to northern waters. This has led to serious differences between the British and Icelandic governments. Is this a beginning of what will occur in the future with increased intensity and extent? In spite of improved and more costly equipment, catches in some areas are declining with increasing expense. Unless checked immediately, the whale from being an endangered species will become an extinct one. The use of Antarctic regions for food storage in years of surplus, is well within the bounds of practicability. Careless use of the world's supply of food resources could result in shortage, but one can reasonably expect that preparations and sanity will prevail.

POLLUTION

Our pessimists, not without justification, draw attention to the effects of modern industry on polluted land, air, and water. Industry in its processes obtains minerals and chemicals from their original sources against which, by the natural processes of evolution, mankind has developed some immunity. These are then concentrated in harmful amounts and/or combined with other chemicals in harmful association. They are then released into the land, air, and water. Industrial waste has caused well-known threats not only to those working in the particular industry, but over a much wider range. The effects of mercury released into the ocean around certain areas in Japan, recently received worldwide publicity. Fish caught in adjacent waters were unfit for consumption. This illustrates the harmful ecological cycle, where the dangerous element gradually increases its concentration from predator to predator till the consequence is serious. But, of course, the problem is not confined to Japan. It is common to all industrialized areas. The Mississippi River has been called an open sewer. It was confidently stated that pollution of the water of Lake Erie was so bad that it would require a century free from further damage to recover. A major source of air pollution is from car exhausts and from the release of carbon during the production of electricity from coal. This statement is all too common: "On clear days you can see . . ." the absence of clear days being largely a result of smoke, gases, and dust from the cities and factories. Recent problems in the increase of toxic amounts of mercury, asbestos, and other pollutants have been highlighted. The extent to which pollution of the air will affect plant and human life is still a matter of uncertainty, but the effect in respiratory ailments is already well known. But having pictured the condition, as seen by the reality, what can be said?

Already practicable and in some degree successful regulations are being enforced to reduce the harmful emissions from cars and factories. Much has been done to reduce the industrial waste and to prevent its release into the air and water. Industry generally has accepted responsibility for improvement. Cities such as London are examples of what determined effort can do. The much dreaded London "smog," a combination of fog and smoke, has largely disappeared. Fish can now be caught in reaches of the Thames from where they had long been absent. We read reports now of fish having been caught in Lake Erie.

One serious position, however, still exists in the primary production, where chemical fertilizers are increasingly common; as well as chemical sprays to combat insect and bacterial pests. The immediate result is improved production from the land. But chemical sprays intended to kill harmful pests are not selective. They often are lethal to the useful species as well, and kill the natural enemy of the harmful species. Men have now learned that any human action that destroys the original ecological balance can be destructive of its own purpose. This process, as well as in the chemical fertilizers, spreads from the point of application, to the animal and plant life, especially the natural fauna. So far no great progress has been made to overcome this difficulty. The destruction of waste from big cities, either by burning in municipal incinerators with further smoke pollution or pouring it out to sea, need not continue. Examples are well known where land reclamation proceeds with the use of city garbage for filling. Is it too much to hope that such waste could be processed by removing the metal from the organic material? This, after appropriate treatment, could then be used as natural fertilizer. Many home gardeners can testify to the very beneficial results of this simple process. Surely when plant and animal nutrients come from the soil, the residues from the cities can be returned to and reabsorbed into the soil. To drain waste into the ocean can be a sheer waste of natural resource.

Atomic waste is at present a matter under furious discussion as to its satisfactory disposal and its possible effect on the ozone layer, so necessary for man's life on earth. With well known authorities differing so emotionally, the ordinary man and woman can at best wait, listen, and hope for some scientific clarity. It must be recognized that all change carries with it some possibility, even the certainty, of risk. The solution is to develop research into the use of safer sources of power, such as solar power.

4

ROME AND MODERN MORALITY

It has been said that it is impossible to judge dispassionately any event in history that has occurred in the last thousand years. The time range might well be extended to any event where the circumstances were similar to those existing today. In spite of this, however, it could be of benefit to examine and compare events and conditions of the past with those of today. Distance from the event may allow a more comprehensive and dispassionate assessment. In this light, some assessment may be made with advantage of circumstances and of conditions which accompany, either as a cause or consequence, the collapse of the Roman Empire and civilization. Though Roman history is the best known to the Western world, studies of Islamic, Indian, or Chinese history strongly support the evidence from Rome.

In any consideration of morality, it must be said that morality is largely a system of social relationships. Kindness, justice, courtesy, and other such virtues apply principles which are established to improve the relationship between persons. It can also be assumed that these relationships were established in early society and were found to support an established social system. We know it is possible to have religion without morality and morality without religion. But early man has normally associated his moral code with religious support to strengthen the impact. Tradition and taboo have always been closely associated. As early societies were of necessity closely associated with nature in the production of crops and in animal husbandry, it is to be expected that the forces of nature were identified with personal attributes and were usually elevated to the level of gods or spirits. This close association of man and nature in small communities tends to develop a religion in which beneficial social customs can grow. Thus, results of idleness or dishonesty were quickly detected. Crops must be sown or harvested when the season dictates. Seasons do not wait. Again as members of such a society are all well known to each other, anyone guilty of antisocial acts would be known to all for what he was. Honesty, industry, and so forth and what may be called the virtues of the home, became part of the approved code. This was strongly typified by the sturdy self-reliant industry of the early Roman. The gods who protected the hearth and the home received regular and convincing tribute. The change of the seasons established a pattern where the sequence of birth, growth, decay, and death were always before men's minds.

With the onset of a money economy, the subsistence economy and the barter system between individuals or between groups changed to the seller-buyer relationship in which close association is lost. History records a close relationship between moral standards and a stable state. No nation or state has long resisted the onset of affluence. With wealth, moral decay has set in. Man is a complex of emotions both good and bad. At a lower financial level each man must spend his time and effort in winning the means of existence from nature. With the acquiring of wealth, circumstances change. Man now has the leisure, the money, and the facilities for indulging his emotions. Money and wealth breed the desire for more wealth. Dishonesty in a dispersed society can be more profitable than honesty—a fair price for a fair day's labor in production. Many of the old religious values stand in the way of indulgence. Men's ideas of religion are then adjusted to suit an affluent society. With this change goes a decline in religious authority. Deprived of the sanction of religion what is there to restrain acquisitive impulses? Idleness becomes the badge of economic success. This deterioration is clearly seen in the history of Rome or of any other early civilization. In the following discussion this can always be compared with modern society. The parallel is painfully close.

In Rome, with military success came wealth largely unearned and unjustified. Loot became more profitable than labor. The small yeoman farmer gave way before the purchasing power of the successful trader of slaves or of other loot from Carthage, Greece, or elsewhere. Cicero, writing in the last days of the republic, says: "Our moral sense is depraved and demoralized by wealth." Thucididies, writing of his observations in the age of Athenian wealth, says: "The cause of all these evils was the loss of power, originating in avarice and ambition, and the party spirit; the one party professing to uphold the constitutional equality of the many, and the other the wisdom of the aristocracy . . . . And the citizens who were of neither party fell a prey to both." Could a better description of modern politics be written? Polybius, a Greek historian writing of the conditions around him in Rome and comparing them with those which accompanied the decline of his own state, wrote: "Some Romans were all out for money, others for unnatural vice, and many for shows and drink and all the extravagance which shows and drink occasion." Cicero, referring to his rival Clodius, speaks of his "armed gangs of toughs" roaming the streets. It must be noted here that Rome had no police as in modern states to maintain order, and that Clodius could be checked only by his own method, a greater force. It is not surprising that in this atmosphere, Julius Caesar, Cicero, Clodius, and many more were all murdered. While these and many more acts of violence were politically motivated, the private morality or lack of it was a cause of the decline. The nature of a civilization depends on the character of its people.

In Rome, the powerful set off in pursuit of wealth—as so often happens today—the quickest means to this being appointment as a governor of a province. It has been said that it was necessary to make three fortunes when governor; one to pay for the expenses incurred in securing the appointment, one to pay the legal costs needed to be exonerated from the charges of corruption committed in getting the wealth, and the third to live on afterwards. The witnesses and victims were far away, the judges were his predecessors, successors, and associates, frequently his own relatives. Charges of corruption and abuse of power are becoming increasingly common today. As wealth increased, so moral standards declined. Women who had formerly been restricted largely to the home now came into society. It is not to be assumed that women have a naturally corrupting influence. On the contrary they can, for various reasons, be regarded as in some degree the guardians of morality. But it was rather, "the means to do ill deeds make ill deeds done." Under such circumstances it was inevitable that customs which respected marriage and the family broke down. Women owned wealth in their own right. Marriage became an instrument of political power and economic advantage. Divorce, as with us, became common. It is recorded that Caesar had four wives, Pompey and Sulla five each. Children more and more were left to the care of slaves who could command neither obedience nor respect. The old virtues inculcated by the responsible head of the household withered away. Corruption and bribery became associated with official position. As unemployment grew, the unemployed rabble increased. Idleness is nowhere conducive to morality. These mobs were always ready for a price, to support anyone who promised to make life easy or interesting. Bread and circuses have been associated with idle mobs ever since. The gladiatorial shows in the arena fed the desire for excitement that only violence and bloodshed can give. The word Lucullus is now almost synonymous with extravagant feasting. Delicacy of dining appears to have faded. Gorging of food followed by vomiting to enable the diner to start again was not uncommon. After dining, drunkenness was usual. As can be expected, indulgence led to boredom in some and disgust in others. To give some meaning to life, better than indulgence, men turned to the mystery religions.

In such an environment the life of the intellect declined. Few or no writers of distinction wrote in the days of the Empire's decline. Juvenal and Tacitus were almost the last of a dying literary elite. Drama sank to the level of mere amusement. A populace, fed on a mental diet of sensation and excitement, had no time for a well planned and developing plot in the theatre. Smart repartee of a dubious morality replaced intellectual themes. Not untypical were the writings of Ovid. He stressed as the objective of the socialite of the day, the care of the body and the elegance of living. Advice was given on care of the hair, the skin, and clothes. His words showed open disregard for marriage vows and a direct incitement to immorality. His books were frowned on by some sections but became "best sellers." His exile by the emperor may have been due to a genuine attempt at control or perhaps because he, too plainly pointed a finger at the emperor himself. Juvenal records indicate that a rage for public spectacles became a mania. Contrary to popular concepts today of gallant young Romans, as in Ben Hur, driving their chariots in the arena, the charioteers were usually slaves whose lives were of less importance than the horses they drove. Betting was rife.

The Roman Empire produced very little of scientific merit in contrast to the Greeks. Education was left in the hands of slave tutors, the "starveling Greek" dating from this age. Under this system, preparation for the life of indulgence and display was of more importance than for morality, philosophy, or service. Under the economic and administration system those who resisted the trend, as did the Gracchi brothers and Cicero, were murdered. It has been argued that by this means the best were killed off. True or false, it is clear that opportunities for vice and corruption increased. If facilities for having anything done, good or bad, are increased, those things will increase whether it be making money, violence, and corruption or service to society. While certain aspects of life in the age of the decline of Rome are not identical with those of today, the parallel is still too close for satisfaction.

So far attention has been given to what may be called the moral decline leading to the collapse. But in considering our administrational and organizational difficulties, can we learn anything from our predecessors? The reasons for the fall of the Roman Empire, as has been said, have been and are being discussed with considerable insight and scholarship. To try to add to this would be presumptuous. But, accepting some of the explanations as having support from history, we may derive benefit by comparing them with conditions today.

It has often been accepted that while early Rome benefited from slave labor, it ultimately proved ruinous and finally the supply dried up. It is claimed by some historians that its significance has been overrated. But today society has its systems of slaves, slaves who work long hours without consideration of reward and take from the mass of the people the responsibility for much of our arduous and unpleasant tasks. We have our machines, much more efficient and tireless than human hands. Here our position is not similar to the earlier one. Rome also, however, according to some historians, had a fall in population and a lack of manpower. Today the reverse is our problem. Gibbon assures us that Christianity was a contributary factor, but Bury tells us that, "the Christians were just as pugnacious as the pagans." This sentiment would not be without some support from examples today. But the question today is: "How far is Christianity or any religion now a creative force in society?" Anyone whose memory goes back a few decades will readily recall being told: "We are witnessing a revival." There is little evidence to support this. The revival is still to come. Church membership may at times increase but it is influence not numbers that counts. To try to recover the lost prestige and influence, church service has been modernized and popularized. Religion is following and not leading. It is not being argued that church ritual should remain archaic. But have the changes modified society to a noticeable extent? Evidence is again lacking. Further, religious organizations have shown a marked interest in social welfare. It is man's duty to aid his fellowman. It can be affirmed that Christianity is a religion of social relationships. To get to heaven one must bring a fellowman. But if a minister steps down from the pulpit to become a social reformer he loses his position of authority and becomes just a partisan of this or that policy. It is his duty certainly to denounce injustice and injury to the dignity of man. But it is his task rather to enthuse others to social improvement and not to become involved in the party debate. After all, Christ's instruction to his followers was to go forth and preach the gospel. Has religion declined to become an illustration of the second law of thermodynamics? Having spent its initial energy, it is slowly becoming apathetic. Church leaders, with exceptions, now are partakers of comfort; well clothed, well housed, well fed, often over fed, secure, and self-indulgent. They cannot expect to inspire anyone. In this situation we can give some support to Gibbon. Religion has outlasted much of its original impulse. As a social inspiration is it to further decline or to undergo a regeneration?

Among reasons advanced for the collapse of the Empire there is practically unanimous agreement that it failed organizationally both as a cause and a consequence. Today we do not share in the inadequate system of communication on land by horse, on foot, or slow ox cart. With an empire stretching from Britain to the banks of the Euphrates, sound control was impossible. But in their efforts to maintain the Empire they adopted the methods we have followed, the establishment of a vast bureaucracy, first expanded on loot, until finally industry was transfered to the perimeter.

With us it can be advanced that the British Empire and the United States of America, to name only two of the most successful, developed by exploiting the cheap labor and cheap products from overseas. Today, capital is exporting itself to set up business where material and manpower are cheaper. Since England fought two world wars at the cost of her overseas investments, she has fallen to the level of a second-rate power. At the moment, the U.S.A. is, perhaps temporarily, striving to hold her dominant position against rising competition from earlier dependents. Many writers refer to the problem of bureaucracy and its burden on industry. Of special significance for us today is that to maintain this vast system, taxes are continually raised with ruinous effect, especially on the small landowner. The small Roman farmer yielded place to the latifundia. Today we see the same trend. Whether it be the small orange grower in Florida or the cattleman in Australia, a strong trend is growing for the big scale business to replace the small producer. We accept society as consisting of several categories: wealthy owners; middle class men, self-employed or employing the family and perhaps a few wage earners; wage earner, as a third stratum; and, finally, professional men and women who fit uneasily into no particular class.

The small free farmer or craftsman in Rome, it is agreed, was the base on which Rome grew. The parallel with modern society is close. Many good farmers today are leaving their farms, jammed between rising costs on one side, of which taxation directly and indirectly is a major portion, and inadequate prices and unwilling labour on the other. Their incomes are often less than those of a wage earner, and in times of droughts, a farmer finishes in debt and worse off than before. Statistics tell how the number engaged in primary production in the U.S.A., Australia, and elsewhere is declining. These men move with their families to the towns and cities to become laborers or to live on welfare.

Nothing can replace the industry, the creativity, and the satisfaction for the farmer, of the care for the quality of his land and his stock; certainly not the pastoral company which takes no pride in the land beyond its ability to pay dividends to absentee shareholders and owners. One does not hear of neurotic farmers. The vertical organization of the large company has an early economy, but it helps to drive off the small-scale man. Also, as with Rome, taxation falls less heavily on the company. The small man has to pay death duties. The corporation does not die. This discourse on the inequity between the two forms of production could be extended considerably.

To overcome the expense of maintaining its vast system, Roman emperors (as do today's legislators), tried various devices to maintain the system. These can be referred to as creeping socialism, which by their restrictions strangle initiative, ending in lethargy. It is argued that it was not the loss of political freedom in Rome, but the loss of economic freedom, that created stagnation. With increasing government regulation today in all advanced countries, complaints arise on all sides that more and more staff must be diverted to seeing that increasing regulations are observed. Governments round the world are increasingly intruding into the economic sphere by regulation or by participation. Some regulation of industry is obviously necessary, but which are we to have? All planning consistent with liberty or all liberty consistent with planning? To an increasing extent planning is overcoming liberty. He who would sup with the devil of government control must indeed have a long spoon or he will be burned.

Consequent with pressure on production to support the state and the idle drones of the cities, comes the money lender. Roman banking was less effective than today, but sufficient to restrict if not to strangle the economy. Reference is to be made in a later chapter to the colossal burden of debt in modern society. By this means a vast system of nonproducers must be maintained, fed, clothed, and housed in luxury by the efforts of others. It would seem that where money and power flourish, so do the forces of corruption. Politicians, businessmen, and criminal investigators as well as the criminals, again and again come before the courts on charges of dishonesty and abuse of power. One seldom hears of the poor retired politician, due to the fact that politicians usually give themselves very satisfactory pensions. It is not argued that politicians and businessmen alone are guilty. Trade unions also can be charged with abuse of power and position. What is argued, however, is that if democracy is to meet the current challenge this evil must be reduced by exposure and reform.

It is recorded that in Caesar's day, of forty-five patricians, only one was even represented by posterity when Hadrian came to power; and this in about a century and a half. The quality of the citizens of the Empire had declined. Government had fallen into the hands of a new rich and industry into the hands of a new race. We cannot argue that a craftsman from Gaul or Galicia was genetically inferior because of his stock. Neither can we argue that current migrants to U.S.A., Europe, Australia, or elsewhere must be genetically inferior, but what is obvious is that they bring a new culture and a new purpose. This is of itself not necessarily bad; we can argue that in some respects it is a gain. It is advanced, however, that unless assimilated into the indigenous population, little enclaves of disunity arise. The migrant of, say a hundred years ago, differs from the migrant of today. Formerly he came unaided, imbued only with the idea that by his efforts alone he might improve life for himself and his family. Today he can have his fare reduced to a negligible amount; he can go to a government hostel and he can at times be an immediate recipient of social welfare payments that will enable him to live at a higher standard than ever before. And all this till a benevolent government finds suitable work. Again these men and their families with, fortunately, general exceptions, do not have the same sense of loyalty to the country of their adoption. There are many facets to this situation, but fundamental to a coherent society is that the children at least should be absorbed into the new life. Divided loyalty, though natural and deserving of understanding, is of doubtful worth, as witness the situation in Canada, Ceylon, Malaya, Fiji, Africa, and elsewhere. The Soviet Union recognizes the possible consequences of regional loyalties as an evil to be eradicated. All must become loyal Russians.

Finally, historians raise the question as to how far education and culture can be spread throughout society. If we can judge a person's cultural standard, it must be done not by seeing how he gains his livelihood, as Aristotle would have it, but how he spends his leisure; how, when he has satisfied the needs of his daily existence, being released from necessity, he chooses to relax. It is unquestionably good that he enjoys athletic performance, his own or, in moderation, as a spectator, or watches life through the pages of literature or the television screen. But if he goes too frequently to watch others race and play, such vicarious enjoyment conveys little benefit and can do much harm. If one surveys the popular magazines on our book shelves or listens to what appears on television, it is clear that what is catered to is the superficial and artificial stimulation of the moment. There life is always portrayed as interesting, exciting, and stimulating. The world of reality by comparison is drab and disappointing. Taste is deteriorated, and life becomes unsatisfying. Is it without relevance to note that after Cicero, very little of literary worth was produced in Rome. Writers and poets today seek the excitement of sex and the distorted comparison. Art, perhaps because of competition from the camera, has deteriorated to trying to picture not the object but the artist's impressions of it; and of that there is no objective standard of criticism. The grotesque in art as in literature is the companion of decay. Formerly children only were treated to fairy tales, but the modern fairy story of the space traveler with galactic adventures and the limitless power of his invention, has replaced the giant and the fairy's wand; and this is for adult consumption. A society raised on such a debilitating mental diet will have no strength or desire to resist the inroads of modern barbarians. Indeed, they may be referred to as modern barbarians.

5

MODERN PROBLEMS AND OPPORTUNITY

THE MIND OF MAN

What a piece of work is man . . . . In action how like an angel . . . . In apprehension how like a god.

—HAMLET

While admitting that some difference of opinion may be allowed concerning the angelic quality of certain of man's actions, the apprehension is the part to be discussed at present. According to the discoveries of Dr. Leakey and his associates, the mind of man in the species *home erectus*, began its ascent at least two million years ago. This ancestor, if we accept him as such, was the possessor of three gifts. He had a certain type of brain, a tongue, and other equipment permitting speech, and a manipulative hand.

This hand, firm yet flexible, was the instrument which carried into effect much of the ideas and concepts of the brain. The speech apparatus permitted the formation of sounds conveying something more than the mere rudimentary expressions of fear, anger, and affection. Thus, through speech, primitive man was able to communicate to others and so accumulate and transmit the ideas of his mind. But last and most important, man had the gift, unique among all his animal contemporaries, as far as we know, of a thinking mechanism, the brain. *Home erectus* in common with his contemporaries had the receptors of hearing and sight, and though his ears and eyes were often inferior to theirs, he alone had the ability to examine, to assess, and to adapt both the environment and his reaction to it. In short, with his brain he had the ability to reason and to learn. Paleontologists tell us that certain creatures alive today show no variation from their ancestors of millions of years ago, and the bones of others bear mute witness to the penalty exacted by nature for failure to adapt.

With this brain, insatiably curious, imaginative, creative, and perhaps not a little fearful—yet driven by his curiosity—man began to develop crude tools of wood and stone to fit his manipulable hand. Thus equipped, he set out on his long ascent to maturity; by his taming of the wild and such of its other inhabitants which were amenable to his purposes. What then has this extraordinary instrument, the brain, which we take for granted, which we use and abuse to our own pain and dissatisfaction, done for us? It has developed skills which have placed man outside the earth and allowed him to walk on the moon. It has developed ideas concerning how the universe has come into existence, has watched stars being created and dying, and has formulated ideas of the space and duration of the universe which can be represented only in mathematical formulae which by their magnitude are almost meaningless and certainly beyond the capacity of man to imagine. And yet this wonderful brain has developed instruments of destruction which threaten its very existence. For the first time man now has the capacity to destroy himself. Why? As a partly evolved instrument only, reason is not infallible. And so with the gift comes the price, the inevitable liability of error. Man, not yet freed from the drive of his animal heritage, must endure all the consequences of pain and suffering. Yet by trial and error he may progress.

Any athlete knows that to keep his body at maximum capacity he must continually subject it to strain; to develop it he must undergo increasingly demanding effort. Without this the body efficiency will deteriorate. It is here affirmed that this principle applies also to the mind. It is interesting to contemplate an epic of the growth of man's mind urged on incessantly by a "voice" which will not allow him to rest in his primitive intellectual slime, but drives him relentlessly onward and upward to that peak of understanding of which he is potentially capable. Regrettably no Milton or Dante has yet arisen to perform the task. It still remains for some unborn genius to do so.

It has been said that the mind of man has developed as the result of the necessity of finding food, and is therefore no more fundamentally a fact-finding implement than is the snout of a pig. Be that as it may a rather extravagant statement, the idea of the "painful process of thought" is not an exaggeration. Like an animal, man all too readily relaxes. The need for food and some minimum of interest may be sufficient; ease and pleasurable sensation take over. Under such conditions the mind, like the athlete's body, deteriorates. And it is all too obvious that modern civilization, having freed man from the pressure of much necessity, is becoming an all pervasive influence in this direction. We are engaged more and more in frivolous, foolish, and destructive pursuits. To an increasing degree the minds of all, especially the young, are fed a mental diet, an insult to a reasoning mind. Television, publications, sport, alcohol and drugs, beauty shows, and horse racing and gambling are turning people more and more away from those things necessary not only for progress, but for the very existence of civilization. We see too frequently the cult of the slovenly body, slovenly dress, and slovenly speech. Cliches and slogans are substitutes for thought. There have been civilizations before ours, and many theories are advanced which seek to explain the cause of their decay. Even a cursory consideration of the fall of the classical civilizations of Greece and Rome, among others, will find some twenty possible causes all of which with some support from historical evidence may be valid. And among these is the spiritual decay, the decline of firm commitment to moral values and the purpose to achieve. Affluence with them, as with us today, allowed the population to relatively relax, to enjoy the emotions and the senses. Food in the so-called Western world is easily obtained. Social service and welfare payments have in large measure eliminated the necessity to toil for the means of existence; for food, clothing, and shelter. If one studies the full impact of current social theory it becomes clear that social security, while in some aspects highly desirable, is a mixed blessing. There is strong and convincing evidence that in countries such as Sweden and Russia where social security is a government responsibility, the people are turning from boredom to suicide and alcohol. Boredom is the first sign of decay both for individuals and for society. Social and economic problems are becoming the province of the expert and the government.

Every general knows that an idle army is a menace, liable to outbreaks of disorder and insubordination, and liable to disrupt the society near which it is placed. Moreover, as a fighting force, men often lack the physical fitness when action is needed. Special exercise and marches thus become part of the system to prevent outbreaks of disorder and to maintain the physical and mental standards necessary for specific tasks. Is the mind of the population less subject to deterioration than is the body?

YOUTH AND DISSENT

It is not surprising that youth today are the subject of much evaluation, criticism, and condemnation. Doubtless Stone Age man commented that the youth of that age lacked the ability and courage of their parents in slaying a sabre-toothed tiger. But what could be something of a surprise is the extent of the criticism and the range of the cause. The dissent of youth from the standards of their parents is common to all ages, but as a phenomenon, what is unusual today is the variety and the volubility, the publicity given and the degree of justification for that dissent. Youth may be considered as consisting of several classifications. Doubtless numerically, the greatest number are those loosely referred to as conformist. They display no more than normal opposition to adult values. They will readily fall into the niche society expects of them in the actions and occupations of their groups, and as such they get no more than normal criticism.

The sections of youth that come in for criticism are those that are seen as disruptive of social and national stability or the seed of the future. Their dissent may also take either of two forms: the radicals, who see it as the function of youth to mold society "nearer to the heart's desire," and the idealists who see no future in reform and for whom the words alienation, estrangement, withdrawal, noninvolvement, counter-culture, and so forth, are part of their vocabulary if not of their thinking. As part of their protest against the adult world they adopt all forms which help to distinguish their separateness. Thus consciously or otherwise, they are readily identified by a certain uniformity of behavior and attire. They subscribe generally to incongruous and ill-fitting clothes, often a wild unkempt hairiness, and on the part of the male members, unkempt whiskers. In short, in their revolt against conformity they have established their own conformity. Where not too inconvenient, bare feet are the "in" thing. Within the system some variation is allowed. Thus to some, bodily cleanliness receives much attention and the long hair is brushed and combed with great care; whereas for others with a body odor most repellent to normal persons, soap and water is an anathema. Certainly, wandering, unkempt men are no new objects in society. They are referred to in the literature of all ages and doubtless will be so in the future. But apart from periods of famine, their numbers are unique to this age. In endeavoring to assess their impact on the future of society, it is necessary to discover the cause of their development. Is it merely a bubble on the surface of society or is it the seminal forerunner of the New Age? Certain broad causes are readily observable.

In endeavoring to assess possible causes it is, of course, natural to begin enquiry where the child himself begins, in the family, in the home, and with the parents. It is most obvious but necessary to stress the changed role of the parent. In earlier generations families of ten or twelve or more were far from uncommon. Thus, as a member of a large group, the child at an early age learned discipline, at times unconsciously imposed by the competing rights and desires of others. An only child, or one of a small family, sees himself to a greater degree as the focus of parental attention. One can indulge individual variation to an extent not possible within a large family. Moreover, the parents of today see their role in a new light. Apart from the financial ability to give the children much that children of an earlier age could not have and at times were not even aware of, parental attitude to child guidance and control has changed. It is not here being argued that this will ultimately be for the better or for the worse, but to assess the effect this will have on the life of the child and so, on the future society.

Much of this attitude can be attributed to the teaching of Freud. As seen by Freud, the child, and also the adult, is psychologically a cauldron of warring impulses seeking the escape necessary for fulfillment and mental adjustment. To be thwarted is to be frustrated, which then leads to a neurosis or rebellion against authority. Thus the child learns at an early age that his urges are permitted an easy outlet. These urges can be either creative or destructive, which for the young are not entirely separate, or selfish. Early habits of conformity are not fixed.

On entering school the child enters a new world with perhaps competing values and habits. It is natural and instinctive for the young child to be imitative. Whereas before his models were his parents, now he is largely motivated by acts of his companions, popularly referred to as his peer group. The old concept of Solomon "to spare the rod and spoil the child" has been replaced by a variety of inducements, mostly pleasant, to approved behavior. In a society based, in theory at least, on the idea of democracy, teachers see their role as in part endeavoring to establish democratic concepts and customs. The child is given a degree of liberty of action and of expression impossible in an earlier age. Much time is also given to the matter of adjustment to the collective. Thus a conflict of values arise causing confusion.

The problems of society are presented as topics for discussion on which opinion and judgment, even when not actively encouraged, are developed. Now if it be assumed that the data of judgment are experience and learning—here defined as having access to the opinions of others—it is obvious that the young child has at best little access to both. Thus the youth is inclined to decide on the desired result without adequate consideration of all the factors between the real and the possible, or the ideal. It was said that between man and his achievement the gods had put sweat. It might also be said that to see the possible clearly, a deal of effort is needed. A primary-school child who writes to the press on matters of social discussion with authority, when experts are divided, has been trained not to think but to arrive at decisions, doubtless reflecting those of parents or or teachers.

Thinking on many matters can almost be synonymous with suspending judgment. As so many of our teachers today are themselves young and with limited experience in the "university of hard knocks," it is unpopular to say that much of our social theory so taught is based on book theory rather than on actual experience in the world. All too often those administering advice on social welfare are young people who have taken a course on social theories and go out to apply them to people who often have a practical experience far greater than their would-be teachers, who after all have had little time to test their theories on their own lives. Is one of the causes of dissent too much liberty too soon? The youth, disappointed in the unattainability of his idea or the problems of its attainment, and the desire for introspection inseparable from Freudian theory, loses hope in practical life and escapes into a subjective state of "inner migration."

It is not too much to say that it is the achievment of modern society that make the idealists' alienation possible. In an earlier age the principle that he who does not work neither shall he eat, was generally applied and perhaps more succinctly and more vigorously expressed by "root hog or die." The idler from choice or difficulty today can be sure of the fundamental needs of existence—food, clothing, and shelter—whether from welfare programs or from family support. And after a period of idleness, introspection, and search for his "identity," he may readily return to the boredom of work in exchange for the necessities of life.

If the dissent is based on the refusal to be a participant in the "rat race" and the evils of modern life, it is agreed that there is much in modern life of the twentieth century that is undesirable—undesired, and not inevitable. But the youth of today who say that "things couldn't be worse" or that life today is worse than that of his grandparents, does so without any support from facts. Cold and hunger were then the lot of those who were even in regular employment. The average length of life has risen from around thirty years to around seventy. The dissent arises not from the conditions but from the vision of a future, part possible and part imaginary, of a more equal distribution of the products of the earth; a society which is not only desirable but should be possible. The alienist-idealist takes the easy, lazy view that society is rotten and peace lies somewhere in a passive rather than a physical effort.

A part cause of this dissent is the effect of the "machine." It is most obvious that for the ordinary worker, keeping up with the needs of a machine must be repellent or at least unattractive. At least the cobbler of the past saw a pair of shoes take shape under his hands from a piece of leather. In reality, however, the picture so admired is anything but complete. The laborer of the past worked long hours, under weather conditions no one works under today, often poorly fed, poorly housed, ill, without the leisure hours of today, and without all the entertainment and facilities that are part of modern life. It is the machine and its assembly line "evils" that have released man from the heavy, repetitive burdens. Our young idealists have heard so much of the joys of creative labor that they feel they are receiving something less than justice if they do not engage in such activities.

Employers are often heard to complain that beginners in industry have the idea that it is beneath their ability to begin at the bottom of the ladder, but should immediately proceed to executive or research duties. Denial of these claims leads to dissatisfaction and withdrawal.

Concomitant with this is the availability of choice. Whereas in the past the son usually followed the occupation of his father, today's youth have the problem of choosing which occupation they will follow. They can, if desired, follow no occupation at all, for a time at least. As a further confusion is the fact that in modern industry the rate of change produces feelings of uncertainty. The skill of the parent who has been a trained tradesman for most of his life can be rendered obsolete by new techniques and machines. The son has a not unnatural fear of being made redundant also. Indeed there is a literature asserting that the operative is rapidly becoming obsolete. The machine does not resent repetitive, difficult, or dirty tasks, but does them better than human hands. The rapidity of change and the need for long training for many skills has had an effect of separating youth from the adult world.

In an earlier age, and in backward countries today, children were brought into the labor field as soon as their efforts could be made productive. Thus the concepts and habits of the existing society were instilled at an age when dependence on the parents was imperative. Today's youth can spend up to the end of their second decade in the process of education often unrelated to any form of productive labor. The youth feel themselves to be adults, better informed and, so they are often told, wiser than their parents. They are impatient to rectify the evils their fathers have passed on to them. Youth are told they are better educated, freed from the shackles of the past, and now classed as adults at the age of eighteen. Yet they are encouraged to go to a variety of counselors to solve their problems. They are trained to depend on others to solve their difficulties. But surely they cannot be both wiser and dependent at the same time.

The nineteenth century can be seen as the age of faith, faith in the supremacy of science, in the ideals of democracy, in the natural ability of man to achieve his millennial destiny. Events of the twentieth century have done much to destroy this faith. Utopia has not materialized, and the closer approach has done much to destroy the glamour. The communist experiment has cast serious doubts on much that was expected to create the new age of peace and plenty. Freud has said that he doubts if civilization can be, or indeed is, worth saving. And Freud and his theories are well known to the dissenting youth of today. The combination of factors has created a psychology of despair. The idealists wander from place to place in search of what they cannot find; and they know not what. They join communes, become devotees of mystic faiths in far-off places, or turn to drugs for a heightened experience normal life cannot give. Work is seen as an imposition. One young letter writer asserted it is a lesser social evil that society should support him than that he should be compelled to work for money. Another went on the air to declare that his aim in society was to abolish work, which destroys one both physically and mentally. That work could be a fulfillment of the creative impulse is utterly foreign to this fantasy.

As an impact on society, the "drop out" has no future; but the effect of the radical is much more important. The young people see themselves as active participants in the making of the civilization to be; and insofar as they persist in this belief, may create a new society or destroy what has already been created. In assessing their significance, a few observations should be made concerning what they are not. As with rebellions in all ages and in all societies, these young people are not typically from the underprivileged but from the middle class—reasonably affluent, their parents often with educational qualifications well above the average. Investigators see no significant association with broken homes. Indeed, the widespread nature of the dissent should rule out broken homes as an important factor. In further assessing their significance it has to be realized that in a phenomenon so widely dispersed, there must be wide divergence of ideas and of application. With these limitations in mind, some elements are still seen as common. Adolescence is the age of experimentation, of assertiveness, and agression among the male of all species; not least among these the human male. A new phenomenon is the degree to which the male has been joined by the female of the species.

Youth is the age of impatience, of intolerance of what is regarded as unjust or restrictive. The force of emotion, with its urge to action, is at its maximum when the restraining influence of reason and experience has not yet developed. They show the typical enthusiasm of the new convert. There is a general scorn of the "old," who may be classed as around thirty or beyond, an age which they realize, but not too effectively, they will soon reach. It is not too much to say that they have the confidence of inexperience. The distance from the broad plain of the future as seen from the height of inexperience, obscures the cliffs and ravines, the problems and dissension to be encountered.

But to return to the origin of their ideas, they are typically of certain family types. Parents are often well educated and of a somewhat radical outlook. Their life-style is normally not orthodox. The children are reared in an atmosphere where divergence is part of the early environment. They are accustomed to hearing radical views presented, and in the absence of equally frequent cogent argument to the contrary, these radically "advanced" views become part of the child's early impressions. Frequently the child is encouraged to read "advanced" books, which in the absence of opposing view, present a biased view to the inexperienced mind. Encouragement is also given to a ready expression of opinions. Researchers have provided some evidence to support the case that the house is mother dominated, the father being in such cases ineffective within the home and living a life inconsistent with his views. Disrespect for authority, as represented by the father, tends to be inculcated at an early age.

Among dominant theories in modern education is a belief in democracy and adjustment to the group. The child learns to expect a freedom of action and expression of his opinions. As referred to earlier, since the data for judgment are experience and learning, caution would suggest that decision be deferred to a later stage. It has often been asserted that the "dissenters" come not from the disciplines of science and mathematics at the universities or practical business studies, but from what are termed the behavioral sciences. This, of course, is as one would expect. Science deals in facts and figures verifiable by anyone prepared to test them. The so-called behavioral sciences admit of no such verification. From their nature the enquiry and discussion as to the nature of society is what the course consists of. Proof is impossible; theory is supreme. Authorities in support of any case can be quoted as desired. In the world of psychology, the theories of Freud are widely considered; and in spite of their pessimism as to the worth of future civilization, individually applied, they hold wide acceptance. Their effect in condemning established authority is strong. While the theories of Marx have had something of a decline resulting from their rigidity and their application in the Russian experiment and elsewhere, the young radicals evade the problem involved. The vital question to be disproved is, "Can the application of Marxian theories be possible without the totalitarian techniques so far associated with efforts to apply them?" The youthful theorists escape by denying this as inevitable or even consistent with Marxism. Thus groups label themselves variously, not so much as Communist but Marxist, Leninist, Maoist, Trotskyist, and so forth. This has for them the merit that no one can point to failure. As seen in some universities, these sections are composed of warring factions bitterly opposed to each other and to the student bodies at large, who prefer to go ahead with those studies which will equip them for adult society. At best there is little clarity concerning what state of society will exist in their visualized future, the immediate effort being to prevent the operation of the existing abuses and inequalities. Leaders like Marcuse teach the doctrine of the "Great Refusal," a combined action by the self-styled intelligentsia, the students, and the "workers" to make the present system unworkable. In so far as those members of these groups would participate in such a breakdown of society, it would be a combination of the theorists, the inexperienced, and the biased; surely not a combination with a good augury for a future social construction and organization.

As a sociopolitical phenomenon the movement appears to have culminated in the late '60s, since when it has declined though still existing and active. In the U.S.A., perhaps more than elsewhere, it comprised elements from the most disadvantaged and "exploited," and as in the universities, from those most "educated" and advantaged. It had or has three categories.

1. Those who as reformers hope to attain their desired goals by modification within the existing sociopolitical structure.

2. Those who see civilization today as basically degenerate and in need of reform of all bases on which it rests. Culturally it is inimical to mankind's needs.

3. As a subsection of these, are those committed to a violent attack on all existing institutions of power as they see them. This is an all or nothing policy, a policy of reversing the status quo, the victims and the "oppressors" to change places. Repudiating the existing "Marxism" of the U.S.S.R., they embrace a neo-Marxism with all the ideals found in Marx added to their own visions. This is to give an Elysium free from all the injustices and compulsions so irksome to them and their visions. It is an antiestablishment movement uniting and using all antimovements in a final triumph. As a revolt against existing authority and custom the use of drugs is encouraged, thus creating a generation of nuisances "and the application of all types of violences to destroy" violence. The universities as they exist and the professors there are condemned as supporters of the structures of oppression and to be resisted by all manner of disruption. All art, music, and literature should picture the triumph of the present victims and the destruction of the oppressors. Rationality is that which has contributed to our "tragedy," and must be replaced by feeling. An extreme form of this idea is seen in the statement: "No universal revolution without universal copulation." Though small in numbers, they can influence others by generally supporting and controlling any agitation against real or imagined grievances. Here they obtain support also from "Leftist" political bodies in an arrangement of mutual aid.

Not unnaturally these young people are inclined to self-dramatization. They see themselves as the avant-garde of the new civilization, manning the barriers of dissent and reform against conservatism, inequality, and injustice. They have acquired an extensive literature devoted to the analysis of society as seen from their viewpoint, and of the techniques to be used in the overthrow of the system. In the methods of setting up committees and organizations which they claim are representative of the great body of students, they have learned much from the tactics of communist cells. As they see it, the university is but a reflection of the instrument of the adult establishment of which it is really a part. Therefore, forceful occupation of administration buildings is natural. Attempts by police to restore order are vigorously resisted, the claim being made that the university belongs to the students. In one case, when the Prime Minister of Australia attempted to speak at the Melbourne University, he was subjected to intimidation and was told that the university belonged to the students and he had no right to be there at all.

This assertion that a university is not subject to normal government authority, is part of a pattern to overthrow institutional authority. The dissent often extends to making demands for curricular decision and governance within the university as a means of settling the dislocation. In their demands of equality, some students have claimed that admission to the university should not be by examination but by ballot, and that no examinations be held during the courses. One would hesitate to submit to an operation performed by a surgeon so selected and trained.

Student dissent and disturbance has become part of the life of all countries, even totalitarian ones. Communist or otherwise, dissent in countries such as Russia and Poland tends to be by older people. Whether declared or not, this disturbance is invariably directed against some action of the government. In cases as in Thailand, it has been effective enough to stimulate a change of government. The Marxist leaning is well documented in the Australian universities. The book *The Australian New Left* was written by eleven contributors all of whom have a history of Leftist experience in university or college, and write from the approved Marxist doctrine. When these dissidents, in later life as journalists and educators, are given opportunity to express their views there is no doubt in which direction their influence will flow. The Australian Union of Students had until recently a unique advantage. Until the West Australian government legislated against compulsory unionism at the university as being illegal, the annual income of the A.U.S. was just a little short of three-quarters of a million dollars. With this they paid known "leftist activists," sent money to overseas forces opposing "reactionary" governments, and paid money into the funds of strikers against the government. In support of the Western Australian legislation the Victorian government has legislated that while unionism is compulsory, the union fees must now be paid to the university administration to be released to student bodies for funding of student needs. A further development has been that at last alienated by A.U.S. tactics and violent entry into university offices and quarrels with administration and students who oppose them, certain university student organizations have been disaffiliated.

At bottom, compulsory unionism is the opposite of freedom of association, long considered as a basic human right. Association becomes forced association, one of the steps to totalitarianism. It is certainly distressing that in universities where freedom of expression should be most valued, such freedom is denied to many.

The reference to other than academic matters, however, brings into clear focus much of what is at the basis not only of radical-student unrest, but of society itself. No one can deny that there is much in society, here or anywhere else, that is in need of improvement. Injustice, inequality, privilege, and prejudice are part of human existence. But this is not to say that improvement is not desirable and possible. Where one disagrees with rebels, youthful or otherwise, is in the use of obstructive and violent means to attain their ends. In the use of obstruction and antagonism the participants have declared, knowingly or unknowingly, that they have abandoned reason and cooperation as a means of changing society. Dissent is inseparable from community life and is indeed a *sine qua non* of progress.

But the history of violence must surely show that in a violent society, leadership falls into the hands and control of the most violent. The abolition of slavery in British countries was initiated by the peaceful efforts of men such as Clarkson and Wilberforce. The institution of Communist rule in Russia was by the means of violence largely engineered by a man who wrote: "Hate . . . is the beginning of all wisdom."

The result of the Russian Revolution is a political system more rigid, more dictatorial, more repressive and less amenable to change than that of the Czars they supplanted. The lesson of history is there to be learned. Gradual change is the price of lasting progress.

THOUGHT CONTROL

At the end of World War II an almost universal cry went up, "what the world needs is training for leadership." And this after the most disastrous war in history, when millions of lives were lost in misery and degradation urged on by leaders, in the disgraceful spectacle of apparently normal men, bellowing defiance at each other behind the fancied safety of millions of armed men. Meanwhile, a third sinister figure waited like a spider in its web for the foolish flies to become entangled; though in this case they actually contributed to the spinning. In reply to the all too obvious fact that leadership had dragged us into war, was the response that what we needed was wise leadership. In short, what they unwittingly advocated was training for wisdom, a very different thing. Training to resist leadership would have been better.

It is generally assumed by writers and philosophers that man has an innate and powerful urge to freedom. This is only partly true. It could be more accurately stated that man has an antagonism against restraint, rather than a commitment to the principle of freedom, either physical or mental. Yet coupled with this enmity is the very widespread urge to follow a leader. The successful sociopolitical system of the future must be based on a sound assessment of these two aspects, an urge to escape from restraint measured against a degree of docility. The success of the leader is based on four main factors:

1. His call to the mass to follow is first an appeal to man's gregariousness. The follower becomes one of a group sharing fellowship, enthusiasm, and a common objective. Mass enthusiasm is a contagious thing admitting of little or no restraint from reason, as witness the heil-Hitler enthusiasm which was all in support of a leader who promised to change history for a thousand years, but who in a few years was dead by his own hand, his schemes and his country in ruins. Regrettably this, though a most spectacular example, is by no means rare. Lesser examples exist all round us. This group sharing gives a most

satisfying sense of power and purpose, impossible of fulfillment in isolation.

2. The new leader, the new avatar, must have that quality now so popularized by the indefinite words of charisma and mystique. Part of this quality is boundless self-confidence with a personality and persuasiveness that convinces. All that is required is for the followers to believe, to follow and be guided. They are the glorious instruments of an ideal which they see but vaguely and of a way that the leader alone will make clear as the journey proceeds. To serve him is to reach the highest peak of their possible fulfillment. The leader alone has the knowledge and the authority.

3. The leader comes with a revelation from above and beyond. Whether he be a Moses or Muhammed, Jesus or Buddha, the revelation by the leader is the source of the plan. This is not to decry in any degree the Ten Commandments or the Beatitudes, the teachings of the Koran or the Four Noble Truths of Buddha.

4. A latecomer to the mantle of avatar, Karl Marx, could not, being an atheist, avail himself of the supporting authority of Yahweh or Allah, but had to rest his plan on the insecure earthly foundations of science and philosophy. Nevertheless, Marx yields to none of the earlier leaders in the fourth requirement, authority and completeness. Rejecting all his earlier rivals he claimed to enunciate fully and thoroughly the essential elements, the cause and the cure of man's social ills. The revelation is full and final. In a reversion to the discredited methods of past indoctrination, the followers of Marx use to the utmost all the techniques of censorship, repression, and elimination of rivals, both human and ideological. Possible converts are of three categories: those who are readily persuaded of their errors and so conform; those who may be persuaded by reason or submissiveness only after a long subjection to the doctrines and disciplines of the new cult; and finally those who by their previous convictions and customs are so committed to the errors of their earlier ways that hopes of "enlightenment" are non-existent. These are eliminated as an illustration of the penalty of persistent error, and as an inducement to others to the "persuasion" of the new doctrine.

It has been said that man being unable to reason out a

problem for himself desires to be told. The "truth" having been accepted fully, he goes outside to argue and disagree with anyone he meets, ready to prove to everyone where they are wrong. His conviction having been strengthened and his emotion aroused by opposition, he throws up a wall of emotion between himself, his reason, and the problem. Like the prisoners of the Bastille after its capture by the revolutionary mob, who few in number objected to being disturbed in their placid isolation, our convert resents reasonable discussion in his mental prison of certainty. The approved writings are supplied at times as compulsory reading. While the above may not give the full picture, it contains more than a few grains of truth. Truth is to be found then not by the process of reason but by searching the sacred texts. The search for truth is confined to search in the utterances of the leader, all further writing being but an elaboration, elucidation, and application of the rules binding on those unable to discern the truth by their unaided reason. Fortunately, the ages of the burning of heretics are past, and former religious antagonism has in some degree been replaced by toleration and, at times, cooperation. Also, fortunately, it is impossible for people who think for themselves to arrive at a unanimous conclusion, though an acceptance of basic principle goes far towards achieving that end.

Here the conflict between freedom of expression and censorship arises. No one will disagree with John Stuart Mill, who stated that freedom of speech is not allowable to the extent that one may shout "fire" in a crowded theatre. Nor can we accept as justified the freedom of any to publicize a simple process for making a deadly poison or an explosive substance. Public action and public expression must be restricted by the needs of the public. Is the expression beneficial or harmful? This, of course, is the criterion any dictator claims to apply. The real test is by whom and in what circumstances is the judgment made and applied. As Socrates might have said in answer to this problem, "knowledge is the only good." It is probable that the word knowledge in this connection is better translated by the word "wisdom."

It is no part of the thesis here to discuss the case for and against the limitation of freedom of expression and action. Sufficient for the present is the presentation of the fact that here is a difficult social problem for the solution of which no simple rules are complete. Freedom of expression is under threat from two sources: from those who would protect those roles and values which may have outlived their use; and from those who would restrict access to information that might jeopardize the interests of their own views, disregarding that any expression of ideas should be allowed. Like all freedoms, freedom of expression, as of action, can be destroyed by excess. The danger of thought control is there, though not perhaps to the degree described in Huxley's *Brave New World* or Orwell's *Nineteen Eighty-Four*. But in an era of rising passion and polarization of policies and prejudices, aided by the technical skill and the power given by a growing knowledge of man's psychological composition and how it may be manipulated, the danger is real enough to demonstrate the need for countermeasures.

THE ROLE OF THE GIFTED MIND

The former English anthropologist, Sir Arthur Keith, said, were it not for the existence of some thirty names in world history we would be living still in the Stone Age. No one would, of course, have expected Sir Arthur Keith to name them. What he was doing in persuasive words was to emphasize the fact that human progress depends on the existence and discoveries of its intellectual men and women. The possessor of a high intellect may use it in either of four ways.

1. He may waste it in the search for the pleasures of the senses. He neglects the tasks of continued effort, choosing instead the ease of the idle. His ability has been lost to himself and society.

2. He may use his capacity, and frequently does so, for the accumulation of wealth. He becomes the head or the driving force in some industrial or commercial organization. He has used his intelligence to give him a sense of power. This of itself is neither good nor bad but depends on how such power is used. To an unappreciated extent, it may result from the desire to create, just as much as are the efforts of a painter. The organization is the child of his brain.

3. He may join a cause which he sees as being for the good

of mankind. He becomes a leader in a religious movement or may initiate one himself.

4. He may join a political or social cause. This at best can be of great good for mankind. At worst, it produces those disastrous leaders of which the world has had so much recent painful experience.

So the genuinely intellectual person must be strongly aware of the dangers of partisanship. Partisanship and objectivity are incompatibles. The true intellectual must keep a delicate balance between the Scylla of prejudiced partisanship and the Charybdis of aloofness and unconcern. As a member of society benefitting from the results of social relationships he surely has the obligation to contribute according to his ability. He must use his mind to understand fully the problems of mankind without becoming too closely involved. To understand he must come down from his ivory tower lest he see mankind in his own image, and not in the light of what may be possible, conditioned by the limitations of the marketplace, and the needs of the people in it. When progress has been made, his is the task to see that satisfaction and lethargy do not halt it. Progress may become ossified or be diverted by those who are unable to understand or who divert it to their own ends. Nothing of human creation can be considered as perfect and final. It is the task of the truly creative brain to discern the flaws, to publicize them and to stimulate further development. Perhaps never before in the history of mankind has the need for this type of mind been greater. Civilization is at one of the great dividing lines on the road at least equal to any in past history, enslavement to dogma and control or to liberation and expansion of the spirit. The opportunity, the facilities, and the knowledge for both roads are at hand. Has mankind the wisdom to understand his grand position, the opportunity to question and to escape the procrustean bed of propaganda and conformity, or of the delusion of innovation? Much of mankind is still illiterate, an untapped reservoir of ability; most still lack the training to beware of false prophets and alluring slogans with appeal to the emotion and not to reason. There is enough technological skill and knowledge available today to enable all men to have access to the book of knowledge and the physical needs of adequate food, clothing, and shelter.

It is perhaps ironic that now that technology has placed leisure and affluence within sight and almost within reach of everyone, that scholarship alone lays no claim to the right to short hours and easy effort. We may aid the learner with all the devices of microfilm libraries, condensations of desired or needed information, and push-button devices to illuminate. Still, learning can come only as the result of long hours, days, and years of intensive study. Herein lies an overlooked danger: Can a student be blamed for desiring the pleasures of leisure and affluence which he sees his contemporaries enjoying, while he must deny himself these in return for long hours of concentration? The amount of learning now available is so vast that only by concentrated effort throughout life can anyone obtain anything more than a small part of the mass. Perhaps on this rock the ship of civilization may flounder, temporarily at least, and to confuse the metaphor, spend another forty years in the wilderness to enable a more virile race to emerge. Hopefully this is not to be the fate. As encouragement, it has been said that the reward of greater income be paid to educators, philosophers, and scientists. It is doubtful if this would have any benefit, or it perhaps may even have the reverse effect. Surely any great discoverer gains his main satisfaction from a task well done and a new discovery made. Society could at least give to the thinker the prestige that is his due. It can be the duty of politicians, as Lorenzo the Magnificent realized, to encourage and facilitate the efforts of those who were making their impact on the life of the age when he himself could not do so. The need here is for scholars from all over the world to meet, to discuss, and honour the leaders free from political and financial patronage and efforts to direct. Some of these are slowly emerging. A world organization such as the United Nations is well adapted in principle, though certainly not in practice, to this task. The organization of UNESCO is readily available to pool and publicize new ideas and discussion. That politics is evident in these meetings so far is all too clear. It is the task of the scholar to see that no pressure be allowed to obstruct him in his search and presentation of the truth as he sees it. The search for truth can never be completed. All new developments must be presented fully and faithfully for examination, for criticism or approval, before the bar of world scholarship.

We readily realize that a genius can arise despite the environment he is born into. Christ was the son not of a learned rabbi but of a carpenter; Buddha was of a ruling family; Newton was the son of a farmer. Their contributions are incalculable but it is not enough to wait for a genius to arise. Owing to the vast range of knowledge today the task is to give our youth the widest and wisest education possible to fit them for the task of guiding the world of the future. There is no room for quick remedies or complete cures. Education is such that no one can claim to be fully educated. Like virtue or complete truth, it can be striven for but never fully attained. For the continued improvement of civilization what kind of education do we need? It has been said that the difference between a wise man and a fool is that the fool repeats his mistakes, the wise man does not. History has shown the mistakes of the past and how they operate. An idea germinates in the mind of one person. It grows and is accepted by others. It becomes part of the mental equipment and is accepted or imposed by force. It falls to the lot of the successors to maintain, to develop, or to modify the new idea. The successors, lacking the qualities of the originator, whether by lack of discernment and inspiration, of will or ability, or from motives of self-interest, cannot sustain what was started. Decay and deterioration set in often, with accompanying confusion creating the need and the opportunity for change. This is much as the Hegelian dialectic argues, but study of the past shows clearly that "synthesis" is not synonymous with "better." The breakdown of an existing organization provides opportunity for good or bad reorganization. If we are to avoid a reversion to the evils of the past in mental and physical control we must be fully aware of the elements involved, and have clearly enunciated principles to follow lest we repeat the mistakes of the past. The question therefore is what form must education take and what institutions must we operate to guide us.

Any consideration of the role of the gifted mind would be incomplete without discussion on the position of our universities. The professors and lecturers—with some unfortunate political appointees—are people who by achievement and distinction within their chosen disciplines have demonstrated their ability to absorb knowledge. This does not necessarily imply that they are the best qualified to impart information. Without being diverted into an examination of all that qualifies anyone to be a good teacher, one essential qualification is emphasized. There is such a qualification as an academic or professional ethic, without which our schools must fail in the purposes of their establishments. This involves the right to enquire, to discover, to teach, and to publicize the results of their enquiries, subject to no control other than those of rational enquiry and exposition. This implies freedom from external control—economic, religious, and political; but receptive to criticism and discussion from within and without, and serving no objective beyond serving the truth as seen and presented. It must be realized that this places on the professor the responsibility of maintaining academic impartiality.

As no rational person would claim to have attained absolute truth, some elasticity must be allowed even to the extent of expounding what may be regarded as heresy. The heresy of today can be the accepted doctrine of tomorrow. This is not to say that in being heresy it must in time become orthodoxy. Truth must rest on a firmer foundation than that it disagrees with orthodoxy. The academic ethic would require that in expounding the beliefs he holds, the speaker also presents to students other beliefs not in accord with his own, and permits these views to be readily presented, limited by time and freedom of expression. It is axiomatic that we are in an age of political, social, scientific, and technological revolution, but it is not the function of professors to advocate trends, but rather to present all that is known and said, and leave the direction of trends to others. To join a party as a university official is to abandon the status of the impartial search for truth. Partisanship and objectivity are incompatible. In opposition to this is the teaching of communism which argues that all thought must be pressed into the service of the Revolution, whether in art, music, or literature. This attitude rests on the belief reinforced by emotion that in communism mankind has attained truth, final and complete. This is a reversion to medievalism which held that truth had been presented and all heresy must be exterminated by any means available. Unfortunately within the universities there is a body of opinion shared by some staff and by students that the function of the university is to shape society, with themselves the *avant garde* of this progress. These belong to various "leftist" schools of thoughts and organizations. Deriving mainly from Marxism, they share the beliefs of certainty and finality. This is perhaps the greatest evil, and from which other developments follow, of the legacy of Marx. Freedom of speech, as other benefits of democracy, they use not only according to the principles of freedom, but as a device to restrict all speech but their own. They use democracy to destroy democracy. Further violence is used to destroy violence. Though few in numbers their influence is not small. As "activists" they work continuously to carry out their plans, plans which often go no further than the distruption of the establishment. Their influence derives also from the inertia of the majority, who can, however, be roused to support them on specific grievances without realizing that the immediate is but a skirmish and a diversion in a long-range policy. The majority are both assistants and victims.

Our universities stand for certain values within society: to extend the boundaries of knowledge; for freedom of thought and association; and respect for learning and courtesy toward one's opposition. Unless both students and staff have a lively awareness of these values and both support them, they and society will be the losers. What the best of mankind has passed on to us today can be more easily lost than it was attained. What has but feeble support will be lost. Our universities have great powers. With that goes great responsibilities of which the maintaining of the academic ethic is their special role.

EDUCATION

On the position of education today, many conflicting voices are heard. On these matters we are told that our young people are better educated than any previous generation. On the other hand we hear from schools, universities, and businessmen that students all too frequently lack the elementary skills of literacy and [numeracy]. If tertiary and secondary institutions have to set up remedial courses at these levels, it surely must be conceded that too many students enter secondary and tertiary institutions without having acquired the knowledge to profit from them. Basic to this position is the sentimental idea that a child must not be subjected to the discipline of success or failure, but to the "cultural compulsive" of equality. The child is moved through his career without proof being provided that he has attained the knowledge necessary to absorb the next stage. The result is an increasing deterioration, the pupil falls further and further behind his fellows, not unnaturally ceases to try, and becomes delinquent in class and outside of it. Any organization is to be judged by results. Our education systems are no exception to this.

It must be stressed, however, that our various educational systems cannot be held wholly responsible for this. Not our educators alone, but society itself, can be held as partly responsible for what our schools produce. Schools must in the last analysis be a reflection of the world they are expected to serve. Bismarck after the defeat of France in the Franco-Prussian war said, "At last the German school master has triumphed." There, the schools were merely reflecting the policies of the German government as Bismarck directed them. To establish a few principles it is affirmed that the duty of the school is to perform those tasks the parent has neither the time, the facilities, nor the skill to perform. No one expects the parents to teach the children the facts and the processes of arithmetic, the knowledge of history, and so forth. These tasks are passed over to those whom society has trained for that purpose. It has been claimed by some historians that in the centuries of Rome's expansion the father held himself responsible for inculcating in his son those values which were considered necessary for responsible citizenship. Equally, the mother held herself responsible for the training of her daughter. These historians see the seeds of Rome's decay as being sown when these tasks were handed over to a slave. In a changing world, the parent's time and attention was turned elsewhere. The slave commanded neither respect nor authority. Nor was he so obviously involved in the result. Here then is an indicator showing where the parental influence can and must be exercized if the child is to acquire standards of conduct and attitude to others, necessary for society. During those first and most malleable years, the child's world is the home. If, as our psychologists would have us believe, the essential elements of character are established in the first few years of life, the parent is the most formative influence. Surely then the greatest gift parents can give the child is their time. No abdication of this responsibility can be condoned. Within the family circle the child learns those attitudes essential to a close relationship with others.

Education can be seen as having three stages.

1. Within the family, from birth to about age five or six. Here is learned the elementary stage of adjusting to the needs of others. At birth the child is wholly self-centered, but within the family in a simple environment he gradually acquires the habits necessary to fit into a community; his own needs and particularly his desires are limited by the equal rights and desires of others.

2. Stage two is at the school, primary or secondary, ending at about the age of eighteen or less. In a soundly balanced system geared to the needs of society the student must learn that reward and success are linked to effort. Here also should be learned the limits of one's own capacities. The pupil is certain to meet others of his own age who surpass him in certain capacities, and so learns to adjust his ambitions to his own ability. To be a worthwhile citizen both in his school and in later society he should acquire a sense of responsibility. At this stage, education should be directed to learning the skills needed for later occupation. Little, or less than nothing, is gained by putting an adolescent into a learning process from which he will derive no benefit. At the secondary level, if not earlier, is developed the responsible citizen or the rebel. Under the harsh rule of necessity someone must perform those tasks requiring a minimum of intelligence, and whether we like it or not the poor learner is best fitted for it. One certain cause of dissatisfaction and inefficiency is to place a person in a position unsuited to his mentality, whether it be too difficult or too simple. In either case dissatisfaction is inevitable.

3. At the third stage, the tertiary level, a change in current beliefs appears to be essential. It had been calculated that those qualified to profit by a university education are limited to a small percentage of the community, perhaps as low as five percent. The accepted percent is now reliably placed at about twelve percent. But in accordance with current ideas the percent in the community attending universities is far above that level. This has several results: there is considerable waste of manpower and facilities; inevitably, the drop-out rate has increased; and to avoid this the level of performance has, in cases, been lowered, which

is a contradiction of what the university is for. A university qualification is or should be a badge of distinction. If shared by many it confers nothing; the best are rated no better than the mediocre. Distinction is not and cannot be democratic, nor should it be. In accord with the cultural compulsive of equality, students have claimed equality with the teachers. They have claimed the right to have decisive powers on the syllabus, to sit on examination boards, and at times to abolish examinations entirely, *i.e.*, that results good or bad should not be evaluated. In this stand they get some support from certain teachers in adherence to the prevalent belief in the superior wisdom of ignorance. No doubt the disturbance within the universities is not unrelated to the fact that in advocating a university education too widely, admission has included many who are mentally and emotionally unfit for tertiary education. In Sweden it has been claimed that status within society is closely related to I.Q. This would indicate that maximum opportunity has been given for each child to attain that level for which his ability has fitted him. Equality apparently has not been considered.

In a discussion on the place of education in assessing the possible future of civilization, it is essential that consideration be given to previous civilizations as far as they are recorded. History is in essence racial or national memory. Individually, memory is the retained record of experiences by which are guided the actions of the present. Without memory the mistakes of the past would be blindly repeated. Thus it is necessary that if the record of the past successes and failures are to have a value for modern societies it is necessary that our teachers, legislators, and administrators have a sound knowledge of history. Any study of history reveals innumerable examples where society today is repeating what led to the decline and disasters of our predecessors. Anyone with a poor knowledge of history has a poor understanding of life today. Life is seen out of context.

Entire libraries have been written about education, its purpose, its methods, the training of teachers, and so forth. Something has gone astray with the adapting of citizens to the demands of economic and social change. A satisfactory adjustment to these conditions has not been made. To add to these discussions would be presumptuous were it not for the obvious fact that society today, and youth in particular, is in a state of turmoil. Can it be said that society and its problems have reached a climax? The next few years can be creative or catastrophic. Perhaps no better summary of the principles underlying education has been made than the *Ten Points in the Black Paper Basics* put out in England in 1975.

Fundamental to any satisfactory system of education is a sound knowledge of the child's psychology insofar as it applies immediately to education. Surely we all accept as beyond question that an infant as well as an adult is a complex of instincts and impulses, both good and bad, both individual and social. The degree to which the environment permits, encourages, or restricts these impulses will in later life form the character of the child and the adult. Man is neither wholly rational nor wholly controlled by instinct, as is the animal. Psychologists agree further that an essential to normal development is security. To the child, security is based on authority. It is most illuminating to hear a child's reaction and enquiry when he is first presented with a new situation. Without being fully aware of the situation he immediately wants to know what is the law with regard to it. His purpose is to discover in what way he is to adjust to the new environment. He is fully aware of his own inability to grasp the full significance. The law then for him is the word of his parent. How often have we heard a dispute between children ended by the expression, "Father said," or more often, "Mother said." That, due to an innate urge, he often breaks the law does not invalidate this rule. Can any adult wisely use unlimited freedom? Is there a motorist who does not more carefully observe the rules of the road when a traffic patrol is near? And that, even when he is fully aware and experienced in the need for those rules. A child has no built-in instinct as has the animal, to adopt those actions necessary for survival. These must be acquired, and it is on the parent that the duty falls to develop habits and attitudes until the child is able to accept responsibility for his acts. Hence arises the need for firm, tactful discipline at home and at school. Too much freedom for children breeds selfishness, unhappiness, and vandalism. It is enlightening to see a child at school, cheerful, willing, and cooperative under a good teacher, and to see the same child at home, where fits of temper and assertion of independence are used as a means of getting his own way. Tales of disruption, disorder, attacks by students on teachers, and gang tyranny in the school grounds are too common to be ignored. They are evidence of a breakdown of that authority necessary for any organization. The criminal learned to break the law, first in the home and in the school. It is a serious commentary that consideration has to be given to having armed guards to maintain order and safety among students. Discipline and a respect for law and the rights of others is a fundamental need for all education.

As part of the theory of our new "progressive" educators is the idea that competition among students is harmful. Cooperation is the new slogan. This is based on the idea that if one may be proved as superior to his associates, it leads to an unworthy pride in one, and a sense of inferiority on the part of the other. If one has a lower ability than the other, surely the best time to discover this is when the child is young, less likely to be hurt and more ready to adapt to it. Is there any value in trying to suppress the truth? Competition is at the base of survival and growth in all nature. Throughout the area of all games the impulse is to compete against one's associates whether in athletics or at cards. Without the element of competition, interest declines, incentive flags, and standards fall. *The Black Paper 1975* sees the need for improved standards to compete against fierce competition from overseas. To minimize competition in one country is very much like the lambs passing resolutions in favor of vegetarianism, while the wolves remain carnivorous. But beyond national economics, competition is the need of civilization itself. The call today, perhaps at no time in history greater so, is for the discovery and use of our best intellects. Progress depends on the number and quality of our leaders. Therefore we eliminate competition from the training of youth at our peril. This is not to say that competition cannot be excessive or that it eliminates cooperation. But the fault today lies not in excess but in scarcity. The slogan of education should be "aim for excellence."

Closely associated with the previous ideas is the need for some common standard. Unless some such standard exists as by common external examination, how is anyone, student, teacher, or society, able to assess the degree of success or failure? We can measure values anywhere only by comparison and results. In essence all measurement is comparison, comparison with an accepted standard. That a truly first-class teacher may have no great need for stimulus other than the pride of giving his best to his pupils is accepted; yet the example of others surely must stimulate him or her to further improvement and give some legitimate reward for the effort and its result. But unless objective standards are maintained, what a glorious chance is offered to the lazy and inefficient. It is assumed that external examinations are set by practical teachers who have attained some status in the profession. That these are not all wise is true; but the risk of poor performance is much less than the absence of any real objective standard. Without this, neither the student, the teacher, nor society can truly measure the effectiveness of the educational system. To discover this when the child enters the adult world is too late. Remedy here, if at all possible, can be only as the result of much unnecessary effort.

The ratio of children to teachers has been reduced recently in an effort to improve results. This is doubtless very good; but the assertion has been made that quality has been sacrificed to quantity. If one can judge by results as expressed by potential employers' complaints, the charge appears to be proved. Along with the increases in numbers, has come the increase in cost and quality of equipment. Television, with all its possibilities, is universal in all modern schools as a bare minimum. But it can be asserted that a good teacher with poor equipment is more effective than a poor teacher with good equipment. Surely the most valuable piece of equipment available to the pupil is the teacher himself. It is not that education authorities do not try to obtain good teachers, but what is asserted is that methods and aims of education do not produce the result. Administration, necessary though it is, is not education. Education takes place in the classroom or in the laboratory, not in the office. In addition to teaching the particular subject of the curriculum, any competent teacher should be able to advise the student without the need of special counselors, particularly as the teacher must know the student in a way the counselor cannot.

If one makes the statement that schools are for education and not for social engineering, we disclose the difference between totalitarian and democratic education. The dictator knows what social responses he expects the schools to produce to sustain his regime. It is regrettable that much current educational theory is designed to produce a certain type of citizen rather than to equip him with those skills and knowledge enabling the child to be himself. Mankind is always engaged in a competition between conformity and innovation. In much current theory the innovators are leading the way. Indeed it is not uncommon to hear a teacher say in his efforts to attract attention, "Now, if we could only come up with something new." Clearly experiment and change can be desirable, but as always experiment must be judged by results. Educationists everywhere are almost unanimous that the standards of basic educational skills have fallen. Children generally neither read, spell, nor calculate as well as an earlier generation. Doubtless, this is conceded by most "progressives," who counter by the claim that this is of less importance than the result they are striving for, the ability of the child to adapt and to merge his personality with the society around him. Increasing delinquency in all countries gives no support to the success of these claims. It has been claimed that we are in the postliterate age, where reason and logic are less needed; but where feeling and emotion are more to be desired. Indeed the book *The Australian New Left* sees fit to devote a large part to "proving" this. It is agreed that much of what is written there is obviously more emotional than logical, and where so many of the new teachers are not outright inclined to leftist politics they, for whatever reasons, stress rather the failures and inequalities of modern society than the positive achievements. Some like Herbert Macuse openly advocate a combination of students, academics, and "workers" in the *Gretat Refusal*, the attempt to make the present society unworkable by nonparticipation. Just what is to replace it is not clarified. The social engineering designed to develop a character adjustable to a social system where the only known alternative appears to be the repressive totalitarianism of communism has no appeal to anyone who judges means by results. It is primarily the task of the schools to train the child in qualities of purpose, industry, honesty, and so forth, as well as to lay down the basic skills to read, write, calculate, and express himself in clear sentences. To ask a child to consider and judge on social problems which have remained undecided since the dawn of civilization is to ask the child to lift weights too heavy for even strong men. The result is to train the child in the habit of coming to a decision before he has acquired the knowledge, the experience and the wisdom on which decision can adequately be based. Such a process is to do an injustice to the growing mind. It is not normal for a child to have the rare capacity to suspend judgment pending further information and experience.

To further elucidate, the problem's two related principles may be stated. One, economic and social conditions can impose a handicap on the development of the child reared in what are rightly termed deprived conditions. Closely associated with this is the principle that children are not born equal. It might be thought unnecessary to affirm this were it not for the stress now being given to the idea of equality and liberty. For the good of the child and for society no one would seriously doubt that those responsible should use their best efforts to see that each child is given access to the best opportunities that can be made available to him. Yet no one should waste time and effort, and burden the child with tasks and experiences from which his genetic inheritance has decided he is unable to gain any benefit. On the other hand it cannot be decided at an early age what latent potentialities are there in the young mind. It is the task of the teacher to do all in his or her power to see that all the means of developing the abilities are operative. The child of high mental ability doomed to live in an environment restricting the use of his natural talent is much more likely to turn his interests and intellect to antisocial acts; in short to become a delinquent, gang leader, or criminal. At some stage, therefore not too late, the gifted child in a deprived area must be subjected to some process of selection to enable him to achieve what his capacities make possible. That that selection will not always be wise is doubtlessly inevitable, but surely it must be allowed that failure from not trying is likely to be more harmful than from trying.

Arising from the two previous statements comes the following: "You can have equality, or equality of opportunity, you cannot have both." Opportunity implies access to all facilities calculated to train and develop the genetic endowment of the child. At birth, children have a much greater similarity than at any later time. Within this apparent similarity lie unperceived genetic gifts which time and training develop. The physical ones appear more obviously than the mental ones. No one would try to train all children to be skillful artists, or scientists, or mathematicians, anymore than he would try to train all children to run a hundred yards in ten seconds. Under training, a few would succeed. Most would not. The current urge in much of our social theory, though not in practice either socially or politically, is for equality. This mass appeal is based on the obvious disparity in access to the good things of life as between rich and poor. Some have not enough, others it is seen have too much for their own good. So the remedy is presented. Let us strive for equality. No one would advance a case for complete equality but only for some reduction in inequality. This is not under question. Where the problem arises is how far this is either possible or desirable. To raise the level of the lower stage is good but to try to do so at the expense of the higher stage is discrimination of the worst kind. It is detrimental to the gifted child and to society. To require the gifted child to proceed at the pace of others, leads to dissatisfaction and loss of opportunity. It has been affirmed earlier that society needs and indeed progresses in proportion to the efforts of its best minds. Nothing is gained by transferring an injustice from the less gifted child to the brighter one. Freedom of access to the benefits of education will not make for equality of result; it will serve to widen the attainment between the two levels, regardless of any artificial division of class or race. Each will develop on inherent merit. Equality of opportunity is good insofar as the child is able to profit from it. Equality of result is neither possible nor desirable.

As a principle it is affirmed that freedom of speech must be preserved in the universities. Such institutions which cannot maintain proper standards of debate should be closed. The need to assert this is a terrible indictment of the universities so involved, and an indication of the values for which they are established. Above all institutions, the universities are established to give advanced training to the more gifted youth, and to develop scientific and cultural knowledge to the maximum possible. For this to be threatened by mass use of overwhelming numbers is a negation of the purpose. The statement attributed to Voltaire applies here most strongly: "I disapprove of what you say but I will defend to the death your right to say it." As mentioned earlier, we recently saw the spectacle of an Australian Prime Minister being compelled to take refuge from the threats of a violent university mob. Subsequently the statement was made that "he had no right there; it is our university." A short while later a scholar widely recognized throughout the world was denied a hearing because of his association with ideas to which the "advocates" of the rights of freedom of speech objected. Freedom of expression claimed for themselves was denied to the opposition. Ochlocracy is no substitute for reason. It is a most ironic contradiction that many of those who oppose freedom of speech at the universities are supporters of a Marxist-Communist theory which denies the right of freedom of expression. A condition of promotion within the Communist system is acceptance of official dogma. It is not without relevance to note that under communism little of any noteworthy scientific progress has been made. It has been said that the only case where intolerance is justified is to be intolerant of intolerance. While this statement is in need of some justification, it could yet be argued not without some justification that freedom of speech should be denied to those who themselves would deny the right to others. If people were susceptible to pure reason, the unrestricted use of free expression would involve no dangers. This, as has been discussed elsewhere, raises the question of censorship. Cases where such limits to free expression may be justified have been quoted. But specifically at a university level one is not entirely free from the supremacy of emotion over reason. And surely the students who would deny the prime minister of a country the right of free speech to members, on the grounds that it is "our" university, are showing an extreme example of emotion preying on reason. At least such people who would use mob power to such a degree should be restricted not by persuasion but by greater legal force. This leads directly to the matter of dissent and insurrection. Its limits can be discussed more fully later in the context of social philosophy in general. Meanwhile, it is affirmed that universities are to be considered, above all others, as places where reason and freedom of expression should be superior to emotion.

In a discussion of this nature an outline of a proposed curriculum would be inappropriate. In addition to the practical skill to enable the child to perform the adult role, the aim is to concentrate on those aspects where understanding is involved. This requires that the student be brought into contact with those minds and achievements which have made civilization. Without understanding and appreciation of the possibilities of decline, little hope can be held that the future can build on the past and the present. Can youth be made to realize the situation that will confront them when they make it? Here is the essential problem with education today. Without vision the people perish.

DISSENT AND DISOBEDIENCE

Reference has been made to the words of the Arabic philosopher-historian Ab'n Kaldum, in discussing the causes of the rise and fall of a civilization. In addition to what has been quoted, is his idea that social phenomena are subject to laws that operate, though not with the same rigidity as in the natural sciences. This view is also shared by the English historian Arnold Toynbee and the Japanese Ikeda, both of whom accept the view that the historical process exhibits a pattern, though not an inevitable sequence. It is in support of this view that the following is written. That we are threatened by decay and disintegration is widely accepted today; but ideas differ equally widely on the causes, the cures, and on the imminence of the danger.

Reduced to its simplist form, it is contended that these dangers fall into three main categories:

1. War and destruction by atomic power.

2. The terrible burden of debt increasingly weighing on citizens of all countries, and the increasing burden of control inseparable from our financial system where purchasing power comes to us almost wholly as a debt.

3. An aspect not as yet discussed in any detail, the problem of dissent and disobedience now so widespread throughout the world. It is the nature of democracy, or perhaps better, the abuse of it, which is under criticism.

It must be made clear that dissent is part of the process of all democratic procedure. Civilization is always subject to the two forces of conformity and innovation. Conformity can be likened to a fully built house. It has been built to meet a need. Conformity embodies principles of associative living, which have proved to have survival values as institutions. Conformity is the building blocks in the structure of civilization. But these can have the defect that they may have outlived their usefulness; or they may not have been entirely satisfactory at the time of their first implementation and the defects have become more obvious with time and change.

Here then lies the case for innovation. But it is no more valid to accept any innovation than it is to accept all conformity. Change has to be tested by results and experiences, aided by careful examination. Where innovative urge results in disobedience, a different argument arises. The amount of disobedience tolerated is related to the threat it poses to the system or the organization. Thus in Communist countries and organizations, disobedience is regarded as similar to mutiny in the army, or heresy in the early church. Dissidents may and do find themselves in "reeducation prisons," incarcerated in asylums for the insane, or executed—as with military discipline.

Disobedience is expressed in various forms in democratic countries. It has taken the form of armed revolt; trained, armed, and indoctrinated from abroad. That the innovation may be justified must always remain in doubt if it has resulted from force. Change by force proves no more than that it was backed by superior force and rests not on the merit of the change. It is a terrible condemnation of the use of force when one remembers that much of recent change throughout the world, and still in process, has been accompanied by atrocities that far outrival the efforts of Ghengis Khan or Tamerlane. Change gained by force has to be maintained by force and repression. Progress lies not in that direction.

A second and perhaps more widespread disobedience arises from indoctrination. If citizens, particularly our youth, are continually subjected to discourses on the evils of society and the justice and possibility of a better society, disobedience against the state follows. It is not argued that injustice and inequality should not be mentioned and condemned when necessary, but what is argued is the wisdom of the statement: "The truth, the whole truth, and nothing but the truth."

If one wishes to present a one-sided version of any human association, it doubtlessly can be shown to be good or bad according to which side was presented. Almost all countries today are the scenes of demonstration in opposition to some undesired part of government. The participants are often sincere, but the leadership equally often is animated by motives not shared by the mass. Leaders are generally Marxist or leftist inclined, with the object not of removing the injustice but with the purpose of establishing some form of "Anti-Capitalist" system. In marches down the streets of Melbourne and other cities, in what were called "moratorium marches," the presence of "leftists" was most marked. Spurious arguments were used to justify their action. It was commonly heard that "the streets belong to the people." This is true, but in claiming that as a right, they denied it to other people wishing to use the streets for normal purposes. It was not taken by a right but by the use of mass occupation. A further justification was that, as the city council had held up the traffic to celebrate the return of a world boxing champion, the marchers were also justified in doing likewise. It might be argued that the extension of a bad practice does not make it a good one. But more fundamentally it is a question of wisdom on the one hand and power on the other. By its constitution a city council has the power to direct and control city traffic. This is essential to orderly movement in the city. That the action of the city council may or may not have been wise is arguable. Their authority is not under question. The two cases are seen to have very little in common. A result of the marches, even if not intended, was to adversely affect government authority.

In most, if not all, countries today students are disobeying constituted authority, as has been discussed in some detail elsewhere. Sufficient to say here, is that these are frequently instigated and organized by students of a variety of "leftist" groups, but who all agree on the need to overthrow the present system of government whether by direct or indirect means. Combined action of this sort would turn the universities and colleges from being centres of dispassionate discussions, learning, and enquiries, into centres of propaganda and violence.

Reference is to be made to the long-range effect on civilization of the increasing burden and control of capital accumulation and its inevitable burden of debt. But at the other end of the economic system is the growing power of trade-union leaders. By various devices and propaganda they have built a system giving them considerable control over members. Indoctrination of a quasi or fully totalitarian theory has been developed. Sitting astride the forces of production, they have elevated the strike as a legitimate means of obtaining what they want. Few union members have the courage to work if a strike has been called, at times not even knowing what the strike is about. As the result of a trade union official being arrested for creating a disturbance in court, Melbourne was treated to the spectacle of seeing unionists going to work sites and calling out the battle cry, "All out." Men obediently left work to find out later what it was all about.

Regrettably this is not an isolated circumstance. No unionist with any regard for his safety, his association with his workmates, or his right to work, dare cross the tabu of the picket line, regardless of who has decided it should operate. The union leaders give much attention to "Capitalist compulsion," and not without some cause. But no one can deny that despite high-sounding words, they are showing an intolerance and disregard for the suffering of an innocent public, at least equal to that of those they are condemning. To an increasing extent, union power is coming into conflict not only with employers but with the government and the laws. No society can long endure the repudiation of its laws by its members. A solution open to unions, capital, and management is outlined elsewhere and has proven successful in operation where applied. If employees were to take shares by purchase and not by gift, and received not only wages but an agreed share of the profits, the cause for strikes would disappear. With the considerable amount of money now available to unions, it would be a simple matter for them to set up and operate their own industry in competition with other forms of ownership. To date they have shown little inclination to prove their arguments by demonstration of their own "superior" system of collective ownership.

While, so far, consideration has been given to open disobedience, a more subtle and perhaps more serious form is seen in the open defiance of formerly established moral codes. Regrettably the word morality is too commonly taken to be synonymous with sexual morality. Important though this is, morality properly applied includes honesty, industry, respect for others, and acceptance of established codes of behavior. In any study available to us of a declining civilization, there is most convincing evidence of an association between affluence and changed moral values and behavior. In addition to causes in common with previous civilization, modern civilization has certain additional forces calculated to assist decay. Science has "liberated" greed, and greed feeding on ambition and power has spread more widely than ever before in history. It is possible to operate these evils to a degree never before. In addition, two doctrines have given "rational" justification. The theories of Marx teach that it is perfectly just to take by force and violence what in the opinion of Marxists stands in the way of their objectives—as has been quoted elsewhere. This is such a simple and satisfying belief that it would be surprising if it were not applied to any situation as well as in the political and industrial situations. The theories of Freud explain the human personality as a warring complex of impulses largely sexual. Restraints of these impulses, known as frustrations, bring later disturbance and expression in various forms of dissatisfaction and violence. A natural consequence of this is an increased indulgence in sexual activity accompanied by, or without, violence. To combat this, current theory is that sex "education" is needed to explain the process and remove emotion. Results show the reverse effect. They would suggest that the "education" is not having the desired result. In fact the so-called education could be better described as sex stimulation, the unfortunate children having it brought to their attention to be studied in school, literature, and on television—which brings it into the home whether parents like it or not.

The effect of wealth has made regular work less necessary. Both time and money are available to enable people, especially youth, to indulge their emotions to a degree hitherto impossible. In general there has been a spiritual decline. This is not necessarily applied to a religious decline. Those impulses and instincts which mankind shares with the animal kingdom are being released. Decline is easy. To strive for nonmaterial values requires effort and self-denial. License is of the jungle, and must lead to conflict and disaster. Liberty requires self-restraint.

In justification of social and political disobedience, it is customary to do so on the fact that many rebels of the past became leaders of progress later on. Indeed, many of these have become the heroes of democracy. But in opposition to this can be quoted many rebels of the past who fortunately did not attain their objectives. To see oneself as a rebel is not necessarily to see oneself as being in the company with the great figures of the past. Instead of being on the side of the angels, one may be on the side of evil. Much use has been made of the integrity and authority of conscience, in that obedience to conscience is more fundamental than obedience to law and order. Justice is greater than the law. In justification for disobedience many people opposed participation in the Vietnam War. Insofar as their efforts contributed to the success of Communist forces they must also accept some responsibility for the consequent atrocities in Vietnam, Cambodia, and elsewhere, and the plight of refugees arriving in Australia, the United States, and other countries.

It would be interesting to hear how these same consciences have reacted since then. It would appear that conscience as a guide to action could derive some benefit from reason. It is accepted that justice can be of greater value than law and order, but without law and order justice would have little chance of operation. The purpose of law is to guarantee, if possible, the operation of justice. Again, if we justify our disobedience on the grounds of conscience, we are setting up our conscience in opposition to the consciences of others whose actions and authority we disapprove. As indicated above, conscience alone can be a poor guide to correct action no matter how impelling it may be. In particular, it was quite obvious that many of those who opposed participation in the war were favorable to the success of Communist invasion. Finally, it can be said that good intentions are not enough and are not an ultimate in political wisdom. Disobedience to the law is a dangerous precedent, to be used with the utmost caution.

It cannot be stressed too often that in man's psychological makeup, there exist certain internal conflicts. One which is finding frequent expression today is that between the desires of the individual and the pressures of the collective. Understanding and wisdom should realize the benefit and limitation of each force. Civilization, or any association, requires some restraint on members in exchange for its benefits. Against this restraint through the ages, and recurring strongly today, is the advocacy of anarchism—though under varied names. It is in effect a revolt against the compulsion of necessity. What is seen as restraining them is regarded as a form of violence, the institutions of the state, the courts, the democratic requirements of election and the institutions of religion. What is advocated is the release of the spirit in instinctive spontaneity, a dethronement of reason and logic to be replaced by the "genius" of feeling and emotion. It exalts the simple life of the Middle Ages, the uncomplicated life of the peasant farmer, the self-controlled guild of the craftsman creating the self-expressive works of his own hands and his simple, unsophisticated pleasures, and, ultimately, unrestricted emotional outlets. In Freudian terms he would substitute the id for the superego, a return to the unrestricted urges of the animal. The rebel seeks escape in mystical beliefs and joins communes in far-off places. But the picture, so alluring, is far from correct. More so than today, the citizen of the Middle Ages was under compulsion. He worked long hours, was poorly housed, poorly fed, and under climatic and other conditions not tolerated today. His health was by comparison poor, and medical treatment, where existing, was inadequate. In consequence his life was short and his mental horizon, limited.

The advocacy of anarchy takes two forms. There are those who expound a reasoned case, based on much thinking and scholarship, in devising institutions which they hope will reconcile the conflict between the one and the many. But the active anarchist of today, though he may not so label himself, cares little for reason and logic. Advocating the release of the impulses he easily turns to violence to resist violence; the destruction of anything which is a product of the establishment—institutions and people in positions of authority. The elimination of violence ends in the apotheosis of violence. Recent history supplies overwhelming evidence of the results of trying to cure mankind's ills by destroying the opposition. Moderation is preferable to demolition.

6

FORMATION OF THE MODERN MIND

PROBLEMS OF SOCIALISM

If anyone cares to study current socioeconomic theories and practice at any time in history, it becomes evident that change is attributable to the reactions against what are seen as the causes of the undesirable conditions of the particular period. With the wisdom of hindsight, it seems evident that those theories and practices are such that they are best adapted to justify the ethos of the society at the given period. But interesting and informative as the development of such theories might be, it is not the intention here. In tracing and discussing these socioeconomic trends, the objective is not to examine them as such, but to examine their effects on life and behavior at the relevant. A complete survey would of course go back to the beginning of history, but it is affirmed that for an understanding of society today it should be sufficient to go back to that great turning point in history known variously as The Renaissance, The New Learning, The Birth of Modernity, and so forth.

Equally interesting and valuable though it might be to recount the causes which led to this change, anyone who wishes to do so may select from a mass of information and speculation available. Similarly just as no one can say at what precise time the darkness of night gives way to the light of day, so the onset of the Renaissance was no sudden, catastrophic event. But consensus could doubtlessly be reached that the first trickles had merged into a flood by the fifteenth century. This new age was seen as a flowering of learning, religion, science, literature, art, discovery, and other such virtues. A vital, if not the most vital, element in this was the opening up to Europe of classical learning; the thoughts and practices of the best minds of Greece and Rome, which now owing in part to the invention of printing, could be readily read in the original. Just as when a flood gate is removed, the water previously held in check, rushes out overwhelming and sweeping away much of what is in its path and establishing new levels and situations; in like manner the Renaissance broke down much of the ideas, customs, and traditions of the Middle Ages. Men's minds, or at least the best and most creative of them, were released from the shackles that had previously restricted them. For this impact, the most significant for our study were in scholarship, religion, and science. The New Learning and its approach to thought is generally referred to as humanism. This attitude saw men's minds not as an expression of authority, but as free to roam over the whole range of ideas; that man was no longer the servant but could be the creator, the creator of a freer, better world. It cannot be assumed that this was an immediate and spontaneous growth of democracy. On the contrary, as exemplified by Erasmus and his contemporaries, humanism as such did not directly disturb the minds of the masses, but was seen more as for an elite of minds capable of appreciating and benefitting from speculating on the nature of man and existence.

It would also be interesting and informative to examine the relative significance on changing beliefs and practices of the ideas of the thinkers and of the practical urges of men whom the socioeconomic conditions affected adversely; those underprivileged who suffered from inequality, injustice, and poverty. But it is unquestioned that the theories and ideas of the intelligentsia give direction, justification, and purpose to mass movements. In this way humanism opened up a new field for the emancipation of the modern man to speculate and build on what classical learning had begun.

Religion, as expressed in the Reformation, was to a greater

degree a mass movement than humanism. As religion was practiced perhaps by all men of the Middle Ages, changes in religion more affected the minds of men. Again, it is not to be assumed that the populace to any degree discussed the validity, or otherwise, of the *Ninety-Five Articles* of Martin Luther, or that Luther initiated a democratic movement. As is normally the case, the rebel against the status quo is also the authoritarian in defense of his own ideas. But the general effect was the breaking down of mental barriers of the past; the stage was set for a new pattern of belief and action. As evidence, several new theologies and religions came into being.

Acting both as effect and cause of the new approach to thinking, a new age of science evolved. Without trying to make a comprehensive list of those names who contributed to scientific discovery, the names of Copernicus, Galileo, Newton, and Bacon are here significant. Bacon's contribution has significance for us in that he tried to link philosophy, long held to be respectable, to the new idea of science. The valuable effect of this was that it showed the earth not as the center of the universe but as a rather small part of a much larger and grander whole, this giving a much more adequate insight into man's place in the scheme of things. But, moreover, it emboldened man with the belief that the secrets and systems of the universe could be revealed by the application of reason to observable phenomena. Reason applied to science and mathematics, so it was held, could solve all the problems of nature. It was not long before this spirit of enquiry turned to the nature of man himself and the society in which he lived. At an early stage, and important, for this new brand of enquiry, were the writings of John Locke; but for the flowering of the field we must turn to France. This new development can in one sense be said to have ended the age of the Renaissance, and in another sense to have been the inevitable result of what the Renaissance began.

Be that as it may, for the purposes of our study, the significant elements of this Age of Enlightenment were focused on religion and the new discipline of sociology, of which the word, and the early stages of thought, were developed by men such as Comte. In accordance with the theory earlier expressed, much of social change is but the result of the swing of the pendulum, a reaction from the undesirable of the status quo. According to this mentality, if the old is defective, its opposite will be good. Hence, for the evils and injustices of the past, the blame was attributed to the authority of the rulers and the powerful; and in religion, to beliefs in general, particularly those of the Roman Catholic Church. As so much of the organization had yielded to scientific enquiry, it began to be logically assumed that belief in a God must come under scrutiny. The concepts of theism gave way to that of deism. The condition of mankind on earth itself queried the existence of a just God who took a participatory interest in affairs on earth. Was it more logical to see the universe as a system once wound up, set in motion, and then left to fulfill its destiny in accordance with its initial systems? From this grew the idea that, since the laws of Nature were gradually yielding up their mysteries to the forces of science, was there any need for the concept of a God at all? The concepts of agnosticism and atheism increased in general acceptance.

Parallel with this, and since then closely associated with it by one school of thought, was the idea of democracy. Since the world was full of inequality and injustice, this state must clearly be caused by those who made the laws governing society, those who set the standards, and who obviously benefitted by them to the detriment of the many: the poor, the uneducated, the underprivileged . . . the majority of the population. So if these evils were due to the actions of those in government, control by the populace would be good. An interesting example of this change in belief is to be seen in the writings of Jeremy Bentham. At first he argued that a better social system would result if the power was placed in the hands of a wise and gifted élite of which he saw himself as a member. Though it was not explained how these would be chosen, Bentham had in his earlier writings worked out to his own satisfaction a system which would produce the desired improvement. The chosen lords and merchants would do this; in short, the upper classes had all the necessary qualifications. Not being able to convince his associates of the merits of his ideas, he turned to the masses. They he then endowed with all the qualities needed for his plans.

No one better exemplifies this confidence—unfounded by any evidence available to him—than does Comte. He maintained that progress would result from the superior moral quality of the masses. He wrote, "This [the newer and better society] at least will be the case as soon as philosophers in the true sense of that word, have mixed sufficiently with the nobler members of the working classes to raise their own character to its proper level." Later he says, "It is in the exercise of the higher feelings that the moral superiority of the working class is most observable;" and again refers to the "noble and spontaneous instincts of the people."

In the light of the then recent excesses of the French Revolution one could wonder what persuaded him to this view of the masses; and more recent history can at least cast serious doubts concerning the masses today. It would appear that some of the philosophers of the Age of Enlightenment were not as enlightened as they supposed themselves to be. Today, probably few would argue that one section of society is inherently more moral than any other.

Prior to, but consistent with these views, are those of Rousseau whose private morals do not show any spontaneous nobility. As he lived in an evil world where ownership of property was in private hands, clearly here was the source of mankind's ills. He states, "Mankind is born free but everywhere he is in chains." And again, "The first man who dared to take from the common ownership a plot of ground, fence it in, and say 'this is mine,' he is the villain responsible for the end of the state of nature." Rousseau does not explain how this innocent child of nature came to indulge in such an "unnatural" act.

That the views of Rousseau and Comte are the views of very few today must be evident to all; but their significance lies in the fact that Karl Marx, who may be regarded as the last and most extreme thinker of the Age of Enlightenment, inherited these ideas and built his system around them. For him, the proletariat alone in their superiority, could destroy the forces and personages of the old regime and establish the Communist millenium.

EVOLUTION OF DEMOCRATIC REPRESENTATION

People who live under so-called democratic institutions are so accustomed to the processes, that they give little or no thought as to how the idea originated, how it operates, and what its justification is as a form of government. To a far lesser degree do they realize, historically speaking, that it is only a comparatively recent development, that it is under serious threat, and that it is being replaced by various types of nondemocractic governments. Unless citizens who do not wish to see it disappear and bestir themselves in its support, it may indeed disappear. It may therefore be wise to briefly record how the system arose.

While the evolution of democratic representation occurred in several countries of Western Europe, the process in England alone is considered. In other countries the process was much the same. Contrary to a common misconception, the origin of our system of legislative representation owes, in its beginning, little or nothing to the ideas of Greece and Rome. These ideas made their impact at a much later stage when the Renaissance opened to the West, windows onto the earlier civilization. When the Anglo-Saxons and Jutes invaded England after the Roman departure, they set up their own systems of law and order. Under the rule of the kingdoms of the Heptarchy, law, insofar as there was a system, was implemented through village moots, shire moots, and hundred moots, who settled, as free men, such disputes as arose; basing their decisions on custom and tradition. After the repelling of the later Danish invaders by Alfred, the witenagemot was established—the meeting of the wise men—to aid the king. By the time of Edward the Confessor, this had reached the stage of an advisory body with an elementary bureaucracy of administration.

William the Conqueror displaced this with his own system of feudalism where he required the aid, militarily and otherwise, of his more important nobles and tenants. Under Henry I, the Curia Regis developed a more effective instrument of administration but not of legislation. Considerable development was made under Henry II, but it was not till the misrule of John followed by the inability of Henry III as a boy to govern firmly, that the barons began to exercise some initiative. After the Magna Carta, which the barons and clergy forced John to sign to preserve what, after all, were their own interests, they set up what John in frustration called "four and twenty over kings," to see that the king was held to his promises. In 1265 the barons under Simon de Montfort further asserted their power. Simon, owing doubtless to the weakness of his position as the ruler of England after Henry was displaced, called representatives from towns and shires to assist, not so much as legislators, but as supporters militarily and financially. But it was Edward I who in 1295 called together what has since been called the Model Parliament. In calling representatives of nobles from the shires and of burgers from the towns, he initiated what has later become the House of Lords and the House of Commons. Representatives to meet the king when called were voted for on a property basis and at first seen as merely instruments of the king's will—both for the administration of justice and for the raising of revenue. When called, both groups of representatives if they had a grievance, presented a petition. Partly from a sense of justice and partly to put the members in a friendly and so amenable mood, the king could grant their petitions. As time went on, the representatives came to realize they had a bargaining position against the king. This bargaining position, to become known as the Power of the Purse, was perhaps the main instrument in checking the power of the monarch.

Under the Lancastrian Kings, some attempt was made to stabilize this influence; for everyone knew that the king's position depended on rival noble support. Under the authoritarian rule of Henry VII and Henry VIII this power declined, but under the rule of the sickly, youthful Edward VI it again revived. By the end of the reign of Queen Elizabeth, clear signs existed of an impending clash between ruler and parliament. Inheriting, as they did, a belief in The Divine Right of Kings, James I and Charles I were ill-equipped to meet the conflict. Among other causes, the Civil War was to decide this issue of who was to govern England. This decision was reaffirmed finally by the rebellion of 1688 when the crown was offered to William and Mary.

Under George I and George II the authority of parliament grew partly as a natural result of the process of yielding to the pressure of events and partly due to the fact that the two kings knew little of English conditions and perhaps cared less. As a by-product of this, there developed the Party System, that safety-valve and curse of modern Parliamentary governments. The name of Robert Walpole stands out for his contribution to this development. The system consolidated over the next century. With the rise of the Chartist movement after the Napoleonic War, change was made in the type of representation, payment of members, universal suffrage, and so forth. The position at present is much as the end of the nineteenth century saw it, votes for women coming after much agitation after World War I.

Variations of parliamentary systems exist. Parliaments may be unicameral or bicameral. Elections may be by "first past the post" preferential or proportional systems. Upper and lower house members may have varied powers. Governments may be presidential, with powers varying from country to country, or monarchical, with no legislative power whatever. Judged by results these differences appear to have little significance; no one system being an outstanding success to the extent that the other nations tend to follow the example. On the contrary, current trend is a reversion to the old system of centralized power and control. Insofar that voting operates at all, it is only for the approval of such representatives as have been selected by the central authoritative system. As has been stated elsewhere, only about one in six world governments allows free nominations for elections—with the candidate's right to canvas his own claims and to criticize the opponents. Democratic election, after but a brief trial period, faces the threat of being condemned as a failure.

OUTCOME OF THE AGE OF ENLIGHTENMENT

If one can regard the eighteenth century as the age which witnessed the culmination of the ideas of the Age of Enlightenment, the nineteenth century can be regarded as the age which saw these ideas in application. To recapitulate, what were these ideas? Briefly, there was an atmosphere of optimism. The shackles of the past had been "exposed" for what they were. The great forces of emancipation for mankind were to operate through reason, specifically science and mathematics. By understanding Nature, man would enter into the age of peace and plenty created by Reason. The future was bright. This application had by the end of the nineteenth century transformed life in those countries which had embraced the ideas. Education was widespread, often free, compulsory and nonsectarian. Newspapers were a fact of daily life, familiarizing men and women with events, not only at home, but from abroad as well. Lending libraries had brought literature into the home. The universal franchise was well on the way to general acceptance. Parliaments were democratically elected and controlled. Industry had changed from a mainly manual process to machine operation which took from the muscles of men the more burdensome and boring tasks. Increased use of natural energy had brought prosperity. Trade unions were now in existence, permitting the views of the laborer to be heard. Factory acts had taken women and children out of the mines, and fixed hours and some conditions of labor for all. Joint stock companies had been formed by which, investment having been made more secure, accumulation of finance capital was made possible as well as enormous industrial expansion. By overseas investment and by continuation of colonization, Western civilization had spread throughout the world.

But this optimistic picture of the progress of civilization was beginning to show some serious flaws. Greater wealth had allowed an improved sharing of the good things of life, but there were still slums at home and starving natives abroad. The mystery of nature still remained a mystery, and indeed, there were signs that suggested that a previously discredited belief in a Supreme God might not be entirely false. Education to a primary level was general, but the "educated" citizen showed little signs of improved rationality. His vote was given according to a fixed-party allegiance rather than according to the rationality of the situation. Newspapers had become powerful instruments for forming public opinion, by selection of news items, editorial comments and the banality of the emotional appeal of the advertisements. Everyone had a democratic right to a free expression of his opinions with or without regard to a serious study of topics under discussion. Religion, having lost much of its authority, began to lose its prestige, in spite of some stimulation and efforts of movements begun earlier by such men as John Wesley and William Booth. The Tractarian disputations had emphasized the schisms within the church. As a counter to this "free thinking," the infallibility of the Pope was clearly enunciated. While factory acts had done much to ameliorate conditions of labor, they had not brought equality between classes. The theories of Karl Marx, promising to give what the Age of Enlightenment had claimed to be possible, were becoming a force in labor, industry and politics. The right to strike had brought serious confrontations between sections of industry and government. The spread of Western culture had almost completed its impetus and signs were not wanting that the upward swing of the pendulum of white supremacy was completed and going into reverse. Altogether, it was becoming obvious that the age of peace, plenty, and rationality was not just over the horizon. Many began to doubt if it were attainable at all. The benefit of so-called progress was beginning to show another side of its face. The conflict struck in the twentieth century, the first great halt being brought about by World War I.

If we can regard the eighteenth and nineteenth centuries as the ages of creativity and growth, the twentieth century has so far been the age of destruction and decline. Former stable states, policies, and ideas have been disrupted. The First World War was not so much a war between armies and navies, but a war between peoples, a war of science and production. While the Central Powers suffered military defeat, the damage to all Europe was terrible. The map of Europe had to be rewritten. Old empires disappeared; new nations took their place. England, which had won the war at the cost of her overseas investments, began the dismembering of her empire. The United States, which had gained financially by selling materials of war to her allies, emerged as the world's supreme trading nation. Japan became a growing force in world trade and politics. Germany and Spain established authoritarian regimes thinly disguised, or without any disguise at all. But the most significant development was the establishment of Communist Totalitarianism in Russia, based ostensibly on the theories of Marx in the abolition of private property and centralized control through the organization of the Communist party.

World War I can be seen as a preliminary to World War II. War became a threat not only to national existence, but to civilization itself. The havoc wrought on the participants was unprecedented, whole cities began being bombed out of existence. War had come into the home. Events are too recent to need retelling. The United States' prestige and power increased. Russia, continuing the age old policy of expansion under the Czars, extended her control further into central Europe. The threatened further expansion has been discussed elsewhere. The boundaries of communism were pushed west and east by the Red armies.

Europe made a remarkable recovery, due to the energy of its people and aided by American money, food, and other assistance. The process of decolonizing grew rapidly. By force or consent, England, France, Holland, and Portugal withdrew from their colonial possessions. Africa, in particular, became the cockpit of warring tribal factions. The new states exchanged not words, but the facts of democracy for aggressive dictatorships. Much of South America is in a precarious balance between dictatorships of the Right and the Left. The U.N., established with various instrumentalities hopefully designed to assist in ending poverty, ignorance, disease, and international tension, has fallen far short of that objective. The U.N. itself has become a battleground of opposing purposes and very much the means for implementing ideas and policies for national aggression and expansion.

As an addition to the former problem of declared wars, undeclared wars are almost continuous, mainly resulting in Communist advances or in countries depending on Communist support as dependent satellites. Any dissenting minority inside or outside a country is assured of arms and supplies to overthrow the existing non-Communist rule, all in accordance with the declared methods of "détente."

Concurrent with, or consequent of, this endless strife, has come a disrespect for the law and constituted authority. Marx has said that the proletariat are not only entitled to overthrow government by violence, but that it is the sole means by which they can achieve the objectives of communism.

In leftist circles there has developed the idea that obedience to the law merely supports the degenerate Capitalist system. One is bound therefore only by such laws as one approves. Terrorist groups therefore acting on such theories, whether from conviction or from opportunism, have become a common phenomena throughout the world. By training and access to arms they are able to hijack planes, buses, or trains, kill any who oppose them, and demand ransom and release from prison any of their associates who have been captured. And all this in the name of a newer and better world. One hesitates to accept their assurances.

So far there is only one case of these terrorists being refused asylum in a country of their choice.

As a result of "liberation" by conquest, a significant world problem is the plight of refugees from Communist and other dictatorial countries. Efforts are made to rouse world sympathy into receiving these unfortunates. If an equal effort were made to arouse opinion on the cause of the refugees—mainly expanding communism—the extent of the flow might be reduced. On the contrary various countries and even the World Council of Churches, have sent assistance to the "take-over" regimes, under the thin pretext that the aid is for the relief of suffering and not for military purposes. The terribly misguided logic is obvious.

7

SOCIALISM

In any consideration of socialism, it is first necessary to realize that it has two aspects: its organizational and its psychological bases. One immediate difficulty is due to the fact that nowhere is socialism in operation as a political system outside the Communist countries; about which consideration must be deferred. There are in many countries, many institutions and controls compatible with what is broadly considered Socialist. This is very fortunate in that it permits a view of Socialist experimentation without society having to commit itself to full implementation, thus avoiding finding itself in a possibly irrevocable and regrettable situation. In the absence of a comprehensive and generally accepted definition, the idea used hereafter is that socialism consists of the public ownership of the means of production, distribution, and exchange; that is, the absence of all private ownership and of all means of acquiring an income. Arising from the foregoing, it is clear that in practical application, socialism has its impact socially, politically, and economically; each part of which must be considered not in isolation but as three closely associated sides of the one topic.

Beginning in its modern form some century and a half ago, it originated in a revolt against the injustice and inequalities which were part of the society in that age. To counter these, it was held that what was essential was a fundamental alteration of the entire governmental and social systems. Primarily, so it was argued, the root cause was the ownership of private property which enabled, by the greedy, the grasping, and the selfish members of society, the exploitation of man by man, to the detriment and degradation of the many. More precisely, this state of affairs resulted in irregularities in the free market; for psychologically, the mainspring of man's motives is the profit motive. From these "obvious" causes it was clear, according to the theorists, that the remedies would consist in applying the opposites. It was argued that the stimulus to activity would be not the profit motive but service to one's fellow man; private ownership would be replaced by public ownership and the free market would be replaced by a planned economy.

The conditions operating today are a far cry from the conditions operating at that time. Without replacing the existing socioeconomic system, ideas compatible with socialist thought have made significant changes by modifying the old political philosophy of laissez-faire. From the Socialist stand these changes may be seen in what can be loosely referred to as the Welfare State. Abject poverty, illiteracy, endemic illness, and the worst features, have been reduced. For the remedying of these ills, in addition to the efforts of men such as Lord Shaftesbury and Robert Owen, changes were in part due to the efforts of the sufferers themselves. The first signs were the establishment of voluntary organizations for the improvement in the conditions of employment of laborers. Prominent among the events along this progress was that of the much publicized "Tolpuddle Martyrs." This resulted in the beginning of trade unionism. The second stage can be seen in the advent of mutual-help societies as in the cooperative trading societies. The third stage is in legislation where by labor laws, factory acts, taxation, and social services, a much greater degree of equality in the quality of life has come into being.

Along this road, two examples stand out as expressing the new ideals; one is the motto of the French Revolutionaries, "Liberty, Equality, Fraternity," and the other is the words of the United States Constitution which state that "all have an equal right to life, liberty, and the pursuit of happiness." These two statements can be seen as a clarification and condensation of the Socialist ideal. Their limitations can be considered at a later stage.

In the use of the above words some elucidation of the exact meaning is needed. For the best minds, as exampled by Jefferson, equality was not seen as uniformity but allowed for diversity. Equality was visualised as absence of privilege: in equality of opportunity; equal access to the benefits of education, health, and occupation; to varied channels of self-development; to free use of leisure; to equality of work security and promotion; or briefly, access to the best that life has to offer. It must be stated that these ideas are those that came to be formulated gradually over the years. Among the wage earners in general, perhaps the greatest appeal for freedom would be freedom from the drudgery of work, especially in the unskilled and repetitive occupations. Such work offers little for the creation of interest or independence in any significant degree. The employee is referred to as "the slave of the machine." While generally accepting this viewpoint, there is little to indicate that drudgery can ever be fully eliminated from work.

This aspect is strongly emphasised by Karl Marx who, without any personal experience of the problem, referred to man's alienation from his work. He goes so far as to see a preposterous ideal, that a man if he so chooses, should be able to hunt in the morning, fish in the afternoon, rear cattle in the evening, and criticize after dinner, without ever becoming hunter, fisherman, shepherd, or critic. Such an absurd concept in modern society could arise only from childish idealism and inexperience. However, having rejected the Marxian absurdity, the real case for some degree of freedom remains. Freedom can be seen as freedom in choice of goods, of leisure use, of occupation, of some choice in the amount of work to be done, and freedom to escape from being "a cog in the machine;" in short, freedom from industrial and economic control. The degree of practicality of this idea is deferred to later pages.

The acceptance of the idea of fraternity, is somehwat more vague and more idealistic. It can be seen best, perhaps, in the concept of fair shares. How, and by whom, the sharing can be decided is as yet an unsolved problem. Enforced agreement with the authority of the state as enforcer, however acceptable, must rest on authority and not on fraternal sharing. This then becomes an encroachment on freedom. The concept appears to be too idealistic for any significant application.

As a political philosophy for the betterment of life, socialism has a strong emotional appeal. Despite the fact that in modern societies most men acquire most of what they really need, the appeal based on the inequalities of the past still exist. Men like to picture themselves as progressive thinkers in the van of progress. For many therefore, Socialist thought is blinded by a mist of emotion. Evidence of the results of Socialist principles is all too often ignored. It can surely be assumed as a truism that no human idea or plan is so good that it is perfectly sound and without possibility of improvement. Based on this assumption it then becomes appropriate that, after stating the ideals and objectives of socialism, we now consider how far these ideals are realizable in application.

As stated earlier, we are fortunately in the position of seeing this, in some part at least, in the modern welfare state. This enables society to see results without having to commit itself to what must be regarded as an experiment. The committed Socialist would argue, in responding to criticism of his doctrine, by saying that for effective application it would be necessary for socialism to be applied fully and on a world scale. To this, one must object that a disastrous situation could be created by failure of the theory. And surely if man's intelligence cannot manage the economy on a smaller scale, there is less hope that success would result on a larger and much more complicated scale.

What then are the points of criticism? As said earlier, socialism can be assessed from social, economic, political, and psychological positions. It is not expected, however, that as far as propounded, socialism would significantly alter basic parliamentary practice.

As a major factor in its satisfactory economic system, socialism sees forward planning as an essential element. Having in mind the accepted desirability of freedom, immediately one is faced with the dilemma which may be expressed as, "How much planning consistent with freedom, or how much freedom consistent with planning?" The two concepts encroach on each other's spheres. Forward planning envisages an investigation conducted by some authority as to what are the expected needs of society for the period under review; in regard to all items of food, clothing, shelter, entertainment, and so forth, both for home consumption and for export to purchase goods needed to supplement internal production. The magnitude of the task by some central authority is surely frightening; and the consequence of miscalculation would surely result in useless surplus or harmful shortages, or both. The low standard of living in Russia, despite an extremely rich natural endowment, gives little encouragement for other countries to follow. In England, after World War II, when ideas of planning, which had received stimulus from the urgency of survival, became more important than freedom, examples were frequent where a farmer was dispossessed of his land for refusing to grow the crops directed by the planning authority; even land that had been in the family's possession for generations. It is to be noted that the penalty was imposed not for failure to produce from the land but for failing to produce according to a Government official.

By contrast what equivalent penalty could be imposed on a striking railway worker who not only refused to put the railways—which he did not even own—to their proper function, thus causing considerable inconvenience and loss, but moreover, refused to permit anyone else to do so either? This inconsistency is compatible neither with equality, freedom, nor justice. Can central planning be possible without these complications? A Socialist might say "yes." It is the task of the Socialist not merely to affirm this, but to prove it. The Socialist experiment in Britain is so far a terrifying example of declining productivity. To put it negatively, government controlled industries are not noted for their efficiency.

It is frequently argued that lack of success of Socialist policies could be cured by extension to a worldwide range. The prospect of a world economy subject to centralized planning must surely daunt any but the most idealistic and impractical advocates. Advocates of socialism look to other means of forward-planning success by financial means such as taxation, loan funds, price control. It must be accepted that each of these mechanisms is a blunt instrument to perform a highly complicated and delicate process. Insofar as each of these has been in operation, it cannot be denied the results so far are far short of success. Taxation as a means of redistributing wealth has reached the stage of confiscation. In the case of many companies, when the company tax and the income tax on the individual shareholder are added, taxation is more than half the profit of the company. This idea of taking money from the one who earns it and transferring it to others is having the effect of deterring production. The phenomenon is too well known to need examples. This is not to deny that taxation is a necessity of any society, but Socialist policies are reaching the stage of bankrupting the people they are designed to serve. Taxation for welfare falls on the poor through prices.

Depression, unemployment, and inflation show no signs of diminishing with the increase in state control. Both taxation and loan policies have the defect that they fall equally on the "just and the unjust," on desired forms of production and those not desired. Selective taxation would depend for its success on the wisdom of those in authority, and an authoritarian attitude of government policy. Insofar as it has been applied to such products as alcohol and tobacco it has merely increased the price while concurrently there has been an increase in consumption. Application here does nothing to support a widening of the practice. Tariff policies are a part of most government laws throughout the world and are a source of conflict within each country and between governments everywhere. If, as advocates hold, this could be overcome by a world central authority, in addition to the problem of size, it ignores the problem of the weight of size against the need of smaller units in influencing decision making with the exponential result of the inability to adequately handle the task.

Wage adjustment has been in operation for many years in most Western countries. Increases in wages in Australia are, in theory, fixed by an independent arbitration system, which when first created, was hailed as a major achievement in settling the conflict between employee and employer as to the just wage to be paid. Judged by results so far and the satisfaction of the wage earner, no one can be too enthusiastic about the system. The reason is that it did not remove the cause of the difference. A suggested method by which this may be achieved will be discussed later.

At present, conflict is endemic, strikes are increasing in number and extent, and wages and prices are engaged in an endlessly spiralling pursuit of each other. Strong unions go outside the system to obtain increasing overaward payments and conditions. Efforts in bringing prices under some form of control, though long a policy of the unions, has so far achieved no discernible measure of success in checking price rises and antagonism between the parties. Moreover, arguments by both parties and the government have resulted in a litigious attitude with an increasing readiness to dispute even minor matters. Rules become more important than production. This matter is so important and extensive that a more adequate treatment must be deferred. Money manipulation, or more properly, purchasing power control, through borrowing and variation of interest rates, is extensively applied as part of planning. This has the effect common to all forms of such planning policy of hitting with little discrimination in selectivity.

As discussed later, financial control and borrowing due to the falliability of human prediction is a direct and inherent cause of "boom" and resulting depression. Theories of control are many; but the clear fact remains that unless recurring boom and depression can be halted, society faces the prospect of collapse. It can correctly be advanced that the evils just referred to are problems of both a Capitalist and a Socialist economy. If a Socialist economy has improvement to offer, it falls on the Socialist to show how or where this can be demonstrated without restriction on liberty, equality, and so forth. In more general terms, financial control has the additional defect that it limits investment and initiative to those that are approved by authority. Controls all too frequently are the genesis of ideas to evade, to be checked by more and still more control. The resulting picture is that of props supporting props in a crazy and insecure structure.

To all these defects as seen in society today, the Socialist has an answer. It is argued that if industry were transferred from private to community ownership, a changed environment would result in a changed attitude. Fraternity would then triumph, once the cause of antagonism had been removed. Men would no longer be animated by the profit motive but by service. All effort would contribute to the common good. No Socialist would argue socialism would usher in a state of perpetual peace and brotherhood, but that major causes of dissension would be removed for a vastly improved quality of life.

How would this be implemented in industry? The main theory advanced is known as "worker participation," or more completely "worker control." This concept ignores large areas of society where application would be impossible. This can be seen as democracy in industry. It can be assumed that new conditions create new problems. Unless one can see worker control being exercised by plebiscite of all involved, with frequent disruption, such control would be exercised by elected committees. This would compound a defect of democratic election where election depends all too frequently on popularity and ability to talk persuasively: personality rather than ability would come to the top. A further defect of democracy, both in the political sphere and in the worker control in industry, is that so much of the decision to be made needs skilled technical knowledge and experience.

Moreover, management, like any other aspect of industry, requires years of training, experience, and capacity. Would the good technician prove a good manager? Would the decision of the representative be subject to veto by the ill-informed and the biased? Fortunately the answer to this has been given by events in Russia for any unbiased observer to see. In the early stages following the Revolution, much verbal waste was produced in support of worker control. It was soon discovered that skilled management could not be subject to employee control. Today great emphasis is laid on discipline and obedience to the decision of the management. In short discipline in industry is as important as in any other organization. Employees must be told what needs to be done. This is not to say that control must be dictatorial. Discussion and agreement is both possible and necessary. But the root cause of employer-employee difference will remain unless a fundamental change is made. But insofar as this is a problem in socialism, the difficulty remains. It is frequently argued by the Socialist that socialism would substitute the aggressive, ruthless profit motive for the motive of service to mankind. The employee would be animated by a desire to give of his best. This has been summed up in the slogan, "From each according to his ability, to each according to his need." Men would be spurred on by pride in reputation and prestige, and approbation by one's fellows.

How far has this belief been seen in successful operation in socially owned instrumentalities such as the railways and the post office? It is all too clear that the public for whom the service is maintained, no more than the employees, have no sense pride or effective participation. The extent to which Russian official propaganda is devoted to this theme without any appreciable result gives little support for a belief in its effectiveness. What reason is there to support the idea that this regrettable absence would disappear by an increase in its scope? An undesirable condition does not become a good one by extending it.

A further criticism of the idea of worker participation is, how far is the employee desirous of using his reason and effort in this direction? To what extent does he wish to participate? It is a pungent criticism of democracy, that for parliamentary elections in Australia, voting is compulsory; and in elections where voting is not compulsory total votes fall as low as 30 percent of those eligible to vote. Indeed, in trade-union affairs, the vote has fallen as low as less than 2 percent for the election of a senior official. Conceivably the long range psychological effects are more consequential than its organizational ones.

As a basis of all civilization and nations is the character of its citizens. Genetics apart, this is dependent on the philosophy underlying its system. What effect on the character of its citizens can socialism be expected to have? Here again by good fortune rather than by conscious understanding we have seen something of this reflected in reaction to such welfare regulations as we already have. This effect is shown both on those who operate the system and those on whom the regulations apply. Controls of any sort require administrators who quite naturally dislike seeing their directions being flouted. Thus we have the bureaucrat, who becomes more and more authoritative and less receptive to individual variation. A capable administrator or scientist objects to having ragged edges to his plans. Operations are conducted on masses leaving little or no room for the desire for latitude to express their own individual personalities.

Under socialism, government would become more and more centralized and liberty would be more and more suppressed. It must not be forgotten that man's struggle for freedom has been usually against governments. As authoritarianism increased, so individualism would be suppressed. Of greatest value to society is the variation and unpredictability of human nature. Thus mankind, without conscious direction, is engaged in mass-scale innovation and experimentation. Its opposite is rigidity and ossification. Citizens would less and less accept responsibility for their own actions. Fulfillment of policy would increasingly be considered as government responsibility and officially due to "circumstances beyond our control." "Tis a poor thing truly but mine own," is not untypical of all people. Thus, if a person has created something by his own efforts, he tends to feel a sense of pride and satisfaction. If the result is provided "free" by a government, the tendency of human nature is to be critical and less satisfied. Further, the effect of bad leadership would increase in proportion to the scale of operations. As with politics today, he who exudes confidence in himself, now grandly styled as charisma, and can promise freely, is the successful man. Leadership falls into the hands of the demogogue. Recent history has thrown up many examples of such men.

In addition, two opposite effects could result. Firstly there would always be a "rebellious" element, who refused to accept control. These dissidents, as in Russia, would be punished for no other reason than that they expressed the inherent desire in man for self-expression. So far as the system was successful, men would lapse into a servile population. A developing civilization lies in neither of these directions. Finally and most seriously, socialism, in setting up the system of control and authority, inadvertently or deliberately lays the foundation for communism. It is not without reason that Russia stresses most repeatedly that socialism is the first stage to communism.

It is affirmed that even if it were possible to eliminate from man's personality impulses of competitiveness, assertion, and so forth, it would be unwise to do so. Even if these impulses were unnecessary in human relationships, there would still remain the competition from nature. In nature, man is not only a cooperator and manipulator, but is as much a victim and a tool. True these impulses can be in measure diverted and redirected, but they still remain necessary while man continues to live on earth.

When all has been said on the merits or otherwise of the Socialist concept, it has to be accepted that the impact of changing circumstances is changing life. No longer can a man push further and further into the wilderness to carve out for himself his own little kingdom and escape the restraints of society in exchange for those of nature. Deep in the complex of human nature is the impulse to create, to strive, and to choose for himself what path he will follow, what kind of life he will live. It is that impulse which drove him, like a distant but faint call, from the depths of ignorance and savagery, to a life where, in part at least, he is able to see his place in the whole scheme of evolution. Here lies the urge to better things, to understand, to enquire into the nature of truth, and to live by the discoveries he has made. Here lies the urge to freedom so deep in the mind of him who said: "Give me my gaunt frame, my empty belly, my ragged back, but give me my freedom." And all this was a cheap price to pay for his freedom.

Change in the encroaching of man on man, the ease and frequency of communication and close contact, make some limitation on the rights of all to act as they please. Mill has defined liberty as the right to do as one pleases, subject to other people's rights to do likewise. It seems obvious that the encroachment of society on the freedom of the individual will become closer. Here lies the danger of socialism. Unless this limitation is clearly seen and stated, the mass of mankind will become no more than the tool of the manipulators. Such a system would be unendurable and unenduring. Man would again have to fight for his ragged back and his gaunt frame as the price for his individuality. Such a regimentation should not be necessary. But, the price of freedom is eternal vigilance.

8

THEORIES OF COMMUNISM

Running parallel to the theory of socialism, is communism. For an understanding of its impact on society in modern social thought and practice, it is necessary to devote some time to the origin of communism as it is now in existence. Though not the first to advocate it, modern communism can be considered as the expression of the ideas of Karl Marx. Resulting from these ideas, we have various groups claiming to be the pure expression of Marxism, execrating any orthodoxy but their own. Thus we have the Russian, the Chinese, and the Jugoslavian systems in operation, and groups labelling themselves as Marxist, Trotskyist, Leninist, and so forth.

It must be conceded that when discussing Marxian thought certain difficulties arise. Much of what Marx wrote had application to, and was intended to have application only to, events at the time of writing. His work shows a deal of variation between ideas expressed in one stage and those expressed later. Moreover, his work was unfinished. Despite this, there is continuity of thought throughout on his basic ideas. And it is the responsibility of the advocate to prove that the repression and violence with which the name of communism has almost become synonymous, are not the inevitable and inescapable results of trying to apply his ideas. Whole libraries have been written on Communist theory and practice. It is intended to add to this only to the extent necessary to allow a clear picture of the results as shown in history over the last hundred years. Contrary to the adulation of his disciples, it is asserted that Marxian thought is based on bad history, bad economics, bad morality, bad psychology, and without any knowledge of genetics whatever.

Marx has telescoped history into four stages, each according to the modes of production: slavery gave place to feudalism, which in its turn yielded to capitalism, and in its turn will inevitably be supplanted by communism. Presumably, no further progress can follow. If one can identify a Capitalist society as one where wealth in its various forms, and in consequence, power, resides in the hands of a few possessors to the detriment and deprivation of the many—as Communist theory would have us believe—then there have been several Capitalist societies in the past, and instead of communism following, it might be more accurate to say that feudalism followed capitalism. Further, while not wanting to enter into a discussion on slavery in the past, it might not be irrelevant to recall that when the Senate asked Cincinnatus to return to government, they found him at the plough in his field. It is also doubtless recalled that Socrates was a stone mason. Enough has been said to cast doubts on the slaves as being a basis of ancient civilization. Also, Marx appears to have drawn his conclusions from Western society only.

On the matter of morality, Marxian ideas are best illustrated by Lenin's application of them at a later stage. It is sufficient for the present to say that Marx was committed to the idea of violence as a necessity of progress. Society could be changed satisfactorily only by violent overthrow. According to this belief Marx is trying to give moral and philosophical justification to violence. Anyone who thinks of the state of society in the days of Marx, in comparison with today, must be impressed with the amazing progress made without violent overthrow except in countries such as Russia, where the progress is markedly less. In the *Communist Manifesto*, Marx writes that the bourgeois have reduced the family relation to a "mere money relation," and the only "nexus between a father and his son is an economic one." Later, he refers to the bourgeois marriage as being merely a system of having wives in common.

No one would accept such ideas today. Any parent would be prepared to deny them. They can be dismissed as merely the splenetic outbursts of emotion and ill will. To fit in with his economic theories, Marx, as is common with social theorists generally, endowed man with those attributes necessary for the implementation of his schemes. Thus he postulated the "Economic Man." If the mode of production determined man's nature then by altering this, man's nature would be altered. The failure of this thesis is best illustrated by the degree to which Russian policy has been compelled to accept previously rejected bourgeois values. In one sense it may be said that the history of Communist Russia is the history of the search for some incentive to replace private gain. Man is not a wholly gregarious animal.

It is in the philosophical theories of Marx that atheism and democracy are most closely associated. It should first be emphasized that the Communist movements stemming from Marx are in no ways democratic, either in theory or in practice. The claim to the name is wholly self-conferred. As an aid to the development of atheism, was the writing of Feuerbach. Engels, perhaps not too accurately, said, "We all became Feuerbachians." But his writings gave weight and influence to the spread of the idea. His concept was that God was merely a creation of the human mind, a mental construct expressing human desires, attributes, and potentialities. These theories fitted perfectly the concepts developing in the mind of the young Marx.

Another concept fundamental to Marx was that expressed by Hegel, whom he refers to as the "Master." Central to the theories of Hegel was what is now known as the Hegelian Dialectic; often wrongly credited to Marx. According to this, physical nature is subject to endless change brought about by the stress of the old—the thesis—coming under pressure from the emerging—the antithesis. Resulting from this comes the new, the synthesis. This fitted perfectly into Marxian ideas of historical inevitability.

In one particular, however, and that an important one, he broke away from the Master. Hegel averred that the highest level of social organization—the state—alone was competent to unite particular rights and reason. Thus he rejected the idea that man was free by nature, as the state was the only means of making man's freedom real. It was in this regard that Marx said he had found Hegel standing on his head, and he put him on his feet. Marx argued that just as man had created God and placed himself in a position of dependence, so it was that man had created the state and not the reverse. The people had created the constitution. While one may accept this thesis with Marx, it is the conclusions he arrives at from this that one must disagree with.

Just as Marx owed much of his early theories to the theories of Hegel, so he owed much of his economics to Adam Smith and David Ricardo. Is it too much to say that in his departure from these masters that his theories went astray? In any discussion of Marx's *"Theory of Labor Value,"* the preliminary point must be made that Marx discusses value of commodities only. Value exists in directions other than in commodities. All natural resources have value, and his concepts must be checked to establish whether this idea admits of agreement here. Central to all his economics is the Labor Theory of Value. This theory he elaborated on more than one occasion, with painstaking detail. Typical of this was his address to the General International Congress of September 1865. In the section referring to "Value and Labor" he says, "The first question we have to put is: 'What is the value of a Commodity? How is it determined?' " He then gives his answer by saying that the "value is determined by the socially necessary labor involved in its production, it is a crystalization of social labor."

In his answer, it cannot escape notice that he poses not one but two questions; the first, *i.e.,* "What is value?" being the more important of the two he does not answer. It is extraordinary that in such elaborate discussion on value he fails to do this but merely explains how according to his theories it is determined. One can determine when water is boiling and how this state was brought about but surely this is not the same as saying what boiling water is. His presentation here is a fine example of how his reasoning has the appearance but not the reality of logic.

But even allowing his theory of labor value, certain difficulties arise. If he is correct, why is it that no one could exchange a worn pair of shoes for a new pair? Is it that the quantity of socially necessary labor had decreased? Why will a man pay more for a house on an elevated site than for one in a hollow? The superior view is in no way associated with labor. Why is it that a stand of untouched good timber is of more value than one of stunted trees? The answers are clear. Further no one can argue that the laborer does not by his efforts add value to the goods, but the laborer is not the only contributor, even in the factory in which he is working. The laborer is the final repository of a long chain of accumulated skills and experience going back in time; as far back as the persons who discovered fire, who evolved the wheel, writing and mathematics, through the discoveries of science, and so forth. Moreover, he is indebted to the whole of society who makes his life what it is and to all of those who directly or indirectly contribute to the increase in value. Indeed it is probably more accurate to say, as has been said, not that the labor determines the value, but that the value determines the socially necessary labor. Thus the value of water to a desert city is not measured by the few cents paid daily by the inhabitants; but that the value is the price of existence. After this has been said, we come back to the unanswered question. Briefly the value of a commodity is its capacity to satisfy a need or a desire. This needs no explanation or justification. If it were not so, there would be no reason in choosing between two articles having the same amount of involved labor.

In stating his Labor Theory of Value, Marx is the victim of his own emotions and the conclusion he desires to arrive at—the crediting to the laborer of the source of all value. By unscientific selectivity, he proceeds by a process which ignores essential facts, to a desired conclusion. For him the value of the commodity has been misappropriated by the employer. The masses, thus exploited by the Capitalists, are entitled to regain the product by whatever means are available. This can be done by eliminating the entire social system and its rulers. Perhaps the most obvious error in the Marxian theory of value, is seen in a look at the varying conditions of production. If one considers the production from a fertile area of land in comparison with that from poor quality soil, to produce an equivalent amount of grain from the poorer soil would require a greater amount of labor. Therefore, according to Marx, the value of that from the poorer soil would be greater than that from the better soil. Inherent in the value is the effectiveness of the labor involved and the quality of the raw material. In spite of their best efforts, farmers have never been able to obtain uniformity in the quality of grain, wool, or hides.

ERRORS IN PRINCIPLES OF COMMUNIST THEORIES

As a thesis having as its theme "Whither Civilization?" a full discussion on communism would be misplaced. But for the student of sociopolitical philosophy it is very relevant to discover, if possible, where and why this modern experiment in associative living has failed.

For the success of any project or idea it is necessary that the underlying principles on which it is based be sound and that the statements are in accord with the reality of the situation. Contrary to this, as has been said earlier, much of history can be seen as little more than the swing of the mental pendulum. If it can be presented, truly or falsely, with sufficient persuasiveness that current evils are due to a certain set of circumstances, then the opposite circumstances will be regarded favorably. Man is perpetually a scene of conflict between reason and emotion, contrary to the beliefs of such men as J. S. Mill, who affirmed that if truth and error were brought together and the case for and against argued cogently, truth would always prevail. Emotion is always a conditioning factor for the acceptance of a new idea. Recent history affords endless examples, in the light of hindsight, of the degree to which people imbued with an emotional appeal, have acted contrary to the dictates of reason and to their own disaster. Hence, an attempt will be made to analyze the principles of communism underlying the Communist experiment in associative living. These principles can be regarded as primary, or causative, and secondary, or derivative.

If one recalls the climate of opinion in Europe around the eighteenth century, there was a ground swell of opposition to the status quo and in particular to those institutions and social organizations influential in society at that time. It is not that economic and social conditions were worse than say in the preceding century, but that the mental attitude was such that there was an increasing awareness of the defects of society and a newly strengthened belief that these evils were not the results of Divine anger as punishment or the inescapable effect of nature which man could not avert. These evils were seen as the encroachment on society of existing defective institutions. So the new scientific attitude seemed to promise that there was no need to postulate the existence of a Divine Being as the originator of the universe, a mystery beyond human comprehension. As the church, and particularly the Roman Catholic element, was associated with privilege and power, the opposite, by the pendulum principle, must be good. Thus, the theories of deism and atheism were increasingly accepted.

A most glaring association of inequality and power was the ownership of private property. This was epitomized, among others, by Rousseau, who in picturesque but unverified words affirmed that all man's evils arose from the event when one man first put a fence round a piece of land and said "This is mine." Marx with greater brevity, but with no more evidence, reduced the evil as being due to "private property."

It appears that little effort was made to discover if, when, and where man existed in such a state of nature, so that no one had any private possessions, and what was his state therein. Rousseau boldly launched into the concept of the "noble savage" who apparently was free from vices associated with property-owning mankind. Herein lie three of the basic principles of communism as first enunciated by Marx: atheism; absence of private property; and the unscientific certainty of the final and complete enunciation of the cause and the cure of the ills of mankind. It is not intended to argue the case for or against atheism but what is affirmed is that man can be animated as much by truth as by "necessary illusions," beliefs which give coherence to man's impulses and identity. This is very clearly illustrated by the ruling elite in Russia who ceaselessly emphasized that under communism there is an inevitably glorious future. On the basis of evidence so far available to an objective observer and many of those who have experienced the effects of the newly evolving society, as well as the experience of human nature in action generally, it can readily be seen that this is used as a "necessary illusion;" but one which so far has done nothing to improve the lives of the people in general. Viewed in one aspect, the history of Russia since 1917 has been the search for some incentive to replace that of personal gain and individual initiative. So, far from succeeding, the acceptance of some material-personal incentive has been compelled as a means of inducing its members to work more effectively.

Authorities from Plato to today have accepted religion as a stabilizing force in society, both morally and socially. That religion has had and can continue to have a regrettable side cannot be denied. But perhaps it can be more accurately stated that the fault lies not in the idea, but in man's failure to reach the standard required by the idea.

Communism as an expression of Marxian ideas, has tried to substitute for the ideal of the objective sanction, the ideal of communism. On the evidence available so far, it cannot be said to have produced anything but deterioration; and until man is able to solve the mystery of existence, the causes and conditions governing the entire universe (one sees little hope of this solution), there is still room for the belief in a universal mind. In conclusion, it is affirmed that the principle of the swing of the pendulum has done nothing to advance civilization here.

Scientific Certainty

A logician once said that he took his examples of logical fallacies from the statements of scientists. This is doubtless a surprise to many. It is surely not without significance that Marx, who had some philosophical training, had no scientific training at all. Moreover, as any reading of Marx will show, he was emotional in his thinking—contrary to what is generally believed of him. Some of his doctrines, but not complete enunciations, are readily available and have passed into the "necessary illusions" of Communist theory, but not of practice. Thus, his acceptance of the Hegelian Dialectic, no matter how accurate in the world of natural phenomena, has no direct and scientific, logical deduction to human affairs. Scientific law, in the days of its early discovery and explanation, is tentative. Typical of this is the statement, "Modern scientific theory compels to a belief . . . " This admits firstly that the theory being only a theory and also modern, the possibility of modification and development if not of outright contradiction. It is, moreover, only a belief. Marx with characteristically unscientific certainty claims to have discovered and enunciated the absolute laws governing society. This absolute certainty is a fundamental and wholly pervasive aspect of the entire system. Failure to accept and apply it in practice is a sure road to failure within Russia. If one can accept credible writers, the people in general, but unofficially, view Marx with derision. Nonetheless, the certainty is repeatedly in evidence as orthodox dogma and used to instill the idea of the inevitable triumph of communism over the Capitalist evil from which it has been delivered. The Party, as the final repository of this absolute wisdom, must be obeyed in all circumstances.

Another belief fundamental to orthodox Communist theory is the Marxian Labor Theory of Value. First, as has been elaborated earlier, Marx argues at length about value, but nowhere defines what it is, being content to prove how according to his theory it is determined. This theory in the light of modern examination has been rejected by economists and is used now only as an emotional appeal to dissatisfied laborers. As part of the derived conclusions, he asserts that man's morality and problems originate with capitalism. If one accepts the Marxian idea of capitalism, it is clear that inequality and evil existed long before capitalism. Indeed, probably no one doubts that both phenomena are as old as mankind. It cannot be overlooked that Marxian theory of value refers to commodities only, whereas many things other than these have value, indeed as have all natural resources.

Again, in seeing history as being an endless conflict between the classes, Marx, with unscientific restriction, does not accept the fact that man, even in his economic activity, has always had a dual relationship, in that while there is a conflict between what the employer claims and what the employee claims, yet cooperation between the two is more a part of the whole than is difference. These and other basic fallacies are part of the problems facing Russian politics and society, in their efforts to manipulate. But the greatest failure of Marxian theory is that in trying to exercise social control over man's productive effort, the rulers have stultified man's energy, his creative faculty, the pride of individual achievement, and the pride that goes with the development of one's own ideas. It is no accident that Andrei Sakharov sees in this the failure of Russia to come up with any new scientific and cultural progress.

Errors of Economic Man

It is a common attribute of reformers to see mankind as possessing those qualities which are necessary to implement the reformers' ideas and which, in large measure, reflect the character of the reformers themselves. Thus, a man like J. S. Mill expects that reason will triumph over evil. Freud, who was obsessed with sex and his own psychologically disturbed nature, saw the relationship of sex as being at the core of man's dissatisfaction and problems. An extreme example of this attitude is Marx. He was obsessed with man as an economic result. Thus he goes so far as to say that the nexus between a man and his son is an economic one. Any father can verify the fact that this is anything but the truth. Since man, according to Marx, is the result of the mode of production, then to alter the mode of production was to alter man's nature. This meant eliminating private ownership of property. Elaborated with fierce emotional intensity and hatred by Lenin, this has become a vital aspect of Russian policy. The failure of this has led to many difficulties, and circumstances have compelled the acceptance of some elements of capitalism with no great success, though perhaps commensurate with the relationship of the dogma.

The idea that man, being fundamentally a social being, would under the circumstances of socialism and communism be sufficiently animated by a desire to work for the good of all rather than gain to oneself, has proved illusory. Man, in Russia as anywhere, is doubtlessly working from necessity. Appeals to patriotism, the inevitability of being part of Communist growth, the picture of the glorious future, the intense propaganda in the education system, the fear of Capitalist aggression against their system, and so forth, are all part of the search for an energizing incentive. The slow rate of growth of the economy bears witness to the lack of success so far.

"A spectre is haunting Europe—the spectre of communism." With this sentence Karl Marx began the opening chapter of his *Communist Manifesto.* Whatever this sentence represented when it was written a century and a quarter ago, it must be asserted with increased emphasis today. But it applies not only to Europe but to the entire world.

As outlined by Nickolai Lenin, its chief designer, as a process it has spread its authority by "subterfuge and stratagem," and by military conquest over Eastern Europe and across Asia, over some dozen formerly autonomous countries. Its dupes and emissaries, openly and by infiltration, have entered into the life of every country on the globe. They have penetrated into the most secret aspects of government, they preach from our pulpits, they openly teach their dogmas in our schools and universities, they use and manipulate the news media of the world, their representatives sit in our parliaments, and they sit on the executive committees of the trade unions—which they avowedly are out to destroy. No reform anywhere in the world is safe from the intrusive tactics to destroy and distort it to their ends.

Misrepresentation, terror, hatred, and violence are elevated to virtues so long as they are designed to extend the authority and control of communism. The meaning of language has been distorted. Conquest has been labelled as liberation. Democracy is now used to describe a ruthless oligarchical dictatorship; elections are now merely processes for appointing party agents. Education is now enforced acceptance of party dogma. Its own dissidents are exiled, imprisoned, or placed in asylums for the insane. Indoctrination where conquest has been made, is by forced attendance at classes, forced labor, or by death to the recalcitrant.

Its agents are active throughout the world as the instigators and participants of dissension, disruption, and terror; as designed tactics. With frenzied haste it is building the most powerful military might the world has ever seen, its equipment including weapons of horror and destruction far beyond anything mankind has previously known. Its naval and spy ships sail all the oceans of the world.

Consistent with the dictum that "religion is the opiate of the people," constant efforts are made in all Communist countries to repress it; leaders often being imprisoned for their beliefs and practices. Its own citizens are denied freedom of movement, freedom of association, freedom of thought, and access to information disagreeing in any way with its own dogma. In places it has built an unscaleable wall flanked by tank traps, barbed wire, electric fences, and guards armed with machine guns and supported by savage dogs, to prevent escape from its control. Walls to keep enemies out have been familiar devices throughout history. This is the first wall constructed to keep citizens in. All its leaders, from Lenin to those in control today, and all official statements (none other than official ones are permitted), preach an implacable, never ending war against all who oppose its dogma, its control, and its controllers. Philosophy, art, literature, and all forms of individuality are put on the procrustean bed of Party control, censorship, and conformity. All culture is reduced to the crushing demands of the Department of Propaganda. The Party poses as the voice and the freely expressed will of the people; whereas it claims also to be the wise informed and authoritarian controllers as well.

The protagonists picture themselves as the avatars of a new millenium when poverty, inequality, exploitation of man by man, and the evils of society will end, under the all-embracing umbrella of communism. In contrast to this allure, the reality as seen wherever communism has taken control is that civilization is faced with the dire threat of a new dark age, when the gains of the past ages will have been swept away in a reign of terror and enforced conformity and submission.

People of the world unite. We have nothing to lose but our gains.

LENIN

As with the teaching of Marx, it is not intended here to give a full analysis of the dogmas of Lenin, but only a consideration of such aspects as have an immediate and influential effect on current political philosophy and practice, and what contribution it can make to the evolution of civilization.

Lenin wrote voluminously, often stressing how according to his methods the proletariat could attain its objectives: the dictatorship of the proletariat, culminating in the Communist state. Most significant and repeatedly in evidence, is his advocacy of violence. Taken from the booklet *Left Wing Communism* are a few quotations: "The hatred is ... the beginning of all wisdom;" "ruthless war;" "a long stubborn war of life and death;" "mass movements, parliamentary and terrorists." Similar expressions recur again and again in his writing. Any other method of achieving communism is impossible. He affirms, "all countries will inevitably have to go through what Russia has gone through, and again, "we rejected individual acts of terror only out of consideration of expediency." "The dictatorship of the proletariat is a persistent struggle, sanguinary and bloodless, violent and peaceful, military and economic." As a means to this end perhaps the most significant quotation reads, " ... if need be ... to resort to all sorts of devices, manoeuvres, and illegal methods, to evasion and subterfuges in order to penetrate into the trade unions."

The degree of their success is measured by the fact that Communists now openly occupy executive positions in the highest union ranks. One of the devices most frequently advocated is the necessity of combining illegal with legal activity, any being unable to do so being labelled as "very bad revolutionaries." He refers to taking advantage of—

> ... every fissure however small in the ranks of our enemies, by taking advantage of every possibility however of gaining an ally among the masses, even though this ally be temporary, vacillating, unstable and unreliable, and conditional. Those who do not understand this do not understand even a grain of Marxism.

In another circumstance he speaks of giving support as a rope supports the man who is being hanged. In the light of such directions what credence can be given to the Russian promise contained in the idea of detente? The answer must surely be none at all. The Communist declarations on this will be more fully discussed later on when considering how far Russian policy is the implementation of Lenin's ideas.

He frequently directs attention to the trade unions for carrying out his designs. He writes of "proletarians schooled in numerous strikes," and "most easily accessible form of organization, the trade unions." As the process of the schooling, he says that "the economic strike develops into a political strike and the latter develops into insurrection." From examples occurring around us, the strike weapon can be seen to be merging the two earlier types, and with indications of gradual application of the final stage. Surely he who runs must read.

The Communist movement always advertises itself as Democratic, but the writings of Lenin and their application in Communist countries, and in some trade unions, show the very opposite. To quote Lenin again:

> Without the strictest discipline, the truly iron discipline in our Party . . . absolute centralization and the strictest discipline of the proletariat are one of the basic conditions for victory over the bourgeoisie . . . not a single political or organizational question is decided, by any State institution in our republic without the guiding instruction of the Central Committee of the Party.

A further summary of the directions given by Lenin is not necessary. In the following he does so himself: "Unless we are able to master all methods of warfare, we stand the risk of suffering great and sometimes decisive defeat."

Though Stalin has been in some degree repudiated, it is worthwhile to show how he saw the methods of Lenin's policies. In *Foundations of Leninism* he writes, "The dictatorship of the proletariat is the dictatorship of the proletariat over the bourgeoisie untrammelled by law and based on violence." Referring to the need for majority support he writes, "No proofs are adduced, for this absurd thesis cannot be justified theoretically or practically." And again, "The revolutionary will accept a reform in order to use it as a means to link legal with illegal work, in order to use it as a screen behind which to carry on his illegal activity."

What then can be said of the teaching of Lenin? It must be said that throughout Communist literature and official statements, Lenin and Marx are linked together as the guide by which all Communist policy must be checked. Surely among all the evil characters of history Lenin must occupy a leading position. His writings show a complete disregard for morality; deceit, trickery, ruthlessness, and violence are the essentials for the enactment of Communist policy. In conclusion, it must be said that communism is not a political philosophy but a campaign of world conquest.

9

MARXIST-LENINIST THEORY IN PRACTICE IN RUSSIA

Having devoted time to the Marxist-Leninist theories, and advocacy of methods to be used, it is necessary to follow this line into its application in Russia. For this purpose it is intended to quote extensively from the Russian book, *Social Science Textbook for the Graduating Class of Secondary Schools and Secondary Specialized Educational Institutions*; the eighth edition of which was published by the State Publishing House for Literature in Moscow, in 1970, and rereleased in the United States by the American Bar Association of Chicago.

This book is particularly valuable as it presents, in most authoritative form, the information, or perhaps better, the doctrine or propaganda to which each Russian child is subjected as part, an essential part, of his learning in his impressionable years. As will be shown, a sound knowledge of what is contained in the book is a prerequisite of successful progress in the school and later society. The purpose of the social studies course is stated to be, "the education of the entire population in the spirit of scientific communism," and it refers to the general sociopolitical and ideological laws governing the emergence and development of the Communist system. For this purpose, two hour-long periods are devoted each week. After this "educational" book has been examined, it will be necessary to show by equally authoritative statements by leading Party and State officials, how far these ideas are put into practice. To its credit, the book devotes a deal of early space to the elaboration and explanation of certain laws of science with which few people would disagree. But contrary to the spirit of science these are presented with most unscientific authoritarianism, where the spirit is not one of enquiry and curiosity, but accepted certainty. This can be illustrated in the following reference to the origin of matter: "Concepts of a universal mind that 'creates the world' are also in monstrous contradiction to natural science . . . how could it create the world from nothing? All phenomena is explained by natural causes."

The natural scientific enquiry would surely be how natural causes came into existence in the first place. This is neglected in spite of the emphatic assertion that results always have a cause. To ask this question and leave it unsolved, as it obviously would be, would of course break the bars of "scientific" completeness. Again much of the basis of Communist teaching is dependent on the Hegelian Dialectic, of the result of competing forces. Following Marx, Russian teaching transfers this from the world of matter to that of human relationships. As has been said earlier, a criterion for the existence of life, as distinct from inorganic matter, is that a constant stimulus does not always produce a constant response. This would imply that the dialectic process does not inescapably apply to human affairs. Nevertheless the laws are thus projected by Marxist teaching. It claims, "Marxist-Leninist teaching reflects reality."

> For the first time ideology commonly understood as a system of social views became a science concerned with studying objective laws of historical development. Marxism is a harmonious system of scientific views about the general developmental laws of nature and society, the victory of socialist revolution. . . .

This unscientific certainty runs through the entire book. Marxist-Leninist assertions are continually referred to as absolute, "verified by socialist change throughout all history," and predicted into the future. This early indoctrination must tend to inculcate a ready acceptance of all teaching presented in the course, a reluctance to suspend judgment, and a failure to consider any other than official statements as interpreted by Communist teaching and beliefs.

In applying the laws of science to society, the statement is made that the toilers in association produce more than the total of individual efforts, and further, that society's growth results from learning about all the treasures mankind has produced. One can accept both of these rather obvious statements, but the deduction made from them is subject to serious logical doubt. This is the law of, "Dialectics, the teaching about universal interrelation and development in the world. . . . Within a given phenomenon or within a society . . . a correlation producing the single law-governed process permeating the world."

It should at least be open to question that reason operates only according to the laws of physical matter or that Marxist-Leninist theory alone has been confirmed by the entire practice of social development of the internationalist revolutionary movement. Having "established" the association of human and material relationship, the next affirmation is that "Marxist materialism is organically related to Dialectics, Marxist philosophy as a whole therefore has been given the name of Dialectic Materialism." This is followed by the unquestioned statement, "Materialism, as a rule, is the philosophy of the advanced progressive classes in society . . . the foundation of the working-class-world view." As indicated earlier, the problem of the mystery of existence having been solved as a statement, it would appear not satisfying to all minds. Idealism as associated with religion is here rejected: "Religion is a fantastic distorted image of the world in Man's consciousness. . . . Clearly these ideas [ideas on religion] correspond perfectly with the ideas of the exploited classes since they distract the toiling masses from the revolutionary struggle." In passing, attention might be drawn to the Four Gospels and the teaching of other religions, which have at times quite a deal to say on social matters.

Society's Development

As a preliminary to the teaching of "The Doctrine of Society's Development" comes the statement that all the problems of social growth and world events "are all answered by Marxist teaching on society's development by historical materialism." A little further on comes the assertion, "Labor is the sole source of all the riches created by mankind in the course of its history." It surely is not irrelevant to refer to earlier statements against activity in a vacuum, and how by dialectic we learn that later development grows from earlier circumstances, by pointing out that the source of all riches is the earth itself. Next we are told, "Thus man's social existence determines his consciousness." And through all runs the preconditioning of the productive process. It is surely relevant that all societies, regardless of social and economic life, have developed religious beliefs.

Following the preliminary presentation is a brief survey of man's production and social evolution—which is referred to as a form of socialism based on scarcity—to modern capitalism. Two points may be made. First, social organization suitable to primitive existence does not necessarily apply to all forms of society; a fact which Marx himself points out. Also, at the primitive level man had not evolved sufficiently to make any great degree of property right either necessary or possible; but to the degree effective in such a society, property rights in hunting equipment, territory, and so forth did exist. That property rights have increased, but not created, inequality is not followed by the conclusion that private property should be abolished. No one advocates the abolishing of motor cars because people are killed by cars. The cure is not to abolish private property but to regulate it. More detailed reference to this matter will be made later.

Several pages are devoted to exposing, according to communism, the evils of capitalism, with its antisocial motives and results, and contrasting it with "Marxist-Leninism, our society's ideology which reflects the society's interests."

This contention gains no support in practice as seen in the writings of Solzhenitsyn and Sakharov, who with many other dissidents, repeatedly refer to the members of the Communist party as a privileged self-creating élite. In support of itself, the Communist party asserts, "The great October Socialist Revolution is an outstanding event in mankind's history." This doubtlessly has a deal of truth, but that the results of the event are those the Party claims, gain little support from events since then. Indeed, from records it is proposed to show that it created one of the most totalitarian systems the world has ever seen.

The unfortunates compulsorily studying the social-studies course are told:

> "Since they [the Capitalists] possess the means of production, the exploiting classes wield great economic powers which they use to impose their will on society. Any action directed against the interests of the exploiters is held illegal and prosecuted by law. Social relations in a class society are regulated by law and judicial norms expressing the will of the ruling class.... The ruling class has the organs of power in its hands such as the police, the army, the courts, and prisons ... the state is the instrument of class domination by the exploiters of the exploited.... Despite the right of universal suffrage, power is held by the wealthy bourgeois.... It is not reluctant to use bribery, fraud, and falsification in order to prevent the toiling masses from ruling the state."

All this is contrasted to a Socialist Democracy with "equality before the law, freedom of speech, of the press, of assembly, inviolability of the law . . . ." In spite of this, it is common knowledge inside and outside Russia that "slandering the state" is a punishable offense subject to the penalty of imprisonment, and even of committal to a mental institution where drugs, perhaps appropriate to mentally disturbed, are administered. The existence of an underground press is well known and is repressed more severely than in Czarist days. With regard to the repressive nature of Capitalist society, the unfortunate student does not know, unless by illicit means, that Capitalist governments are quite frequently elected by votes mainly derived from employees, where men and women from the shop floor and the shearing shed often attain cabinet rank and have been known to become prime minister. The student knows nothing of the great mass of labor laws protecting the conditions of employees.

That class struggle is the motive force of all history in all exploiter formations can easily be refuted by men such as Erasmus, Luther, Newton, Copernicus, Descarte, and a host of others among whom economic motives were perhaps wholly absent. After such a distortion of Capitalist society and processes of history, many pages are devoted to the idea that mass "effort and revolution has been and will be necessary and inevitable to achieve the aims of Marxist-Leninism." It may be said with certainty that in history, no critical period can be found in which the masses did not take the decisive part." And again, "There is no area of social life in which the decisive role does not belong to the masses."

By reference to the controlling role of the Party in Russian social and political life it can readily be seen how little the rulers of Russia believe their own teaching. This aspect is to be discussed more fully at a later stage.

Decline of Capitalism

In typical fashion each chapter of the book opens with a significant affirmation glorifying some person or aspect of Communist life. Thus, "having brought to light the laws governing the production and distribution of material goods, Marx showed that the causes of the unavoidable downfall of capitalism and the victory of socialism are rooted in the economics of social life." As a description and elaboration of capitalism he quotes John Bunyan who lived two hundred years before Marx: "Everything becomes the object of buying and selling, homes, land, honours, rank, counties, kingdoms, desires, pleasures, conscience, honor, wives, husbands, children, masters, servants, life, blood, bodies and souls." One is compelled to wonder how far the Russian student believes this fantasy.

Several pages are devoted to a picture of Capitalist society. A full reply to these misrepresentations would be tedious and purposeless. One typical statement should suffice: "Under capitalism the products of labor are the private property of those who do not produce them or spend a single minute of time in their production." That owners of property do not spend one minute of time in production is too inaccurate to need to illustrate its absurdity. The statement condemns itself.

It is interesting to show the self-contradiction displayed when the Labor Theory of Value is enunciated: "The consumer value of bread, butter . . . lies in the fact that they satisfy people's food requirements." Later it is given an illustration: "If two commodities are made one of which would last two years and the other five years that form B would be more advantageous."

Would one be justified in saying that this would be identical with that forbidden word "profitable?" There is nothing to indicate that more labor time has been spent on one article than on the other. It would seem that there is in "advantage," a value or something other than labor time. To illustrate further it can be said that a pair of shoes made from leather from different cattle or from different parts of the same hide would differ in quality and so the production would differ in value. Examples of this sort could be multiplied. In spite of all effort by farmers, no one has yet, after not minutes but years of effort, succeeded in producing meat, hides, or wool of identical quality. Several pages are devoted to discussion on values, some of them being sound, but the conclusion that "capitalism can and will be defeated by creation of the new much higher productivity of socialism," can get no support from the lower standard of living in Russia. Clearly, some part of this production is being devoted to the building up of a military system—perhaps the greatest the world has ever seen—to the detriment of living standards.

Some pages are devoted to the role of money in exchange. Reference is made to gold and paper money in that area. But anyone familiar with monetary theory and practice knows that the greater part of exchange is done by the mechanism of records of such exchanges shown by figures in files. Following this, several more pages are devoted to explaining the Marxian Theory of Value from a biased and selected array of statements. It condemns the idea of surplus value. But as is obvious to anyone who gives even passing thought, that unless value of goods produced is not greater than consumption in the process, no economic progress would be possible. Under any system, profit is merely the excess of production over consumption, and no economic system can endure without it. It is affirmed that "many proletarians subject to the so-called assembly line used in the capitalist production system turn into invalids at forty or forty-five."

> Plans devised by capitalist states are not binding on privately owned Capitalist companies. Redistribution of the national income by the device of the state budget plays a major role in the enrichment of the monopolies . . . through taxation . . . the toilers bear the whole burden of militarism.

It is by these and other analagous statements that the growing Russian student is persuaded to believe that the whole Capitalist system is bad. Can statements be further from truth? Following this, great play is made of a picture of toilers of all countries uniting to throw off such a system to join world communism, the old system being forced "more frequently than ever to the use of bayonets to preserve its rule." A grudging admission, however, is made that "some qualified workers there are able to own private automobiles and private small family homes," and again, "some do live under material conditions that are not bad." It is not irrelevant to say that small family homes in countries are much larger than those in Russia.

In the section devoted to "The Historic Mission of the Working Class," the following statements occur. These are made not to rebut them, but to show what the unfortunate Russian child is taught to believe.

> The proletariat, the most advanced, the most revolutionary class of bourgeois society, the proletariat . . . the most conscious . . . the best organized great army of toilers, subject like himself to forced labor. . . . By taking part in strikes the proletariat learn by experience . . . are weapons in the struggle against the class enemy. . . . As Marx said they have nothing but their chains. . . . A struggle of millions headed by the working class which is led by the Marist-Leninist Party. . . . Vengeance on exploiters for their criminal acts against the toilers.

Innumerable examples of similar expressions occur with wearying frequency. They are there for anyone wishing to have a picture of what the Communist strives to have his youth believe.

Under the heading "Economic System of Socialism," some thirty pages are devoted to a somewhat theoretical and idealist picture of USSR economy. However, a few relevant quotations are made:

> Houses for example may be rented at speculative prices. . . . Sale of commodities for personal use have been marked by rapid growth. . . . The law of the planned balanced development of the economy. . . . Five-year plans are

drafted according to the directives approved by the Party and the Government . . . the final-plan variant is approved by the USSR Council of Ministers of the USSR Supreme Soviet. . . . System of planned prices . . . it is done to control demand. . . . *Kholkoz* prices are not fixed by the state but are based on supply and demand. . . . They [factories] must make some profit. . . . Because of lack of material incentives the collective members lost interest in production."

One is not surprised by this.

Sociopolitical System of Socialism

At an early stage in the explanation of the above comes the statement: "The Communist party created by the working class organizes and directs the development of society." But in contrast to this, at a later stage comes the statement, "Admission to party membership is granted only to individuals." As a prerequisite to granting admission there is made a "detailed enquiry into a evaluation of his merits." If the party is not satisfied "understandably it has not only the power but the duty to reject his application." Understandably also, it is clear that the Party allows into its ranks only such individuals as give evidence suitable to the Party requirements. This being so, it is somewhat impossible to reconcile this position with the claim that the Communist party is created by the working class. Rather it is clear that the Party is an oligarchical system, the membership of which is not subject to any public election or restriction. It appears also that society consists of "three divisions," but surely not classes:

> the working class . . . the collective farm peasantry . . . who are gradually approaching working conditions and culture of the working class . . . and the intelligentsia. . . . All three build the new world hand in hand with the workers and peasants and serving the people's interests in its higher obligations. . . . No political privileges are attached to belonging to the working class.

But affairs in the system give ample evidence that privileges pertain to others in the society. Russians like Solzhenitsyn and

Sakharov repeatedly stress that the system has created a powerful privileged elite. "Union republics . . . may enter into direct negotiations with other states and exchange diplomatic representatives with them." Some uncertainty exists as to the precise meaning of the words "other states." If this means within the USSR itself, this is possibly true, but one has yet to hear of the diplomatic representative of the Ukraine, Georgia, or any other union member, having diplomatic representatives abroad. In spite of the claim that the republics are "autonomous," there is an admission that "particularly tenacious and harmful are the remnants of the nationalistic attitude." We are assured that "these harmful traditions have their effect," and "must be fought with utmost severity." We are not told, but no doubt the centrally controlled Party takes a lead against this most important threat to national unity. One is compelled to ask just what "autonomy" means in Communist terms. " . . .It is imperative to have a means of communication within the family of fraternal peoples." All Russian-Soviet people have freely adopted the Russian language as this means. Statements made by many who have escaped from Russia certainly discredit entirely the claim to having freely adopted anything.

In the explanation regarding what is referred to as representative organs, what is omitted or glossed over is more significant than what is said. Thus, "all state agencies derive from the Soviets, receive power from them, and are under their control." " . . . . Suffrange is universal," "voting is by secret ballot," and "candidates for deputies are nominated by the people."

Accepting these statements as accurate, it is to be noticed that candidates are nominated by the people, but what is not said is that nominees must be approved by the Party before public voting occurs. Further, nothing is said about the fact that one name only is accepted for public vote, and the most that anyone can do who is opposed to the candidate is to vote against him. Under such circumstances it is certain that the Party choice will be elected. The presentation of candidates, freely advocating their own views and criticizing those of the opponent, is of course unheard of.

In modern, non-Communist, parliamentary affairs this would not be referred to as an election at all but merely a device for ensuring the success of the party objectives. Concerning this

Solzhenitsyn says, "for forty years there have been no genuine elections." Moreover, when these representatives arrive in Moscow it must not be supposed that they legislate for the community. Their object is to endorse the directives of the Communist party during the preceding years.

When it says the Supreme Soviet chooses the government, one is left to wonder what is meant by the word "government," since it is stated that the Party is all powerful and all pervasive. It is stated that Soviet citizens enjoy broad political rights and freedoms: "freedom of speech, the press, assembly and association, and demonstration. . . . Organizations are furnished with printing presses, supplies of paper, publishing houses and newspapers, radio, motion pictures, and television." This aspect is so significant that a special section will deal with it later. For the present it can be said that masses of official evidence contradict it. One can give complete approval to the statement, "There are no rights without obligations, no obligations without rights." It would seem from much of the practice that many of the rights exist in theory only and not in practice.

The laws in labor relations show a close systematized relationship.

> . . . Every new worker signs a bilateral agreement known as a labor contract . . . management issues a service record book to the new worker. All information (family name, first name and patronymic, age, education, date of employment, profession selected, position held), is entered in the book. He is not allowed to make any alterations or additions. . . . Reason for dismissal must be registered exactly. . . . Socialist production requires unconditional strict labor discipline. . . . Socialist labor discipline is inseparable from conscientious and prompt fulfillment of the production manager's orders. . . . Violations of labor discipline are punished. . . . The local trade-union committee signs a collective contract with the management.

When one considers these requirements, it is painfully clear what control this arrangement has over the employee.

Regulations go on to say, "In calculating wages," the method is by "the rate system . . . based on wage scales. . . . The piece-rate wage is the best method of establishing the complete, direct relationship between the results of a worker's labor and his earnings." Obviously to induce greater effort "time and output norms," are in use. It seems there is needed something more than furthering the glorious cause of socialism and Socialist emulation. In other words, private gain is the best method, just as under the evil Capitalist system. All this is under the leadership of the Party.

In youth training, the *Komsomol*, in which "our country's youth spend more than ten of the best years of their life," is a "league of Communist youth closely tied to the Communist party" and is "an inexhaustible membership source for the C.P.S.U." Many pages are devoted to recording its efforts and achievements as a stirring incentive to all youth. Listed are many "voluntary organizations [which] operate on the principle of social self-help." As expressed, the "Communist party binds together all these social organizations and unions according to their activities." It seems that self-help stands in need of guidance.

While "Socialism has gained victory in all spheres of society's life and activity, it has prevailed completely," and "capitalist encirclement is therefore obsolete and without meaning." In consequence, "The conversion of socialism into communism is an objective law-governed process." In this process the "problem of private plots which of now the Kolknov peasants cannot give up . . . since they contribute to the fuller satisfaction of their personal needs." These "are to end. . . . The future of these plots is perfectly clear, they must disappear." Any visitor traveling in Russia can vouch for the fact that those working on the private plots show a degree of energy not obvious on the collective farms. Also as a reason for their existence is the fact that of produce sold on the open market, a considerable amount comes from these lots. Clearly they serve a very useful purpose.

In the section devoted to the "Material Basis of Communism," much space is devoted to saying how much better this ideal state is than the Communist version of capitalism. Division between intelligentsia, peasants, and workers"—one wonders if the intelligentsia and peasants do not work—"are to be brought closer together by changing the nature of manual labor, bringing it nearer to intellectual labor." Then all will work "with selfless labor for society's good." Under such a state the bourgeois claim that "laziness is deeply rooted in human nature" will be proved false as "slanderous accusations." All will learn to see "constructive labor as the highest aim and meaning of life." Strangely enough, "thousands of toilers will be able to compel the 'do nothings' to work conscientiously.... We must wage a battle against idlers, loafers, swindlers, hooligans, and the violators of community rules." It would seem that the expression that "victory in society's life has prevailed completely," must be used with some elasticity. "The new man and woman" will not cover his walls with magnificent canvasses whose proper place is in a museum. It leaves open the question as to whether there will be cheap prints or bare walls. According to "the predictions of the Marxist-Leninist scientific theory . . . the state will wither away." However, "authority will exist" in spite of this. As a conclusion we are told, "the withering away of the state is a complex social process . . . and will not immediately reach the necessary organizational perfection." Doubtlessly, all can agree about the "complex social process" bit. The cynics also will no doubt be relieved to know that immediate perfection is not expected. Also, those who would aspire to a nobler, "purer" life will be encouraged to know that some improvement can still be made, enabling a greater meaning and purpose to life. It is to be noted that the Communist states so far have not shown anything of the tendency to wither away. What a wonderful thing is distance, for on the contrary, to the observer outside, wherever states claiming to be implementing the scientific theories of Marxist-Leninism have been established, the opinion is fairly general that they have established totalitarianism with a thoroughness unequalled anywhere else in the world and perhaps unsurpassed even by the ancient Incas of Peru.

Education of the New Man

The heading above "means effecting a revolution [in the fullest sense] in their consciousness and behaviour."

> Yes man can be reeducated. The bourgeois sociologist and moralists are wrong. Human vices will die out with the eradication of the social conditions that generate them. Pri-

vate ownership and exploitation of man by man are the chief ones. . . . No it is not nature that is responsible for human vices but rather the system of capitalism that deforms actual human nature.

It cannot escape notice, that if one can believe the records of history, that vices are older than capitalism. "The dispute about man and his destiny has long ago progressed from theory to practice." For the creation of the new man, "the school, literature, and art, the press, radio, television, and other means of influencing man's minds and hearts, tirelessly popularize the heroism of labor." There will be "honest desire on the part of men to become purer and better, to educate themselves." The new man will first have "the scientific view of the world." "Imagine a person who has no world view. . . . Absurd are the views of bourgeois philosophers." As a "sign of ideological maturity he must know how to identify hostile ideas and dispel them."

> The study of Marxist-Leninism and Party documents is helpful, but most important is the verification of theoretical knowledge by life experience. . . . Duty according to fearless knights of the revolution is not obligation but necessity, need profound conviction, the meaning of life. . . . Socialist patriotism is one of the finest features of human nature. . . . The distinctive feature of Socialist patriotism is its intrinsic bond with internationalism.

On Marxist Atheism the student is told, "an atheist" is "someone who passionately and uncompromisingly struggles against all forms of religion."

> While Socialism has guaranteed the toilers freedom of conscience, the right to practice any religion, or to be an atheist and conduct atheist propaganda, no one in the Soviet Union has the right to avoid the obligations of citizenship by pleading religious conviction. . . . They [the churches] are poisoning people's consciousness, endangering their spiritual and moral growth. . . . In fact communism and religion are irreconcilably antagonistic.

So much for the Christian communism of the Western world.

> Religious holidays, as is well known, are connected not only with mystical rites but also with drinking, fights, and infringements of social discipline. Every Communist and Komsomol member has the duty to expose stupefaction caused by religion. . . . School boys and school girls can actively participate. . . . Religious rantings most often take place in the family circle where society's cleansing power does not reach. It is precisely from there, the family and daily life, that religious superstition must be driven out. . . . Religion represents a stronghold of ignorance.

> The new man will have a joyous attitude to work. As evidenced in—the poetry of work. . . . What an extraordinary surge of energy, what joy you experience when you have worked well. . . . For Soviet citizens work is an honor, the chief content of their lives. . . . Once you have grasped the deeper meaning of your work, understood the social significance . . . the inner readiness for heroic deeds will emerge. . . . Work was like a song.

Examples of heroism under Socialist morality are given. "A Komsomol member risks her life to snatch a child from under the wheels of a train; a volunteer policeman takes a blow meant for another from a hooligan." It should perhaps be known that such examples do occur under bourgeois morality.

Among the relics of capitalism still in existence in spite of socialism having "prevailed completely," there are—"Take for example the type of parasitism black marketing is. . . . Another most repulsive product of the former world is philistinism. Its essence is a total lack of ideology." By contrast one may report the words, "My whole life is a constant striving toward one objective, to become a good person." One young girl is reported as saying:

> She sees her purpose in life as getting married, living in security, and having fun, not in working, after all even horses die from work. . . . It is hard to find words to express one's revulsion at such vile thoughts. . . . Can any one of you say sincerely that his conscience is clear? . . . A person's daily life is not his own affair. No it is not.

On family and marriage the advice would no doubt commend itself to thinking people anywhere, and is an implied criticism of much of our current attitudes in Western society. To quote:

> Marriage based on financial considerations is considered monstrous in our society . . . the moral and ideological foundation of the family—love, friendship, mutual respect and frankness between the partners, community of views and interests, love of work, and care of the children, have acquired all the greater importance.

V.I. Lenin severely condemned the bourgeois concept of "free love."

> The moral and physical impossibility of living without the other person is exactly what love is. It takes time to make love, and a third life results. It is here where society's interest begins. . . . Sometimes young people marry too early before they have fully realized what these obligations are . . . without having learned a trade and completed their studies.

As a guide to the new man, the CPSU has included a moral code for the builders of communism. This in twelve statements is no more than a condensation of what has been elaborated earlier. It concludes, "For centuries communism was a far off dream of the oppressed, and disfranchised. Now it is becoming a reality." When one reads that "it [communism] has prevailed completely," and also reads references to the "prevalence of black marketeers, violators of labour discipline, idlers, loafers, swindlers, and hooligans, and to the existence of private plots which contribute to the fuller satisfaction of their personal needs," the words "prevailed completely" must be read with not a little caution; and it must be borne in mind that many of those guilty of these offenses have known no life other than under the authority of the Communist party.

The Party, Our Helmsman

Some twenty pages are devoted to picturing the CPSU as "Our Helmsman." However, as the social-studies textbook is produced by the State Publishing House for Literature and compiled by a team of five authors, all members of the Communist party and under general Party supervision, the book is revealed as a description of the Communist party by the Communist party for the Communist party—its version of itself. Nonetheless, even a superficial scrutiny is very revealing, both for what it says and what is omitted. At an early stage the student is told: "The CPSU is a ruling party and it is confirmed in this role by the constitution." The word "election" occurs frequently in the account but this refers in no way to election by the people, but within the party hierarchy. These words appear:

> Persons are brought into the ranks of the CPSU by ideological motives, their grasp of the just cause for which the Party struggles.... Admission to party membership is granted only to individuals ... the party CPSU devotes great care to selection and education of *cadres*.... The Komsomol is an inexhaustible membership source for the CPSU, no other single source organization gives so many members to the Party.... Communists join primary Party organizations at their job locations, industrial enterprises, construction sites, *sovkhozes, kholkozes,* government offices, institutes, Soviet Army units, educational institutions, ... There is not a single collective or sector of any importance where no party organization exists.... Thus the party is a party of persons with identical ideas.... Democratic centralism also signifies strict party discipline and subordination of the minority.

Much more to this effect occurs in the chapter devoted to the role of the Party, but sufficient amounts have been quoted to show its essential character. The party is revealed as an unelected oligarchy using all the powers of persuasion, propaganda, distortion, and suppression to maintain its control over the masses it pretends to represent.

When referring to industrial, political, and social affairs, the words "lead," "control," "direct," and "guide" frequently occur.

In fact, "There is not a single collective or sector of any importance where no party organization exists." Internationally the Party claims of the CPSU read: "It is a component and detachment with equal rights in the world Communist movement." One can ask by whom was this right granted other than by the CPSU itself. Further, having regard to the strict discipline of the hierarchical system and events in such places as Hungary and Czechoslovakia, it is clear that the CPSU tries to exercise complete authority, not equality, over the Party organizations anywhere in the world. A glorious picture is painted of the expansion of world communism to its historical destiny under the guidance, control, and assistance of the CPSU. There is no secret about the ultimate objective of world control operating from Russia. The measure of this possible success can be questioned, but the obvious fact remains that the world is in a state of turmoil which has been inflicted by their measures. It is perhaps unnecessary to say that the U.S.A. is the great evil standing in the way of Russian military expansion. To quote: "If the imperialist powers headed by the U.S.A. have so far not succeeded in drawing the world into thermonuclear war it is first of all thanks to the firm and flexible policy of the Soviet Union . . . which is gaining ever-increasing support and gratitude from all peoples."

In reply to this distortion of society both inside and outside Russia, many responsible and informed observers can be quoted, but the reply will be limited to internal sources, to men of world eminence like Solzhenitsyn and Sakharov, and official sources within Russia itself. If it has not already been accepted, the following pages and official source quotations should surely leave no lingering doubts as to what communism can potentially bring to the future of civilization. It is a vast powerful organization of propaganda, censorship, lies, militarism, and ruthless control, run by men who leave no doubt, judged by their words and deeds since 1917, that they are determinedly active in endeavoring to bring all mankind under a ruthless dictatorial system of control. That the task may be too big for ultimate success may be true; but, in trying, they have caused and will continue to cause untold damage to man and civilization.

PEACE OR PEACEFUL COEXISTENCE

In the following pages official quotations are taken from the book *Peace or Peaceful Coexistence*, published by the American Bar Association. These selections could be corroborated by *Warning to the West* by Solzhenitsyn and *My Country and the World* by Sakharov. These are men of world standing in the field of their own studies and they have had first hand experience of the conditions of which they write. The book *Gulag Archipelago*, a series of three volumes, is also available as an authoritative source of information on numerous cases of tyranny and injustice toward people who had the courage to engage in the new crime of slandering the state.

The New Man

The concept of the "new man" growing up and responding to the environment now operating in Russia is a constant theme running through innumerable statements officially put out. Indeed, it should be realized that all statements put out at least have official sanction. To quote:

> A new man is being born; is growing to manhood. He is the builder of communism and will well deserve the honor of being the first citizen to live in the beautiful community of the future.... Socialism and communism enoble man ... The fraternal Marxist-Leninist parties are educating the working people to be active builders of the new world and are instilling high moral qualities in them.... Armed with Marxist-Leninist theory and knowledge of the laws of social development the party directs the life and labor of our country to a single goal.

In the social-studies textbook it is written, "Objective factors ... creating the new man are social ownership of the means of production, socialist democracy." The degree to which evidences of the new man, "free, industrious, unselfish, and purer" is in existence, can be verified by reference to Sakharov and Solzhenitsyn. Solzhenitsyn in his series *Gulag Archipelago* gives innumerable accounts from experiences both personal and from others of the ruthless cruelty applied across the country. Sakharov informs us that the Soviet prison and camp system has "annihilated more than twenty-million people." As a world figure with a scientifically trained mind, he can be expected to speak with calm detached accuracy. Hear him:

> A definite gap has opened between words and deeds.... What is hidden is a sea of human misery, animosities, cruelty, profound fatigue, and indifference.... A multitude of drunkards and individuals gone to seed.... Many people simply vegetate. Drunkenness is epidemic everywhere.... The dissipation and tragic alcoholism of the great mass of the people including women and young people.... The per capita consumption of alcohol is thrice what it was in Tsarist Russia.... In the Russian Republic alone 10,000 drunkards collapse and freeze in the streets every year.... Groaning from the spreading epidemic of senseless brutal hooliganism and crime.

So much for the light of a glorious new day and the new man under the bright sun of communism. As a sign to the West it rather heralds a tornado of darkness and destruction. In spite of the above conditions when referring to specific areas of society, officials can say, "Communism is the most humanistic ideology and socialism is the most just order known to mankind.... Ideals for mankind and clear and liberating hopes can be provided and are being provided only by communism."

The value of the education system in creating the new man is most significant. As has been discussed earlier, *Social Science* is primarily produced for the inculcating of Party objectives in all secondary classes.

A Pravda article summarizes the position as follows: "The Communist Party and our people see in our young people dependable successors, an inexhaustible reserve of devotion to communist ideals." Especial attention is given to ideological training:

> The shaping of a Communist world view in the younger generation is closely connected with the educational, moral, and cultural level of this generation.... The process of

forming the ideological conviction of youth does not proceed spontaneously but requires qualified daily and active leadership.... The entire educational and indoctrinal process in the higher-educational institutions is directed to the formation in the students of a Marxist-Leninist world view ... to be a Communistically convinced people everywhere and always capable of carrying out the policy of our party.... Youth should not be fussed over but trained for militant work.... The Soviet teacher does not just teach. He simultaneously educates his students ... to educate them in collectivism and the ability to work and to instill in them boundless loyalty to the cause of the Communist party.... It is necessary to develop production of books which can help the Party educate all the working people in a spirit of high Communist ideals.... Books are the sharpest ideological weapons the Party and the people possess.... It is necessary to keep this weapon honed and ready.

It is most obvious from the above quotations that the party does not view education as being concerned with literature and mathematics. Education for them is a process of inculcating in the pupils' minds a firm belief in Communist teaching and practice. The degree of the success can be measured by the writing of those who know the process and see its results. Thus Sakharov says:

> The quality of education is low, especially in rural areas. Classrooms are dimly lit and crowded. The concept of free education is not extended (as it is in many non-Communist countries), to providing children with food, school uniforms, and textbooks. There are many deliberate injustices concerning the admission of students to college and graduate schools. Among them, discrimination against Jews is especially well known. But there is equally unjust discrimination against students from rural areas, against members of the intelligentsia, the children of dissidents, of believers, of persons of German origin, and in general against all those who do not have connections.... Almost no German has a higher education.... It is impossible for them to maintain their national culture and even their language is half forgotten.

Since the social-studies textbook says, "There is not a single collective or sector of any importance where no Party organization exists," one readily expects that literature, broadcasting, newspapers, the arts, and books in general play a most significant role in the attempts to create the new man in the social state suited to their objectives. Hence, "The toilers and their organizations are furnished with printing presses, supplies of paper, publishing houses and newspapers, radio, motion pictures, and television." But what is not mentioned here at all is that as in a sector of great importance, "the Party organization exists." And this is not in any unimportant and disinterested relationship. Thus:

> The Party makes use of the entire arsenal of ideological methods to form a new man. These include literature and art, the press, radio, television—all the shock forces on the ideological front.... The Party Congress and the Central Committee it elects determine what is beneficial to the people and what is harmful to them.... True Party management of the artistic process is based on authoritative knowledge on historical experience of the Party.... Management of the Party has been, is, and will be, the absolute prerequisite for a successful development of Soviet arts.... Would it be proper to open the gates of our country to the free entry of publications, films, and so forth, from the Capitalist countries? Everyone understands this would be quite wrong.... In opening the new theatre season, our playwrights, actors, and producers can continue to put into all their creative work the inspired ideals of communism in support of the Party.... Needless to say the Communist artist is in a sense a propagandist, even a statesman. The sphere of his activity can be likened to a sector of the battlefront.

When one considers that the Party provides all the material necessary for publishing and distribution, what is significant is not that the material is provided, but that the Party controls its use. For it is the Party that determines what is beneficial and what is harmful. Censorship by the Party machine in the interests of the Party is as complete as can be made possible. The existence of an underground press proves that a number of people, a growing number, is resisting this attempt at thought control. Sakharov comments, "One of the commonest causes of political repression is the reading, keeping, or passing on to friends of *samizdat* typescripts and books of undesirable content (although they are essentially harmless)." He goes on to give a list of books (most of which are well known in the West), the possession of which, if known, would result in punishment. This punishment as in the cases of Sinyovsky, Daniel, and others can result in long prison sentences for having anti-Soviet books. Others again, as in the case of Val Tarsis, can be committed to mental institutions. "Many political prisoners are nationalists from the Ukraine, the Baltic republics and Armenia."

Even though, as may be, the books are harmless, the principle involved is not; for it strikes at the very root of the authority and thought control of the Party. This of course could not be tolerated. If in a Capitalist country the possession of Communist literature were to become such a crime, a vast majority of the people would be in asylums. The asylums would not be big enough to hold even a small fraction of them. If it were a crime to be "slandering the state," we would all be in prison. The significant fact is that Western-style countries can accept criticism. Communists, as totalitarian countries, cannot withstand the force of open criticism.

As instruments of propaganda and control, what is with us referred to as the media, plays a most important role. Official quotations in support of this are common, only a limited selection from the mass available can be repeated. From Pravda:

> The higher duty of our press is to help the Communist party actively and effectively in the Communist education of the people.... The Communist party has always attached great significance to the press as the sharpest ideological weapon and a collective agitator, propagandist, and organizer.... The journalist is an active warrior in Party affairs. For him good intentions are not enough.... As long as there exists a class society, as long as there is a struggle between communism and imperialism ... there will be no full freedom of information.

The above gives all the evidence needed to show that the

Communist party has no belief whatever in the idea that people should be free to see and read what they please, or that they are capable of exercising wisdom (as the party sees it), in their own affairs. In other words, communism is the opposite of democracy.

The attitude to broadcasting is similar. "Social broadcasting is a powerful medium for the Communist educating of the working people, for the propaganda of the great ideas of Marxist-Leninism." Referring to broadcasts which reach Russia from outside it is recorded: "Some excessively trusting or insufficiently mature young people may thus swallow the poisoned bourgeois bait." The report concludes, "Television, moving pictures, radio and the press must become in the hand of the Party organization an effective weapon in educating Soviet people in the spirit of Communist ideology and morals." It is most obvious that the population of the entire Communist world is subjected day and night to a barrage of outright distortion and falsity.

How far this is successful may be gauged from the reports of R. G. Kaiser in his book *Russia: The People and the Power*. He writes, "I don't think I met any nonofficial Russian who knew the names of even half the members of the Politburo." The fact that he found widespread belief in rumours, indicates that no great reliance is placed on official reports. Concerning knowledge of the past history by the young he quotes the poet Yevetushenko, who in discussing with young people, was amazed to find that they thought the number imprisoned under the Stalin regime might have been twenty or thirty people. If this rather surprising statement is correct it is clear that in creating the society desired, no great success has been achieved. But in suppressing relevant knowledge of the past it is very successful.

Religion

It is not uncommon to find, among clergymen round the non-Communist world, members who are favourably inclined to, if not strong supporters of, communism and what it stands for. One is forced to the conclusion after reading official pronouncements and examples of cruelty toward, and oppression of, religious believers of all sects, that they have failed in their duty in two respects. Either they have equated their own perhaps well-meaning ideas as being those of communism in practice, or they have not endeavoured to read official documents and actions against religious adherence. For these viewpoints there can be little excuse. The facts are available for everyone to read. A further possible explanation is perhaps that their Christianity so professed is a very poor type, or as in the case of the representatives of the Russian churches at the World Council of Churches, almost certainly atheistic; for they, as government and Party officials must, of course, be atheists.

As far as the Communist state is concerned the problem is that as an organization owing allegiance to a power other than the Communist party, religion is basically opposed to such authority. This the Party most clearly sees and expresses. The *Social Science* says:

> But in fact communism and religion are irreconcilably antagonistic.... The struggle against religion is a struggle against religious ideology and morality.... Religious rantings most often take place in the family circle, where society's cleansing power does not reach.... It is precisely from there, the family and daily life, that religious superstition must be driven out.

In support of its efforts, in 1963, the Central Committee of the Communist party established a special "Institute for Scientific Atheism." The case against religion is clearly enunciated.

> Christianity, as is true for all religions, remains incompatible with communism; Christianity and communism, these are two completely contrary ideologies, two entirely different concepts of social life.... If we could and we have to do it, educate the entire rising generation in the spirit of scientific world outlook, then, already in the near future, religious ideology in our country will have been eliminated.... Under present conditions religion appears to be the main opponent.

Quoted in condemnation of Baptist teaching of "love towards all men:"

> They support the principle of all embracing love also to the enemies of humanity.... Criminal prosecution of hostile antisocial elements among religious groups is one of the drastic methods for cutting short subversive activity and weakening their influence on the believers.... With this in mind prosecution and conviction of such persons [should be regarded] as a means of combating banned church and sectarian groups, for alienating their followers, and for doing broad educational work among rank and file members of these organizations.

Sakharov is no less outspoken.

> Among those suffering for their convictions the religious believers constitute a large group. The persecution is a frightful tradition in all Socialist countries but nowhere (except perhaps in Albania), has it attained such scope and depth as in the USSR.... Today the religions have been so humiliated... that they have become appendages of the state.

He gives several names of men who have suffered "tragic death in a labor camp,"... the "brutal murder" of another, and several other similar examples. He describes how "one of the most inhuman forms of religious persecution is the removal of children from their parents to protect them from a pernicious religious upbringing." The course in social studies recounts with pride a case where the children were taken from the care of the parents and placed under the legal control of an atheist member of the family. And in spite of all this the Party can proclaim that freedom of conscience is guaranteed by the Constitution. As Sakharov says there is a wide disparity between words and deeds.

Communist Morality

In any statement of Communist party policy, method, and objective, the word "morality" occurs repeatedly, often accompanied by the words Socialist, Communist, and scientific. It should be clear from the following just what this means in Communist party language. Any reading of the works of Marx and of Lenin shows (particularly those of Lenin who more than any one else set the pattern for Communist ethics and action) that hatred is a fundamental emotion to true communism. "Hatred . . . is the beginning of all wisdom. . . . And hatred for the class enemy is necessary because one cannot be a fine fighter for the people, for communism, if one does not know how to hate the enemy." This concept is clearly expressed and exemplified in official statements and actions. This was most clearly expressed by Lenin in an address to the Young Communist League in October 1920 when he said, "We say that morality is entirely subordinated to the interests of the class struggle" and "morality is what serves to destroy the old exploiting society and to unite all toilers around the proletariat which is building up a new Communist society." Again, in a more recent Party statement in 1965, "The lofty principles of Communist morality to the Communist cause and love of the socialist motherland are organically united with these moral values. . . . Communism represents the highest form of humanism and morality."

This morality in practice is most clearly expressed as follows: "Communists must regard themselves as free, indeed morally obliged to violate the principles as truthfulness, respecting life, etc., when it is clear that more harm than good would be done by adhering to such principles." When it is realized that morality, as previously stated, is that which advances the Communist cause, it is most obvious that anyone who relies on the words of a Communist member, except insofar as it supports Communist objectives is completely deceived.

Communist policy and practice is clearly an illustration of Lenin's direction to use any subterfuge, trick, or stratagem to obtain the objectives. When referring to Soviet action Solzhenitsyn uses such phrases as, "inhuman ideology," "a system which deceived the workers in all its decrees," "the disguises that communism has assumed," "the essence of communism is beyond human understanding," and "both the theory and practice of communism are completely inhuman." And these opinions are from men who know and have suffered harsh penalties for no other reason than that they had the conviction and courage to criticize the outrages they saw around them. As for the "glorious society" of the future, one can only say with the strongest possible hope that the spread of communism will be not only checked but rolled back. As both our writers affirm all too frequently, time is running out.

Communist View of the West

Fundamental to the idea of inculcating in Russian citizens a belief in the superiority of their principles and practice over those of non-Communist countries, is a most wild and unprincipled distortion of them. They are pictured as decadent in the extreme, ruthless, oppressive of the laboring majority, class ridden—with the entire system of society geared to maintain and increase the privileges of the ruling class and the subjection of those on whom their wealth depends and doomed to destruction. Thus:

> Furthermore modern capitalism must be systematically presented as a regime suffering from incurable ulcers and vices, and doomed historically to extinction.... Since they possess the means of production, the exploiting classes wield great economic power, which they use to impose their will on society. Private ownership ... is declared to represent society's unshakable foundation. Any action directed against their interests is held illegal and is prosecuted by law. Social relations in a class society are regulated by laws and juridical norms expressing the will of the ruling class.

When we realize the vast extent of labor laws in all Western countries, the systems of arbitration and so forth, one can only ask, "Can anything be further from the truth?" Equally impossible is the statement, "Thus the toilers bear the whole burden of militarism." Any taxpayer who is not a wage earner as well as those who are, surely can only wonder what is the state of mind of one who could write such a distortion.

Following a denunciation of the Russian Duma of 1912 are the words, "Bourgeois parliaments today are similar, they are mostly composed of industrialists, bankers, high government officials, managers, and lawyers of monopolistic corporations." The unfortunate student reading this will not know that a president of U.S.A. was a peanut farmer. And in many non-

Communist countries, members of parliament can and do belong to parties representative of employees' interests and bearing such names as Labor party; where employees from the shearing shed and shop floor can and do attain cabinet rank. Indeed, Australia has had as Prime Minister one who was a state train driver something not yet achieved in Russia, and another, who was a trade-union secretary. To keep up this distortion, Krushchev is reported as referring to those Russians, who after returning from a visit to the U.S.A. or elsewhere and seeing "one side . . . such a person deludes himself that is bad enough. It is much more if he spread everywhere . . . the wrong views and impressions imposed on him. . . . Such people who have risen to the bait of bourgeois propaganda should be corrected."

And how is this done?

U.S. foreign policy is officially described as the "policy of the big stick," "dollar diplomacy," "nuclear blackmail," and "policy from the position of strength."

> If the imperialist powers headed by the United States have so far not succeeded in driving the world into thermonuclear war, it is, first of all, thanks to the firm and flexible policy of the Soviet Union . . . a policy which is gaining ever-increasing support and gratitude from all peoples.

Countless similar distortions of the West exist. Does anyone need more to show Russian tactics, hate, and distortion?

Convergence: Peaceful Coexistence

Just as in the days before the outbreak of war in 1939 when the credibility of statements by Hitler was under question, so the credibility of statements by Communists are under question today. In those days were people who accepted as reliable, statements by Hitler that he had no further territorial ambitions. These people were prepared to believe, as to do so was much easier and less demanding of effort than if the evidence had been allowed to outweigh the words.

In similar manner, to accept Russian statements has an appeal to many, among them being those who find it easier to accept the line of least resistance and to do nothing. Also, there are self-styled intelligentsia, a number of people all over the world who with a lofty scorn of the governments of their own countries are ever ready to accept the words in spite of the evidence of deeds. Both Solzhenitsyn and Sakharov refer repeatedly to the "illusions of Western intelligentsia," despite the overwhelming evidence of deeds. Those of us whose memories go back to the year before 1939 can recall the slogan "The Common Front," which was a Communist-inspired slogan to unite with Communists all these forces who saw the threat of war. It was to be condemned as a Capitalist brawl about who should exercise control over the masses. In no small degree this was responsible for the poor effort put up by France in the early stages of the war. Following the German attack on Russia, the comrades immediately reversed their direction and marched heroically backward in a holy crusade. After the war the popular slogan became "peaceful coexistence," and now "detente." Like the rose, the name does not alter the nature. To the non-Communist world, detente is seen as a situation where the West and the Communist world can agree to accept differences and will have peaceful trade and cultural exchange with each other. So it becomes necessary to define this grand word in Russian terms. Apart from the innumerable statements by Marx and Lenin and down to the present rulers of Russia and the unending conflict, some people are still prepared to believe statements from Russian sources which claim to aim for a situation of peace. There is some opinion that technological forces will drive the two differences together in a convergence.

What is the official Russian policy? "They ignore the fact that these two countries are diametrically different. They [the technical factors], do not eliminate the basic socioeconomic contradictions between capitalism and socialism, but deepening them, create the objective prerequisites for Socialist change." Khruschev defined it as follows, "The policy of peaceful coexistence as regards its social content, is a form of intense economic, political, and ideological struggle of the proletariat against the aggressive forces of imperialism in the international arena." Elsewhere and more recently, "Peaceful coexistence . . . does not imply a temporary absence of war of a breathing space between clashes . . . an active and intense struggle in the course of which socialism irresistibly attacks while capitalism suffers one defeat after another." It cannot, however, be overlooked that Khrushchev blames the aggressive forces of imperialism. A second writer, N. Shishlin also informs us that "socialism irresistibly attacks."

Events around the world, as those in Angola, Ethiopia, and other countries leave no doubt as to who is the aggressor. What is the latest version as stated by Brezhnev as a time-winning device during which the forces of the USSR and the United States will not engage in armed conflict, but during which the USSR reserves the right to help all people endeavoring to throw off the "yoke of imperialism?"

But what has Sakharov to say on the subject? Emphatically referring to detente, he speaks of "the illusion of some people . . . disarmament cannot be separated from the other basic elements of detente; overcoming the secretiveness of Russian courts, strengthening international trust, and weakening the totalitarian character of our country." He outlines what are the necessary elements of detente, regrettably all absent:

> These include disarmament, inspection, end of secrecy, and free, open communication between East and West. Is there any doubt that this would mean the end of communism as we know it? And the rulers of Russia are most clearly well aware of this.

No amount of persuasion from an outsider or repetition of official statements can be half as persuasive as to the real nature of communism and its objectives, as an examination of the writings of our two authors, both men of international standing and high repute. Nothing can equal the clear logical statements and pictures by the scientifically trained mind of Sakharov, or the moral intensity of Solzhenitsyn. Both have seen and suffered under the totalitarian regime. Both repeat the urgency of the problem, lest the entire world fall under the control of this tyrannical system. What is needed is not more evidence, but will. This, both bitterly regret, appears to be lacking.

Political Future: Spread of Communism

Having devoted some consideration to the matter of mankind's future insofar as is associated with physical conditions, attention can be returned to man's relationship with his fellow man. This as has elsewhere been referred to as the problem of associative living. If even two persons associate for any length of time arrangements for smooth relationship, whether stated or implied, will emerge. In the wider society of the state, these relationships become regulations and laws. Laws are enunciated and enforced (or endeavoured to be enforced), by government. In simple analysis, governments can be divided into two classes: majority rule as in the theory on which democracy rests; and in the various forms of oligarchy or dictatorship and its extreme form of totalitarianism.

In terms of designation, dictatorships are classed as of the Right or of the Left. Those of the Right are distinguished not so much by differing techniques of repression, but perhaps by the attitude to private property and to their opponents. Opponents are usually members of one or more of the Marxist theories or parties. Dictatorships of the Left are readily identified by their declared opposition to private property and their support from local and overseas Marxist parties. Both the Left and Right are guilty in various degrees of suppression of the opposition, freedom of association, freedom of expression, and other rights. Parties of the Right are the subjects of considerable condemnation in the world press and by such organizations as Amnesty International. To be styled a leftist, all that is necessary is for some strong personality to seize government, dispose of his opposition by death or exile, denounce capitalism, distribute some of the property among his followers, derive support from the Communist powers, and call himself a Socialist.

Political antagonism today is largely a matter of implementing the ideas which democracy is supposed to represent as against those of the rising powers of communism. Is communism as a form of government the wave of the future? It is obvious that communism as a form of government, nonexistent though advocated before 1917, has spread in one form or another over much of the earth. What are the prospects of its further spread and why is this spread possible? It is not too much to say that any organization or government which is managing quietly and successfully would not be subject to any serious possibility of being displaced. It has become trite to say that the world is in a state of turmoil. The inadequacies and the injustices are obvious on all sides. In desperate situations, desperate remedies are accepted. Communism promises to abolish these evils, and despite the examples of Russia and other Communist regimes as now operating, people are ready to accept the promise.

This is because of differing emotions held by those who accept the promise. First are the idealists. They see the evil around and hope that under communism these evils will disappear. As has been quoted earlier, Marxist theory condemned religion as the "opiate of the people." It is further condemned as the great opponent of communism, as it rightly is, and as a superstition which must be rooted out. Yet it is not rare to hear prominent Christian clergy who try to see communism as the expression of Christ's teaching. Similarly, there is an effort by some to see Chinese Communism as the modern expression of Buddhism. It is tragic to see sincere people who would equate communism as the practical expression of their ideals.

On the other side, are those whose main motivating force is hate. Lenin the architect of the Russian Revolution, writing on Left-Wing Communism in England said, "The hatred . . . is in truth the beginning of all wisdom." As a motive force hatred is perhaps the strongest human emotion. Violence and death are its methods. In spite of all protests nothing is clearer than that communism, in attaining power, has caused death and disaster on a scale never before seen on earth. Does that auger a desirable life for the future?

People believe, or persuade themselves that they believe, that capitalism is doomed and a gentle nudge or a violent push are justifiable ways of expediting the slow process of history. Any effort to increase the difficulties of government are approved. It is not enough to wait for capitalism to destroy itself or to wait for majority support. Stalin clearly, in his explanation of Leninism, showed his intolerance of majority decision when he said, "No proofs are adduced [for majority decision], for this absurd thesis cannot be justified either theoretically or practically." That this is not a repudiated theory was demonstrated by the Party in Portugal where with a vote of little more than one-tenth of the population they attempted to take control. In addition to the sections advocating Communist methods, there is a third much less well-known group who, ambitious for power and scornful of the mass of the people to be ruled, see themselves as the organizers and controllers of a single world rule. In this they are closely allied with Communist objectives.

Though communism has spread as an aggressive minority movement, except in the limited areas of Kerala in India and in San Merino, it is a worldwide menace. In its "takeovers," the methods are clear. First it must be realized that there are no mass movements in the sense that there is a large body of public opinion who freely and of their own volition, set out to attain a certain result. They are stimulated, brainwashed, threatened, and directed to work for objectives pointed out to them by those who claim to be working for their interests. In the appeal to the people the full intention is not made clear. Reliance is placed on popular slogans: "Bread, Peace, and Land;" "Land for the Peasants;" "Worker Control;" "Patriotic Front;" and so forth. All have done good service. When the governments are established, names such as People's Republic are used. In furtherance of its objectives the party is constructed as a rigidly disciplined organization, hierarchial in system and ruthless in method.

The system is fully spelled out in the works of Lenin and would well repay study by anyone who would understand the movement. Until the parties repudiate by word and deed the tactics and teachings of Lenin, it must be held that a system built on these ideas holds no hope for a better world. Party members are trained in methods of control of subordinates and in the best means of taking control of any organization which may be useful to the cause. Plans are laid well in advance. In short, as the exponents of the system repeat, they are engaged in a war, a fight to the finish. Attention must be drawn to the tactics of participating in popular discontents; fanning them to a flame; if possible, taking a guiding role; doing all possible to rouse discontent with the existing establishment, and having themselves seen as holding a policy out to benefit the good of all. By this means, "by all sorts of devices, maneuvers, and illegal acts linked with legal means, evasion, and subterfuges," as quoted by Lenin, they seek to make themselves respectable.

In practical application, the spread may be engineered from

within or from without. In the first phase of expansion, enthusiasm outran discretion. Thus abortive attempts were made in Germany, Finland, Hungary, Greece, Austria, North Iran, Korea, and later Indonesia, to name a few examples. Experience has taught a new technique. The outbreak of war gave communism its great chance. Red Armies were there to support local effort, whether having a degree of internal support or without it. Familiar now is the method of giving support and training with words, arms, and manpower to uprisings. In those East European countries under Communist rule, the Red Army was either there in fact, or an ever-present threat. Subsequent events in Hungary in 1966 and in Czechoslovakia in 1968, clearly showed that it was not an idle threat. Failure in such places as Malaysia, Indonesia, and Chile showed the error of attempts where military support was lacking. Cuba is an exception to this rule. Later, where strength has given confidence, aid is openly and successfuly given in the case of South Vietnam, Cambodia, Angola, Ethiopia, and so forth.

An interesting development was seen in Somalia where after the Soviet had succeeded in establishing friendly government backing, they were finally expelled after further support was refused. This was no doubt due to the fact that the government of Somalia could see that support was perilously close to control. Now the indications are that as a warning to Somalia and all others who may be watching, refusal to accept "support" will be punished. As the result of military supplies openly given to Ethiopia, Somalia has been defeated in war. The end is not yet known.

In Western Europe the situation is in an unstable and precarious balance. The new attitude, as expressed today, is referred to as Eurocommunism. With various degrees of support the movement exists in all Western countries; strong in France and especially so in Italy. This new development poses several questions. It is voiced as democratic, being more tolerant and cooperative with other parties, permitting freedom of expression and movement, with approval for universal franchise, and opposed to domination from Russia.

The questions which puzzle observers are threefold: Are these expressions genuine or deceptive? Can such toleration be exported to the East? Can Russian Communism adjust itself to the new type and will it allow these changes to go unchecked? The claims of sincere desire to cooperate with others is liable to the charge that we have heard all this before, as in the cases of Hungary, Rumania, and so forth. But in extenuation of these examples, it can be said that the ever-present threat of the Red Army may have nullified any genuine liberal ideas. Further, the experiences of Hungary and Czechoslovakia, where there was attempts to establish "Communism with a new face," would certainly make anyone cautious in accepting the statements as being sincere. However, some evidence is not lacking that patriotism here is stronger than the fear or the wish to be incorporated in the Russian system. Some additional support is given to the viewpoint by the fact that East-West trade is on the increase. Moreover, borrowing by East Europe from Western banking systems has increased considerably; from twenty-four billion U.S. dollars in 1974 to an expected total of 45.3 billion in 1976. Could this indicate a more conciliatory attitude to the West, or is it a realization that only by such borrowing of money, machinery, and techniques, can the East hold the support of its people? Information as to the relative standards of living cannot be held from them. Communist parties, in particular in Western Europe, must be clearly aware of the disparity.

But in spite of all claims of toleration no mention is made with regard to private property. This subject is of course at the basis of all Communist theory. One cannot identify communism as operating within a system of private property. The existence of Communist controlled municipalities in Italy could be achieved with a policy of, slowly and with restraint, hastening all impulsive moves. Time alone can tell. The fundamental question is, "Are the parties more committed to the strictly interpreted tenets of communism, or will national patriotism, supported by some evidence of the benefits of Western style of government, triumph over the existing defects of now well-known Marxist theory and methods?

Can these ideas be transferred to the East? It is clear from official Russian statements and from events in Hungary and Czechoslovakia that such deviation is, or was, anathema to the Russian idea. The increasing publicity given to dissidents, publicity both within and outside, is an indication that perhaps the people may force some relaxation of control. Despite the practice of promotion within the system, depending on orthodoxy, it is impossible to train men as scientists, engineers, and managers without at the same time training them to think on all problems. Recent attempts to hold worldwide party conferences where official pronouncements could emanate with resultant Russian hegemony over parties abroad, have not been successful. If a Communist government could be established in another European country further evidence would emerge. The Russian build-up of war preparations on land, at sea, and in the air, the giving of aid to elements opposing established governments, or the establishing of puppet governments abroad, give no support to any hope that Communist policy of increasing domination is declining. As in the past, the use of foreign policy was proved a successful means of rousing patriotism and diverting attention from problems at home. So if one takes a world view on broad strategic lines, the appearances do nothing to support an optimistic outlook. Sympathetic or pro-Russian influence is strong in the Red Sea region, a main arterial route for world trade. Influence is strong on the East and West coasts of Africa. In these situations the influence of East Germany is not fully recognized. Could the policy be to bypass the retaliatory threat of nuclear war by a tactic of strangulation? The method used in Czechoslovakia, after the difficulty in Hungary, the final penetration into South Vietnam, and the abortive Tet offensive, appear to show to them the benefit of experience. Withhold your effort till overwhelming superiority is established, then strike with a blitz; as demonstrated by the German armies in World War II.

To look more closely, what are the signs to support the idea of pluralism in Eurocommunism? There are its promises and the support for the Christian Democratic government in Italy, its moderate line in municipal government in Italian cities, some criticism of Russian intervention in Czechoslovakia, its difficult attitude to conferences called by Russia, and the assertion that there are many roads to communism. Against this, what is the evidence? There is of course the expressed intention to establish socialism by various means. Socialism is for Marxists today a euphemism for communism, or merely a stage to that end.

In September of 1977, when the union of Socialist and Communist parties in France seemed likely to attain government, the parties finally joined forces only when no other course seemed possible. There must have been strong tactical reasons or perhaps outside influence to affect the decisions. If as has been said, the parties have not altered their attitude to private property and still maintain their strict pyramidal structure of control from the top, we can not be persuaded that the leopard has changed its spots. If the new Eurocommunism is a threat to Russian prospects one would expect Moscow to be critical of French and Italian leaders. In fact, they come in for considerable praise. Again the parties outside Russia, with the exception of the Czechoslovakia incident, slavishly support Russian policy in Angola, Vietnam, and so forth. Moreover, they are highly critical of dissidents like Solzhenitsyn, Amalrik, and Bukovsky.

The French party's policy on Western defense has been described as disruptive and ridiculous. Trade between Russia and Italy is almost a monopoly in some primary products in the hands of the Communist party front organization, Interagara. By this means, considerable funds flow to the Party through commissions. The Party is generally accepted as being wealthy. Further, those countries which have rejected Russian domination as have China, Jugoslavia, and Albania are still rigidly Communist in all essentials. In France, the Party has strongly supported the policy of nationalization of industry, elections to positions of power being by "the rank and file." As in elections elsewhere, this is an established means of seeing that party members or nominees are elected. Communist parties everywhere are strong advocates of detente and critics of it are labelled as reactionary and seeking a return to the Cold War. This is far less than persuasive for those who can remember the predecessors, the "common front" and "peaceful coexistence." The name has not altered the policy. All this is in spite of the warnings of men like Solzhenitsyn, Sakharov, and others as to what detente really means. It is not fully recognized that the Socialists, who could be expected to ally themselves with the Communists because of the identity of objectives, are perhaps the strongest opponents. It is not a matter of reactionaries against progressives, but of the Left being opposed by the Left. What must be fully realized is that Communism is an irreversible process so far. "You won't be able to unscramble the eggs," would certainly urge caution. Reason should certainly urge disbelief of Party promises and full opposition to Communist moves till absolute proof of safety is available. Optimism is not justified.

Just as in the case of Russia in the twenties and thirties, conflicting and favorable reports, many of which have been proved as incorrect though at times widly favorable to the regime, also are in circulation with regard to China. Briefly, the increased population of Hong Kong, usually refugees from Mainland China who crossed despite guarding gunboats, risk of drowning, and other dangers, gives eloquent support to the belief that satisfaction with the regime is by no means universal. Recent events after the death of Mao show the leadership itself is not yet stable. Moreover the reestablishment of Chinese control over Tibet, the little known crushing of the independence movement in Kazakastan, the claim that Taiwan is an integral part of China, and the recent control of the disputed Spratley Islands, would indicate that expansion is not outside the bounds of Chinese ambition. Could the policy of "hasten slowly" till strength is gained, be a part of Chinese strategy? Aid to revolutionary parties round the world strongly supports this view.

10

WORLD INTERNATIONAL ORGANIZATIONS

In the pioneering days of any country the settlers had minimal contact with others. The rights and desires of one did not infringe on those of another. As population in any area increased, so did contact and possibility of conflict increase. By steady growth, there developed the system of laws that protect us while at the same time they restrict us. Similarly, with increased population throughout the world and with rapid communication, the nations are to an increasing extent impinging on each other's interests. This acceleration has been most marked over the last hundred years.

Coincident with this growth have been efforts at some sort of arrangement to minimize possible conflict. The earliest attempts were little more than military alliances to secure each other against, or to help each other in, foreign aggression. But later come organized efforts without aggressive or national intent alone. Thus 1859 saw the beginning of the Red Cross designed to help all victims of war, and so forth, without regard to national identity. Today the Red Cross receives worldwide recognition for its impartial humanitarian acts. In 1874 the International Postal Union was set up, staffed with very few executives and so silently efficient, that one rarely hears of it. Its aim is to aid, when necessary, the dispatch of communications between nations. Its only weapon is that if any nation refuses to deliver mail from abroad to persons within a country, then that nation's mail also will not be delivered. It is very successful. The International Meterological Organization was established in 1878, its purpose being to collect and dispatch information on climate and weather conditions round the world. The Geneva Convention was established in 1865 to formulate some rules of warfare, later to be followed by the Hague Peace Conference which added to the rules. In furtherance of this, the Court of International Settlements was established. This court may decide, without authority, to enforce decisions and disputes among the nations. Success has not been unqualified. The International Labour Organization was established in 1862 with the object of improving on a worldwide scale, wages and conditions of employment. Though recently the object of much political pressure, it has done something to publicize bad labour conditions where they exist. Some unorganized efforts have also been made to regulate world prices of commodities widely used in trade.

But the first real attempt at a comprehensive plan of international cooperation was the League of Nations, set up after the First World War. On the part of its planners, we can accept that the attempt was sincere; though judged by results we must accept also that certain of the member nations' representatives were less than sincere. It is sufficient to say here that it failed largely because the territorial ambitions of some members overwhelmed any ideas its founders may have had. Moreover the United States did not join. But its significance lies in the fact that it expressed a recognition that war was a terrible evil, disruptive of civilization, destructive of life and property, and should have no place in a modern world. War was a relic of barbarism.

The conclusion of World War II saw the establishment of the United Nations, a much more comprehensive and thought-out scheme. Its organization and institutions were devised with admirable purpose. These and its history are either well known or information is so easily obtained, that discussion is not considered appropriate here except insofar as they have been active in attacking world problems. It might, however, not be irrelevant to see, in the first statement of the United Nations Charter, something short of accuracy: "We the people of the United Nations determined...." It is no exaggeration to say that the people were not consulted. The leaders alone decided. The nations were and have been since, anything but united. Among the first fifty signatures those from Germany, Italy, and Japan, as enemies, were excluded. Subsequently, these and the emerging countries were added till the total number now stands little short of one hundred and fifty. South Africa has been expelled. Regrettably the various nations are less united than when it was first established. Arguments are often advanced that it should be abandoned or that certain nations should withdraw. This is often advanced, but certainly not officially, particularly with regard to the United States, who contributes most, financially and otherwise, and is very often the object of attacks of small emerging nations though they are the beneficiaries of help. It has to be admitted that many nations have used it as an instrument of national advantage and aspirations and have done much to bring the organization into disrepute. Its greatest failure is perhaps that it has done little to prevent wars. These have been endemic and threaten to break out on a greater scale than ever. But its various instrumentalities like FAO and UNESCO, have had some success in aiding and publicizing world problems. In the world of international thought, though clearly used at times for narrow and hostile purposes, it is an irreplaceable forum. This alone justifies its existence.

11

DISPARITY OF WEALTH: NATIONALLY AND INTERNATIONALLY

It must be accepted that the believed ease of solution of any problem is proportioned to the distance from it. Bearing this in mind, some attempt must be made to focus attention on the outstanding problems of today. Chief among these is the disparity in wealth throughout the world, both nationally and internationally. It must be asserted that no one would attempt to completely solve mankind's problems. The best that can be hoped for is that they might be reduced to manageable or tolerable proportions. Men, being unequal as they are, will never attain any significant degree of equality in any sphere. Such is not only impossible but undesirable. Considerable evidence exists to support the contention that affluence and an easy life would not end dissent, conflict, or violence. The poor, as an underprivileged group, are not the focus of dissent. It is all too clear that the leaders in any movement, or in dissent, come from middle class, comfortable, and well-educated people, at best animated by what they see as the injustice between the privileged and the underprivileged; or from an urge to power. They use the poor as the instruments for obtaining their own objectives.

It is not proposed to enter into a discussion for and against all the reasons for a greater degree of equality. This is not the problem. Doubtlessly, an overwhelming majority would like to see a greater degree of equal accessibility to the world's goods. The problem is not why it should be brought about, but how it can be done. Disregarding, for the present, the influence of money in distribution, the industrial-economic process can be seen as consisting of four elements. These are first, labour; the body of men and women whose wages or income enables them to buy that part of production to which their effort has contributed. Second, are the owners or managers, briefly referred to as capital, primary or secondary, whether in plant or raw material. Third, is the body of administrators of all types necessary to the maintenance of any system. Fourth, after man has satisfied his essential needs of food and shelter by the processes needed, he turns to leisure pursuits, loosely referred to as entertainment and luxury.

It is assumed ideally that each group takes from the total of production that portion to which its contribution entitles it. In this analysis everyone is seen as employing everyone else. Should anyone of the four take an undue proportion, one or all of the others must go short. It is repeatedly said that women have been forced into industry to maintain a standard of living. Without here in any way supporting or disapproving of women entering the work force, it should be clear that the wages paid today could easily maintain the living standard of a few years ago. It would appear then that our purveyors of luxury and entertainment have taken an undue amount from the pool of production. We need a new car, a new refrigerator, more entertainment, a bigger house, more and more expensive clothes and food, and more holidays. These wants are not to be condemned of themselves, but with the emphatic proviso, "Can we afford them all?"

A very humble example, well known to all, should illustrate this point. Years ago, sliced bread was unknown; today unsliced bread, except for special types, is almost unprocurable. In the period of transition, unsliced bread could be bought for little more than half the price of sliced variety. Today we pay someone to cut our bread, for which service, no doubt, a good profit is made. The householder who buys sliced bread and complains of the price of bread is contradicting by acts what is said in words.

Similar examples are known to everyone. Briefly, former luxuries have become regarded as necessities. We are all trying to live on a television standard. To maintain this, people load themselves with a burden of debt, money which could be earning interest. Debt is now used to pay interest.

A fundamental fact, overlooked by most, is that each producer can at normal rates produce more than he or his dependents can consume. During the war period when great numbers of the best manpower were away destroying each other's lives and capacity for production, and many of those left behind were engaged in producing means of destruction, there was in spite of some scarcities, no real absence of necessities. In fact, as in the case of England, as a result of the increased employment and the enforced policy of controlled distribution, it was claimed that the poor were better off. Further in spite of the numbers of unemployed today who must be fed by the efforts of others, there is no real starvation. It is readily conceded that those unemployed would, if they had the means of doing so, increase their consumption.

Yet all this is surely evidence that in all moderately advanced countries a surplus of goods could easily be produced. Indeed, primary producers are frequently advised and constrained to reduce their production. Others again complain that they cannot dispose of the wheat, meat, or wool they have produced. The fault lies not in the range of production but in distribution. In the area of secondary production, it is claimed that a depression results from an over supplied market, "capacity production." It would seem that a solution would lie in shorter hours of labor. This solution the trade unions strongly support. But if hours of labor were reduced at the same rates of pay per week, costs of goods would then rise and labor would take a disproportionate amount from the pool of production. The unemployed would gain nothing. Any suggestion that wages, incomes, and profits be held stable by law is met, not unexpectedly resisted, by vigorous protests from those concerned. Costs and prices must be geared to profits and not adjusted artificially.

Is there then no solution to the problem? As has been repeatedly said there is no complete cure to any of mankind's problems. While there are two forces in production, management and capital on one side and labor on the other, there will always be disagreement on what proportion should go to each. Marx, with myopic understanding, saw a simple solution, abolish the owner. Measured by life and living standards in those countries that have tried to apply his ideas, in comparison to "Capitalist" ones, the cure has proved worse than the disease. Yet in the chapter on labor relations, a system of easing the difficulty has been outlined. This may be of either of two ways. One scheme is based on the idea that employees receive in addition to an agreed wage an amount according to the added value as a result of their efforts, with a later payment based on profits. Also if employees by various means were induced to buy (not be given), shares in the business, much of the difference between owner and employee would disappear. The entire staff could then see clearly the irrationality of keeping up wages, *i.e.*, costs, when sales, *i.e.*, incomes, are falling. Adjustment to the business cycle could be predicted and anticipated. That this would not solve all problems is clear, and any attempt to apply the idea to all industry would be fatal. As a method it would be wisest to leave it to be proved on the basis of economic efficiency. Any government able to free itself from the economic straitjacket of theory could easily devise methods of assisting this development. Also trade unions, with the money now available to them, could easily establish their own businesses and so demonstrate the efficiency, or otherwise, of their own management.

One difficulty, increasingly widespread, is that government is taking on added responsibilities to pay; for which we pay increased taxes to the extent that for many people taxation is the greatest expense during the year. Taxation, both direct and indirect, is a cost on production and so must go into the price of the goods sold. It was calculated years ago that there are fifty taxes on a loaf of bread. Here is a serious problem. All organization feeds on itself. Is "Parkenson's Law" absolute? Among the consequences and causes attributed to the fall of Rome, and other nations also, administration and debt are generally both recognized. It is affirmed that it is costing too much to run the country. Increase of manpower in the administration side of society is too well known to need emphasis or to quote statistics. In the case of a business that increases its administration at the expense of the production side, the result is bankruptcy. This principle has as much application to a nation as to a business.

The full impact of government intrusion into the lives of the citizens will be discussed later. But with the extension and complexity of the organization so the difficulty increases. The approved practice of building a national economy on exports can be ultimately a short-sighted one. The experiences of England, the United States, and Japan show this. As the excess of exports over imports grows, a high standard of living results. Results may be twofold. With the high standard comes increased costs of production, which prices exports out of the world market. Or in defense, importing countries raise tariff barriers or set quotas which have the same effect; with ill will as a byproduct. Improved productivity at home merely heightens the competition. A too favorable trade balance is self-defeating and just as harmful ultimately as an unfavorable one. Until nations realize that building an economy by pushing exports is self-defeating, trade wars by competition or by guns are inevitable.

MONEY IN THE ECONOMY

As a preliminary to a discussion on the influence of money in the economy it is necessary to make a few statements which are expected to have general acceptance, but which are not normally subjected to any consideration of their significance.

1. We engage in work to supply a need, in economic terms to supply a market; *i.e.*, to exchange goods or services with someone who has exchange power in goods or services.

2. The G.N.P. must expand. Any country which does not increase its total production in any period is judged to have failed.

3. To expand a business it is a usual practice to borrow.

4. For exchange purposes we have two forms of media: government currency in coins and paper issues; loans from bankers. The latter comprise by far the greater amount of purchasing power in society. A smaller amount, of less significance, exists in promissory notes and so forth.

To follow this up, it is necessary to know clearly just what money really is. This might at first be thought to be considered as unnecessary, but it is held that the full effect of money is lost just because of our familiarity with it. At one stage in the growth of civilization, wealth was measured in corn, cattle, and so forth. This, though sound in principle, was defective in many ways, but for our purposes here, in that it did not readily admit of exchange. So coins were used, which by their various advantages, replaced the prior barter. It is not appropriate here to give a treatise on the history of money, but to refer only to certain elements relevant to our purpose. Among the different concepts and uses of money, the relevant one is that money is a medium of exchange. When functioning, money is readily accepted as exchangeable for any commodity desired in the exchange.

A prime difficulty arose with the development of modern banking. Some systems of banking existed previously, but the beginning of modern banking is associated with the name of William Paterson who in 1694 proposed a scheme to the English government by which it was shown, "The bank hath benefit of interest on all moneys which it creates out of nothing." It could reasonably have been that our Mr. Paterson might have been more tactful to disguise the fact of money being "created out of nothing." No person today, at all informed, has any doubt about this; though it is not to be assumed that the acts of creation could be wisely used indefinitely. Judged by results, it is not wisely used as it is. It is not limitless. For our purpose, the words "purchasing power" rather than money are to be used as giving a clearer description of the function. As has been said, purchasing power or exchange media is derived from two sources. First it consists of coins and paper documents produced by the government, closely and rightly regarded as a government monopoly. But the greatest part of purchasing power results from loans from banks. Once put into operation their purchasing power is indistinguishable from that of any other source.

To understand the full impact of borrowing referred to in point three above, it is necessary to follow the process of borrowing. It begins when an industrialist or other person wishes to expand his business. He is confident that greater production will yield greater profit. He approaches a banker. He in turn investigates the possibility of increased profit and if satisfied agrees to the loan. This has two aspects. First, he has injected additional purchasing power into commerce. Second, he assumes the debt to be incurred in purchasing the material and so forth needed for the expansion. The borrower is in debt to the banker.

The banker of course secures himself from loss by holding collateral, *i.e.,* he obtains a lien over the borrower's property. The borrower hopes by the increased investment to be able to pay the interest on the loan, someday to repay the principal, and also to increase his own income. So far as the process has gone, this increased purchasing power for goods not yet produced will have caused a disparity between purchasing power—or money—and goods.

This is of course inflationary. In theory and in part practice, borrowing and repayments cancel each other out and the relationship between money and goods is stable. But nowhere do facts support this. An expansionary period means that borrowings exceed cancellations as any examination of statistics show. This process goes on till the market for goods is over supplied, giving what is euphemistically called "capacity production". Prospects for increased production and sales have fallen. Several results occur.

It must be borne in mind that the increased expansion was built on debt by the borrower and by income of the banker, *i.e.,* the purchasing power comes into circulation as a debt. The principal and interest debt remains unaltered. As sales fall, less wages can be paid. Unemployment and depression follow. Now a depression is not a visitation of nature like a drought or a typhoon, but the direct result of man's own actions; basically when it is due to misjudgment or greed by both borrower and banker.

This predicament leads us to ask why must production expand? This is to question the third of our basic assumptions given at the beginning. To ask why must production increase is equivalent to asking a group of dedicated Christians why they worship God. It is rank heresy. But still, "Why?"

Expansion means greater production and consumption of goods and services. But is this necessary, especially if it is to result in booms and depressions? In countries such as the United States, Europe, Japan, Australia, and so forth, living standards are not in any urgent need of improvement. We could get along very nicely if what we already have were more evenly divided. Expansion means increased use of diminishing world resources. It is mining the planet and hastening the day when depleted resources will of themselves reduce expansion.

To be guilty of further heresy it can be asked why must

society, both private and government, go to private citizens, the bankers, for the issuing of the media of exchange? This involves an explanation of the role of central banking, known in the United States as the Federal Reserve System and often referred to as the Bankers' Bank. In the United States this system was established in 1913. It was said to prevent recurrent financial panics inherent in the former system. Briefly, policy is in the hands of the board of directors, members of private banks nominated by the private banks and appointed for fourteen years by the President. Their meetings are entirely secret, even from the President and the Treasury, and it is on their decisions that the supply of purchasing power increases or decreases. Increases are made by the simple process of writing out a cheque, drawn on the Federal Reserve System itself, with which to buy government securities. Sellers of these securities depost these F.R.S. checques with their own banks in virtue of which further loans and debts are created. It has been reliably calculated that as the result of an initial creation of $1,000,000, over $6,000,000 comes into circulation in loans and debts.

Formerly the currency of a country had to be backed by gold, but in 1933 the gold standard was abandoned in the United States so that credit creation has now no brake other than the opinion of some men who stand to profit from it. It is most obvious that the F.R.S. has not prevented financial crises as it was promised. Instead, booms and declines of varying intensity, occur with increasing rapidity.

Two queries are obvious. Are these board members incapable or unwilling to halt the spiral of booms and depressions? Further, as they are all in the business of lending in their own banks and in a position of prior knowledge of rises and falls in prices, is anyone naive enough to believe they never use this knowledge to their own advantage? Money is power as everyone knows, and as a result of this system, inflation and national debt have increased enormously, especially in the last forty years or so. It has been reliably calculated that the total worth of the United States is some $2 trillion while the total indebtedness is $3 trillion, *i.e.*, the debt is 50 percent greater than the asset, a position shared in varying degrees by other countries. So the central-banking system has brought about the mortgaging of national assets at an increasing rate. As the main lending institutions are the privately owned banks, society is in debt to people who have a monopoly of power in imposing public debt, owed to themselves, at the cost of merely writing the required figures.

Apart from the theory of "capacity production" as a limit on the issuing of bank loans—debt, there, is what is euphemistically referred to as excess liquidity. This term in the average mind obscures the fact that if depositors were to ask for cash to replace deposits, the banks would not have sufficient cash reserves to do so. Greed has outreached caution. Thus, we could see the spectacle of depositors in numbers demanding cash which the banks do not have. This position is normally avoided, as few people ask for cash at the same time. So the circumstance does not arise as it did in the 1929-1931 depression.

As figures shown elsewhere indicate, bank liabilities are in a precarious situation. Should any large group of depositors, like OPEC change their banks, the United States banking system would collapse. United States government, bankers, and individuals, have been mortgaged to the limit so much so that reputable authorities are on record as saying they expect to see another world depression in the near future. The possibility of expansion in the undeveloped countries is being used as a means of postponing this event. But should these countries realize that if they can issue and control their own currency, they can also issue their own credit, this avenue of postponement would be cut off. Must society sit passively and wait for the disaster to arrive? The cause and the cure are both well known in informed circles.

The anomaly of unemployed people, when there is work to be done in slum clearance and so forth, derives from two factors. In normal employment, a person produces more than he or she and the dependents consume. There is thus a surplus of goods available. The second is that purchasing power is not geared to production which should generate its own purchasing power. As is well known, the amount of purchasing power in any community is determined by the central banks. We then have the absurd anomaly of the banking system producing debt-money for the unemployed to enable them to have the purchasing power for the surplus goods. The claim that the banks do gear the supply of money to the goods available is disproved by the obvious fact that the goods are in surplus supply and the purchasing power is not available. As this is debt-money, it must be repaid to someone. The position then, in the long run, is in no way relieved. A parallel absurdity is that the greater the wealth the greater the debt, an anomaly if ever there was one. The existing system whereby central banks create and destroy purchasing power must be reformed for a stable economy.

In a matter of such significance, why must the power of creating purchasing power be taken from the government and given to private interests who thereby accumulate a terrifying debt owed to themselves? If the note issue is a government monopoly, why not the issue of credit also? No one would put this power in the hands of politicians who could most certainly be expected to use it for vote-catching purposes. But if our bureaus of statistics can measure the rate of inflation to a decimal point of accuracy, could they not also measure the amount of purchasing power needed in the community with equal accuracy? By this simple process, the onset of an inflationary spiral would be seen and checked before its consequences could operate. Needless to say, this system would end the power of the loan-debt financial structure to continue to pile up the huge debt burden now threatening to cause the collapse of modern societies.

Money is essentially a medium of exchange and as such it should reflect the amount of goods and services available in the community. It is wholly unnecessary and artificial to have it geared to gold or any other commodity. By a process of creation based on statistics, the amount of purchasing power would be freed from the desires of both bankers and politicians.

An effect of this system of bank loan-debt not fully, publicly realized, is its effect on the government's foreign policy. International relationships are largely a matter of facilitating international trade. As our elected representatives are not international financial experts, they are accompanied by experts who are. These men, of course, are in the business of international banking, and it is on their advice that trade relationships are concluded. In consequence, foreign policy becomes a matter for bankers' decisions, people who cannot be expected to lose sight of their own interests. How many people know that during World War II the allied banking system, as represented by Sir Montague Norman, was in regular contact with the German representative, Dr. Schacht, meeting him in Switzerland? The explanation given was that otherwise the situation would become chaotic. The ordinary citizen could be excused for thinking that this made the situation appear more chaotic.

Professor Armen A. Alchian has been quoted in the press as saying that for 3,000 years or more, growth of national money supplies "has been almost the sole cause of inflation." In the Middle Ages it was a device used by impecunious or unscrupulous rulers, by a process known as debasing the currency, with disastrous results on the people. Inflation is a process whereby the wealth is taken from those who have earned it and transferred to those who have not. Inflation, as expressed in rising prices, causes a demand by wage earners to cover increased costs. These increases also go into further prices. Strong unions in a monopolistic labor position can, by strike action, force employers and governments to increase wages. This inflates costs, and so prices, still further. Sales must fall off and so unemployment increases. The worst sufferers are those retired people who, living on formerly earned wealth, see their assets declining in value. To relieve the situation, the government comes to the rescue. Unemployed and the aged are paid social-welfare benefits. These are paid from taxes on those who are still earning or by "deficit financing," *i.e.*, by printing money. Bureaucracy must of course be increased to handle this, and the vicious cycle is intensified. Government becomes responsible for various public needs such as housing. These activities lead to a system of government control over the lives of the citizens and a dependent, complaining, and dissatisfied population, claiming as a right that they be kept by other people and with all too often no or little incentive to work. In short, it is some form of socialism; not by legislation and consent, but by financial manipulation and debt. More and more people are working to pay taxes to maintain government control and to create a dependent population. Does anyone believe that those who control our money supply are not fully aware of this? Are we to believe that it was not designed or utilized of deliberate purpose? A vast, informed, and persuasive literature exists giving evidence that this is so. Are we to meet communism in the process of establishing a one-world system of control? Adler's theory of the will to power has been fully substantiated.

The matter of international exports and imports would be sufficiently complicated without the added complication of money. International trade is not unlike some 150 men round a vast cistern, each adding to and taking from the water supply. All desire a stable level but tilted just a little in each one's own favor. The results can be visualized. Each strives for his own gain and blames others for disturbing the balance. The international loan-debt system is plagued by the problem that the borrowing country may not be able to meet its commitments, *i.e.*, to pay interest on the loan, to make the economy more productive, to permit reinvestment with renewed or increased borrowing, and to supply home consumption. Loans can be, and at times are, repudiated. The borrower may delay interest payments, which if continued, would amount to the same thing. Borrowing countries may renegotiate the loan or obtain a new loan which, substantially, is little different. It is seen then that borrowing countries develop only so far as they can go into debt to lending governments, world bankers, or the International Monetary Fund. Frequently, when interest payments are at risk, the lender steps in to secure his income. Usually this involves giving directions as to how the country is to be more efficiently governed and usually involves lowering consumption on the home market. This, as in Peru, has caused riots by protestors who, not unnaturally, object to lowering the standard of living to benefit one already much better than their own.

The trouble in Zaire, further highlighted their financial situation there. Considerable sums have been advanced to the government of that country. Zaire's export income depends largely on copper exports from the Katanga area. Should invasion from Angola be successful and the province be detached from Zaire, repayment of loan-debt and interest would be seriously jeopardized. This goes far to explain the interest of the Western world in this country. Unpredictable world economic conditions can and do upset the judgment of lender and borrower alike. Owing to unexpected oil-price rises and a mild world-trade recession, fears are expressed in some quarters that borrowings have been too great for satisfactory interest payments. Thus, in the years 1973 to 1976 sixteen less-developed countries had between them an overseas debt increase from $45.41 billion to $83.66 billion, an increase of some 15 percent in real terms while their combined GNP has increased by about 4.5 percent. Debt has increased faster than capacity to pay interest. Without following this any further, enough has been said to show that as presently operated, development is made in the short run by loading an enormous incubus of debt around the necks of the borrowers.

As has been indicated earlier, exporting countries have endeavoured to build their wealth and economy by their exports which allow them to invest abroad, *i.e.*, to enter into a loan-debt arrangement. A too "favorable trade balance" frequently develops, which is actually unfavorable to both sides, and a variety of restrictions are imposed to restore some equality. The remedy surely is to check the growth before it becomes too troublesome. Not unnaturally, individuals desire to produce more than they consume. But if this means to the disadvantage of the buyer, the process becomes self-defeating. Just as it is desirable to hold a close, constant balance between goods and services and the amount of purchasing power, so also it should be clear that trade balance should be maintained between exporting and importing countries. That country which builds a high living standard by an excessive amount of exports will eventually be in trouble. The history of England and recent U.S.A. and Japanese problems clearly demonstrate this. It should not be beyond the intelligence to see the remedy.

12

THE WELFARE STATE

It is a mere truism to say we are living in an age of social and political change. One does not have to go to Hegel to realize that change gives both risks and opportunities. The Roman writer Horace has expressed it, "Adversity has the effect of eliciting talents which in prosperous circumstances would have lain dormant." What will emerge satisfactorily from this change will be, it is hoped, that social organization which best meets the needs, the potentialities, and the limitations of mankind. At present we may recognize four competing "philosophies," each claiming to be able to develop those institutions and customs which will bring greatest good. These four may be roughly defined as:

1. Communism; a return to the authoritarian control of the past, aided by modern techniques of coercion by physical restraint and by thought control. Despite its failure and its appalling ruthlessness, its methods are producing considerable advances.

2. On the other end of the spectrum are what can be termed the "Liberationists," an incoherent number of people, mostly young and disgruntled, who go no further than the disruption of the existing society without anything but the vaguest ideas as to what system would result. They oppose the concept of the compulsion of necessity. Work is a curse in an age where feeling and emotion are superior to logic and reason. It is not entirely

a revolt against the restrictions of associative living but against civilization itself.

3. Third on our list comes the current form of democracy. It is, after some two centuries, being weighed in the balance and found wanting. It has produced much, but not all its initial enthuisiasts had promised.

4. To remedy its defects rather than to eliminate it, as communism would do, the concept of the Welfare State is advocated.

In considering the Welfare State it is not proposed to add to the mass of information both for and against the idea. All that is intended is to examine some significant current trends and from them, attempt to predict the effect on the future of civilization. The justification of the Welfare State is based on the inadequacies of capitalism as it exists in advanced countries around the world today and the benefits to be gained by removing or at least minimizing its harmful aspects.

The essential basis of capitalism is the right to private property to be used as the owner sees fit. Derived from this is the existence of the "free market" with its philosophical support in the doctrine of "laissez-faire," where each in pursuit of his own interests would in competition produce a generally beneficial result for all. The role of the government is thus limited to keeping the ring clear from violence to life and property. The government which governs least, governs best. Reward would thus flow from effort, and apathy or inability would be penalized. While few if any today would support the doctrine in the form of its earlier expression, it yet cannot be condemned as out of hand. If one looks at the society in the beginning of the nineteenth century and compares it with society today, it is obvious that capitalism so operating made a tremendous change and improvement in the life of the people. Economics, health, length of life, literacy, mobility of status, and so forth, all bear witness to the achievements of modern capitalism.

Yet equally, few would doubt that Capitalist society today (or any other form of society), is without serious flaws. These, it is claimed, the Welfare State can eliminate within the Capitalist organization. Implicit in this is the belief that capitalism has some inherent desirable attributes which it would be unwise to eliminate. The question here becomes not one of planning versus no planning, but of what planning and how much. All government implies and applies the principle of planning. The evils which the Welfare State claims to be able to remove are or may be briefly stated as follows: Clearly the base of which capitalism rests, *i.e.*, private property, is not wholly good. It gives power to the strong in the arena of competition. To succeed, the participant must possess not only the desirable qualities of energy, creativity, intelligence, and a sense of purpose (desirable under any system), but also an element akin to aggressiveness, not to say ruthlessness, which is prepared to push aside those who obstruct. Thus, success is in large measure conditioned by a sense of disregard for one's fellows. Here also, undue emphasis is placed on material objectives which are not always compatible with the highest goals of society. Given the power which wealth and success give, large aggregations of capital, like the multinational corporations, can and do exert undue influence on governments to enact legislation and grant concessions designed to favor the corporations; with little or no regard for the welfare of the whole.

Exploitation is not a word which is only part of Communist terminology. The idea then of the "free market" becomes a blind to cover individual and maybe selfish effort. The market today is not freely available to anyone who wishes to participate, being restricted both by devices available to the powerful, and more so by government legislation on labor laws, factory legislation, and so forth. The market is anything but free.

A further criticism by advocates of the Welfare State is that there is no overall plan to coordinate and direct, and to a degree possible, predict and implement desirable methods and objectives. Capitalism is accused of following the line of least resistance, or more accurately of going where maximum profit is to be found. A common accusation is that when profit falls, capital goes on strike and refuses to produce. It is not concerned with the general good but with the "profit motive." This has the result that there occurs a shortage of desirable and desired goods, and a surplus of others.

It appears that inherent in Capitalist production is the so-called "unmanageable surplus;" with consequent inflation and unemployment. To utilize this surplus, industry develops policies of waste. New models are produced with improvements or mere changes to displace the old models. Vast organizations exist to absorb the waste by advertisement, sales systems, tax consultants, and so forth, all helping to absorb this waste to enable capital to be employed. A large body of psychologists is employed to study how to motivate buyers and to create psychological obsolescence. All of this must go into the price of the articles sold.

Since reward goes to the successful few, the majority are disadvantaged. The person on wage income, especially if the wage is low, lives a cramped existence. Freedom is restricted by the demands of the occupation and the "machine" of industry. If experience is essential to growth, the laborer who tends a machine, rather than develop mentally and spiritually, becomes little more than an animated cog in a system. The opportunity to make one's own decisions is an essential to the dignity and psychological growth of a man. Denied the power to think to an optimum degree, a vast reservoir of intelligence and purpose is lost to society as a whole. Employees are manipulated as commodities to be bought, used, or sold as the employer desires. Inherent in this is the dichotomy of class, a division within society with differing values, opportunities, and access to the good things of life. Dissension is endemic and alienation from one's occupation and one's fellows, places continuing strain within society.

It is of the nature of change that it normally results from pressure imposed by unpleasant conditions, lured on by the prospect of conditions resulting from elimination of the unpleasant, and replacement by conditions nearer to the heart's desire. It usually follows that the "philosophical" support for the new is systematized subsequently to justify its existence. It has been stated by some supporters of the Welfare State that no comprehensive philosophy has yet been developed. But enough of the Welfare State is in existence to enable some observations and perhaps predictions to be made concerning its future success. A very strong case has been made on the superior merit of a planned system over one which responds just to the market pressures. But surely it is axiomatic that, as governments and groups plan, the less need and less scope is available for the individual to plan. That some central organizing is essential to any society is obvious, but if plans are centrally designed there is clearly less scope for the individual to think for himself. In principle the criterion for decision lies between planning consistent with freedom, initiative and individualism, and freedom, initiative, and individualism consistent with planning. It would be a wise central planner who could control his own urge to control the lives of others.

It has been argued in favor of the Welfare State that its policies are based on freedom, democracy, solidarity, security, and efficiency. The limitation of freedom under planning has been discussed. Probably no one other than he who possesses wealth and consequent power would argue against a more equal reward for labor. While accepting the principle that reward should be closely related to effort and the benefit to society; yet reward is too often the result of effort inversely proportionate to the benefit conferred on society. Moreover, the disparity between the size of the reward which relegates one to a restricted access to the good things of life and another to the extent that he lives in extravagant luxury, can have little support either morally or economically. It gives reward, as has been argued earlier, to qualities which are not in the best interests of all. Some attempt at minimizing this inequality has been made by progressive tax scales, social welfare, education and health payments, and so forth. With regard to taxation, it is widely accepted that this has reached the confiscatory stage where employers are driven to devise schemes (and not without some success) to avoid paying the full amount of tax. It has actually been considered that the weight of legal taxation can be borne only by the fact that the full tax is not paid. If the earner is to be deprived of an undue amount of his earnings the source of supply will dry up. Protest is loud around the world that transference of wealth from he who has earned it to he who has not, has generated a highly skilled occupation for tax minimization or, perhaps more accurately, tax evasion. The Welfare State must of necessity exacerbate this position. To misquote a well-known saying, the position could be stated as, "From him who has it shall be taken: to him who has not it shall be given."

In England, the objective of the new society was given as security "from the cradle to the grave." Freedom from unemployment, from the excessive cost of illness, from anxiety, from the penalties of old age, and so forth, and the availability of a good education, without the evil of privilege, are all desirable. But freedom and responsibility it must be repeated are the opposite sides of the same coin. Responsibility is the price of freedom as well as its reward. To be relieved of responsibility is not to be given freedom. Rather it can impose dependence, dependence on the decision of him who is responsible. It is claimed that responsibility devolves on the state. But the word "state" is merely an abstraction without any concrete existence. In the field of social welfare, it is those people with the authority and the power to implement ideas which they hold and support. Is the ordinary citizen freer to decide his own actions?

Is the principle of planning here then so comprehensive? If one looks at the position in England where access to the facilities needed to maintain good health are by legislation referred to as a right, what is its effect? Physical health has improved but on the psychological side there appears to be little evidence of gratitude, but rather a demanding, dissatisfied public, crowded hospitals, delayed operations, and constant dispute with the government. Doctors, all too frequently, are dissatisfied and turn to fee-paying patients.

Again, in the pursuit of equality, what more fundamental social principle is involved? In this pursuit it has been advanced that one objective of the Welfare State is to reduce the arbitrarity found in nature. This is very much like giving training facilities to slower runners and denying them to the more speedy. Does anyone doubt that this would result in an overall reduction in the speed with which races were run? To deprive the best of equality of opportunity for development, is inequality of the worst kind. Society needs, as never before, the use of its highest intelligences on its most difficult problems. High capacity instead of being an undesirable variation is a supreme gift of nature to be developed and used to the maximum.

Sweden is usually referred to as the country which has progressed furthest along the road to the Welfare State. It has the most comprehensive plans, with an obvious gain in the standard of living more evenly enjoyed than anywhere else and a healthy people. But it can be cited on the other side that too much consideration has been given to material gain and the removal of insecurity resulting in a population with a high incidence of boredom, suicide, drunkenness, and sexual immorality. Whatever can be said that these attributes existed in some measure before the current planning, it is evident that the Welfare State, insofar as it exists, has at least done nothing to remove them.

As much of the economic planning has removed power from the owners of industry and transferred it to the employees, it must be realized that this is not a renewable resource. If, as has been stated, the employees will ultimately have a controlling interest, what is then the position of the employer? Will he be prepared to invest capital where others can control it? Of course not. He will either cease to be an investor of capital or migrate to a country where he can control his capital. If this occurs it would be necessary for the state to take over the role of private capital or the employee to assume the role of being their own employers after "acquiring" the property of the former owners. In either case the benefit of private property implicit in the principle of the Welfare State would be lost.

Finally, the position must be acknowledged that all this central planning puts power into the hands of a limited number for whom the position of planning the lives of others has a strong attraction. Man will not evolve as a result of having all his problems solved for him. The challenge and response applies as well to individuals as to nations. One inescapable difficulty arising from the vast extent of knowledge available today is that no one can have more than a superficial grasp of the whole or a deep insight of a small amount. Herein lies the difficulty. Our planners may see clearly a limited field in the short run; but have they the wisdom to measure the extent of their plans?

At the beginning of this chapter, some reference was given to the shortcomings of capitalism. But, if it is of the essence of understanding that both sides of a proposition must be given, reference must also be made to the achievements of capitalism; and this presentation must be given fairly and freely, not on the basis of the idea that there are two sides to every question, mine and the wrong side. First it cannot be denied that under capitalism there has been unprecedented progress in living standards, in economics, education, health, culture, mobility of status, and freedom of expression and association. Perhaps the strongest case for capitalism is that it gives dispersed authority based on private property. To a degree not equalled under any other system, it utilizes to a maximum the qualities of energy, initiative, inventiveness, and endless diversity, without loss of efficiency. Reward is dependent on effort. It assists the freedom of ideas and association. For the consumer there is unequalled freedom of choice, the freedom to decide how one's income will be spent, whether to work more or take more leisure, to invest one's money or to take a holiday. And with all these freedoms goes discipline imposed by the possibility of failure. Under capitalism, as under any system devised by man, there are no absolutes. But we can measure only by comparison. No other system, certainly not centrally planned ones, can express the desires and potentialities of men as we have so far. That it can be and should be improved is undeniable. But in the criticism of its defects and the haste for improvement there is the danger that its achievements and benefits may be overlooked. Hasten slowly.

THE NEW WORLD ORDER

In the quarter of a century or so since the end of World War II tremendous changes have taken place. These may be listed as follows:

1. Considerable economic expansion has occurred. It has been calculated that world trade has tripled in this period.
2. Following the disruption of the aftermath of the war, several areas formerly "owned" by the big powers have gained political but not economic independence. (It must not be overlooked that others have lost their independence.)
3. Considerable urban expansion has taken place producing a greater problem of world food supply. These changes have created a new mental climate of opinion and action.
4. The world is seen as consisting of three divisions: (A) the industrialized world outside the Communist system; (B) the Communist group; (C), the more backward nations referred to as the Third World.
5. The existence of a wide disparity in wealth between A and C is now seen not only as existing but as a problem.
6. The recognition of global dependence between all nations, politically, culturally, and economically.

7. The encroachment of population on diminishing resources has aroused attention.
8. The disastrous effects of a possible third world war are clearly recognized, but little has been done to avert such a catastrophe.
9. In the last decade there has been a serious decline and dislocation in world trade caused in part by the malfunction of the world financial system.
10. The concept of centralized planning has great prestige.
11. In view of all the above, the concept of world planning to effect fundamental changes is advanced from several sources.

In support of the concept of global, centralized planning, various amendments to the United Nations organization have been suggested. In the years 1972 to 1974 working committees were set up by the United Nations to plan the objectives of such amendments; finally emerging as the Charter of Economic Rights and Duties of States. Expanded into thirty-four articles elaborating the prior statements appeared the following fifteen objectives.

Fundamentals of International Economic Relations

1. Sovereign territoral integrity and independence of states.
2. Sovereign equality of all states.
3. Nonaggression.
4. Nonintervention.
5. Mutual and equitable benefit.
6. Peaceful coexistence.
7. Equal rights and self-determination of peoples.
8. Peaceful settlement of disputes.
9. Remedying the injustices that have been brought about by force and which deprive a nation of the natural means necessary for its normal development.
10. Fulfillment in good faith of international obligations.
11. Respect for human rights and fundamental freedoms.
12. No attempt to seek hegemony or spheres of influence.
13. Promotion of international social justice.
14. International cooperation for development.

15. Free access to and from the sea by land-locked countries within the framework of the above principles.

While doubtless the fifteen points are generally acceptable the significant aspect is in their application and how it was proposed to implement them. Consistent with the new theories, the new institutions are centrally planned with admirable regard for those nations whose living standards fall below the desired level economically, educationally, socially, and with regard to health. The disparity between the living standards of the advanced countries and those of the Third World are rightly seen as a problem concerning all the nations in a world of increasing interdependence. The logical deduction from this is that aid must flow from the rich nations to the disadvantaged ones to redress the imbalance. Concurrent with all this is a necessary survey of what may be called world assets and needs in food, population, and resources of energy, minerals, climate, vegetation, air, earth, water, technology, and knowledge among people. In general outline, the plan postulates an improved United Nations developed into a world organization with power to plan a coherent system. As a long-range objective, the aim is to produce world equality as citizens, producers, and consumers; being guided by principles of human rather than economic values into what is termed "humanistic socialism." More particularly, this involves a restriction of existing national sovereignty, and controlled by rules stated by the central planning authority empowered to impose penalites.

Certain areas, as the air and the ocean, are to be regarded as a common heritage to be used for international benefit through a system of pooled resources. No country is to be in a position of total dependence for food. As a means of attaining this, attention must be given to Third World agriculture to produce more effective work systems, improved types of food producing plants, fertilizer use, pest-control systems, and so forth, and the use of more labor-intensive methods to absorb the unemployed. As the use of grain for animal food is wasteful, it should be necessary in the production of an adequate world food supply that rich nations consume less meat. As a further aid to the objective, it is desirable that the growth (if not the actual world population), be reduced to a level of stability. To supervise all this, it would be necessary to establish a World Food Authority.

Since industry has proved to be so important in raising living standards of industrialized nations, considerable obligation rests on the owners of industry who must be expected to do all they can to develop reciprocal trade with the Third World. Industrialists must be brought to see that when the disparity between nations is reduced, so is the understandable hostility felt by poor nations. Since industry develops in today's world by the use of finance, the needed income and cultural transfer must be brought about by finance. To this end it is necessary to establish an international currency, a World Bank, having international deposits with the International Monetary Fund and an international tax system. In this system, voting rights would be democratic, either on a strictly numerical basis or on a weighted proportion. By this means, loans would be made for approved projects with the object of transfering resources to the Third World. International guidelines for this purpose would be laid down. Further, by this means it would be possible to end the gold standard and national reserves, as well as price and trade fluctuations. To facilitate the acceptance and operation of such an international order, an Information Organization would be necessary. This would be designed to create a public opinion explaining the need to reform the United Nations and to persuade the industrialized world of the desirability of transferring some of their excess wealth to the Third World. By this means, the spread of needed scientific and technical knowledge would be achieved. What is envisaged is the development of a global ethic to replace the existing self-centered and competitive one.

Consistent with the method throughout these pages of not devoting a full assessment to the presentation of ideas but rather to an examination of trends and to attempt to forecast the consequences, it is necessary to assess from the foregoing the possible future. Is it without significance that in the fifteen fundamentals presented to the United Nations in 1974, the free flow of ideas is not mentioned; the closest reference being in "respect for human rights and fundamental freedoms," without specifying in any way just what these freedoms are. Without a free news media for the dissemination of conflicting information and viewpoints, the World Information Bureau would be an indoctrination bureau more than an information center.

This regrettable absence becomes more important when attention is given to the UNESCO meetings held in Nairobi in 1976 and in Paris in 1978. The claim that the Third World nations have a right to be informed of their own affairs from their own sources is incontestable as expressed by the wording "free and balanced flow of information" as "the duty of states." But if notice is taken of the supporters of these resolutions, the real motive of the UNESCO meeting becomes suspect. Prominent among the supporters of the idea is the USSR, whose idea of a free flow of information is the publishing only of such information as the Communist party approves in the Party publications; and in which readers and publishers of an underground press, which has arisen as a reaction from extension of the censorship of all ideas other than the officially approved, are punished by gaol or exile. Further, one may ask where in the Third World is a free flow of ideas permitted, including those which criticize the government.

In this analysis it appears that the UNESCO meeting is calculated to the increased control of unapproved ideas by those governments to those countries where the "free flow" of ideas has in fact some freedom. Any system, national or global, which seeks to control the news media is well on the path to dictatorship, if it is not already there. An informed, responsible news media is an essential of democracy; a government controlled one is the instrument of tyranny.

Other statements, as published, are subject to criticism. It must be obvious to anyone that the flow of resources is to be directed from the rich nations to the poorer ones of the Third World, through the mechanism of a world financial structure. This would in effect be giving them access to a well-filled purse, an arrangement which they, not unexpectedly, enthusiastically support and which the richer nations view with something less than enthusiasm. Obviously, also the Communist nations, euphemistically referred to as the Centrally Planned Nations of the Second World, support any plan which tends to denigrate and weaken the "Free World."

Would it be unrealistic to suggest that as a precondition of any loan assistance the recipient nations be first required to put their own houses in order? Disparity of wealth and unequal access to the benefits of civilization is more marked among citizens of the Third World than among those of the industrialized world. Examples of this inequality are there for all to see. Doubtlessly, the duties of the state in the free flow of information would not include reference to this. Among others of the fifteen points, adherence to nonaggression and nonintervention is markedly absent among certain nations of the Third World. In the use of finance to aid growth in the Third World it is apparent that the planners are not aware of the fact that it is the system of loan-debt that is largely responsible for what they condemn in the current financial difficulty.

While one can applaud and support a good deal of the criticism of the existing world structure, in the poverty, lack of education, poor health, and the exploitation by the powerful both at home and abroad where civilization is threatened by the growing concept of setting up centralized world authorities, but which when examined means the control by remotely placed men over the lives of the masses of others; for a man to grow he must exercise his own judgment and responsibility. Assistance is not control.

While it is clearly realized that planning and democracy are not mutual incompatibles, it must also be clear that of central planning, so much a part of the Communist system, we must ask, is there no other way consistent with the dignity and mental development of the citizenry? As has been stated the problem has been described: "What planning consistent with freedom, initiative, and individuality, or what freedom, initiative, and individuality consistent with planning?" Central planning is going far to take from the average citizen the freedom and responsibility to determine his own development.

13

MAN'S PSYCHOLOGICAL LIMITATIONS

In all examinations by anthropologists of primitive man, there is always found some organization, some set of rules, and an ethic, designed to promote the welfare of the society. Organization and order are in inevitable association. However, with the partial exception of Athenian Greece, the only known social organization in the latest century or so has been based on the needs, the limitations, and the potentialities of mankind in political association. That in practice it has to no great degree understood and applied the principles, does not invalidate the concept. In the effort to overcome the four great curses of mankind—war, poverty, disease, and crime—it has achieved some success. Poverty and disease in a quarter or a third of the earth have been conquered to the degree that malnutrition, disease, and plagues are absent as they were known a few centuries ago. From an average life expectancy of about thirty years, average expectancy today is around seventy years. Man has thus challenged nature; though there are not warning signs that a future world, not too far distant, could experience a return to poverty. The threats of war and crime reflect the fact that man has yet to conquer himself in his own nature.

This difficulty arises from the fact that man is governed neither wholly by instinct, as are the animals, nor by reason.

Man's climb up the ladder of evolution is incomplete, which leaves a conflict for control between reason and instinct. Basic to the difficulty is the fact that man is both egotistical and gregarious. He needs, both psychologically and physically, association with others, but his ego can and does obstruct this association. His gregarious urge impels him to join collectives and therefore to become a partisan. Partisanship has a strong emotional appeal and it is most obvious that emotion and reason are incompatible. It is a matter of no small wonder to see how normally quiet reliable people when in a mob, urged on by emotional leadership, can relapse into wild violence, destroying both life and property in a frenzied rage. Is there in man a deep-rooted defect, an urge to destruction held in check by civilized restraint? Evidence from all round the world shows an increase in violence both internally and internationally. Hate and killings as means of obtaining one's ends have in some quarters been elevated to the level of virtue, as in Communist teaching. Its disastrous consequences are threatening peaceful existence everywhere. Together with the creative urge as a sort of opposite is the destructive urge as seen in vandalism and guerila warfare.

In spite of certain portents, much of the advanced areas of the world have evolved from the state of scarcity, with its compulsion of necessity. Under such compulsion, mankind, with considerable effort, has risen, survived difficulty, and shown a capacity for survival as a species, avoiding the fate of the dodo and the brontosaurus. This is part of his genetic endowment; but there is little in this endowment to fit him for an age of leisure.

Given freedom and comfort and little to stimulate his mind and actions, he becomes listless, bored, and rebellious. Any army commander knows that an idle army can be a threat to discipline. If mankind, in the mass, is not to indulge in an orgy of dissipation and disruption, society must devise activities which can occupy the minds and energies. Thus, the idea of "security from the cradle to the grave" carries the seeds of its own destruction. Better the idea of the "instability of security."

Education insofar as it trains for a future occupation has definite limits; but education to develop interest and understanding has a far greater range. Thus the idea of education throughout life could be an aim in societies. None should leave the school system without having developed an active interest beyond the occupation. But it is realized that the question remains unsolved as to how far education and culture can apply to the mass of mankind. Today it is apparent that mass appeal is replacing that of an elite, a distinction restricted only to a limited number, and those, the best of society. Our elite, in the best sense of the word, must lead. Toynbee writes that when mimesis fails, decline and disintegration follow.

Could it be possible to acquire citizenship rights not as the result of living for a given number of years, but as proof of qualification? This standard should be within the grasp of all normal people who aspire, and could be lost, temporarily at least, as a result of disregard of society's rules. Quality cannot afford to sink into mass. As is well realized, man has great capacity both for good and ill. If we define morality as "an accepted code of behavior having survival value within a society," it is clear that morality is almost entirely a social attribute. If violence, corruption, and apathy are not curbed, civilization will have generated the seeds of its destruction. The great need today is a spiritual revival, an escape from the shackles of unrestrained instinct.

PROBLEMS OF DEMOCRACY

In summing up much of the foregoing it is affirmed that civilization carries within itself the seeds of its own destruction. Olaf Stapleton, deliberately or otherwise, in his book, *Last and First Men*, illustrates this most forcefully. Civilization begins slowly but with increasing momentum derived from its good features. But underlying this are the seeds of destruction, though their influence is slow to develop, those human limitations and institutions which may give an early benefit but ultimate harm, which like a drug activates the mind at the expense of its later deterioration.

As has been said, we have been told we are going to have world control either by consent or by conquest. Control may come from either of two sources. It is probably widely conceded that the Western world is not at present militarily inclined. But if one looks at the enormous build up of military power by the Soviet Union and reads the indoctrination compulsorily taught in the schools, there is no room for doubt about the danger and the intention of the leaders. And if we consider the treatment given to dissidents and national loyalties within the Soviet Union—as relics of obsolete ideologies which must be destroyed—it is obvious what such control would mean. Control by finance, as has been discussed elsewhere, could lead the world into a load of debt to those who can and do manipulate the finances of the country. But is either control necessary and the fierce, resulting competitions inevitable?

As an alternate to control we have our theory, or principle if preferred, of democracy. At any time, particularly in times of dislocation, it is unwise to apply without question any principle or process of operation. Democracy has perhaps been best defined as government with the consent of the governed. It is also defined as being based on liberty and equality. It is further claimed, as in the words of Jefferson, that under democracy government starts with the people. If one accepts this, would it be wise to enquire just where does it end? As a following query it could be asked are we satisfied that we have reached the ultimate wisdom in our political philosophy? Judged by results today it can surely be said that there is room for serious doubt and perhaps hope. Obviously, results could be better. Could our institutions function more effectively? The answer must be an emphatic "yes." To argue that imposed control by a dictator or oligarchy would be better would rouse wild indignation and uncomplementary name-calling such as Fascist, Communist, and so forth. However, hinted by implication at the possibility of approving such ideas, it must be said that such governments have been tried and proved a failure. So we are left with democracy, but not necessarily with the exact form we have.

Democracy, as a form of government, is on the defensive. As an experiment of a century or so it has certain defects, as judged by results. Lord Bryce writing in the 1920s could say, "although democracy has spread and although no country which has tried it shows any signs of forsaking it, we . . . are not yet entitled to hold that it is the natural . . . and inevitable form of government." He saw indications "that some day might reverse the process." Impatience or something else has certainly done this. Today among some 145-150 members of the U.N. a mere two dozen are democracies, in the loose sense that they allow party opposition and criticism in government.

Why then has it been so dramatically reduced in application? Apart from the fact that democracy has not produced the results expected and promised there are several causes. First there are, and no doubt always will be, ambitious men, ambitious to lead and control. This is a strong part of man's animal heritage placed there for a desirable purpose, but in man, at least, not always used to man's best advantage and indeed, as frequently illustrated, to his picturesque disaster. Parallel to this is the impulse of some to be led. The reasons for this have been elaborated more fully on earlier pages. Briefly, they are the difficulty of reasoning oneself to a conclusion, the desire for certainty, enjoyment of mass emotion and all the euphoria that goes with it, and so forth.

To a Greek of the fourth century B.C., our system would not be classified as democractic at all. Every free born Greek had the right to participate in all discussion and to vote on its acceptance. But today, as was already evident then in some degree, numbers and distance make this impossible. So modern democracy, perforce, has devised a method of representation. This raises a problem. Is a representative in a position merely to express the wishes of his constituents? Apart from the endless process of ascertaining this and accepting a majority decision no matter how repugnant to the representative, there is the further problem of how far the majority is competent to exercise a decision.

If one were to ask for a Gallup Poll on, say, the question as to whether it would be sounder to apply a monetary or a fiscal policy to contain inflation, it is probable that most or many would not know what the question was about. It is not so much a matter of democratic right as of knowledge or wisdom. When finance economists differ furiously as they do, and as we know, fail to control inflation, surely the uninformed must hesitate. The process of governing a country today is a most involved operation, in which our most experienced brains convey no conviction of expertise. Here is a vital problem of democracy. National and international relations, legal, commercial, political, and so forth are involved to such a degree no one appears to have a clear and generally accepted solution. Must we then accept the solutions of our "experts?" Have we elected our representatives to positions where, as with our legal and medical advisers, we regard them as empowered to use their knowledge and experience to our best advantage? In fact this is largely what we do. This is the position so cogently argued by the English statesman of the eighteenth century, Edmund Burke. The obvious danger here is the existence of a docile population and an authoritarian rule. Can the electorate be educated to the degree necessary for informed judgment? It is clearly doubtful. Democracy here has apparently encountered an antinomy.

This brings us to a further difficulty. Gustav Le Bon, in *The Mob*, raises the matter of the effects of mass emotionalism. Jose Ortega y Gasset in *The Rise of the Masses*, perhaps better translated *The Rise of the Unqualified*, discusses another aspect of it. Both remark on the extent to which emotion in the individual, and more particularly in the mob, overrules reason. It is not to be thought that mass emotionalism is an attribute of the proletariat only. Le Bon discusses the phenomenon as being as much a part of the psychological endowment of the professor as of the man in the street. But recent history has given painful proof of the power of the impassioned orator to sway the mob. If we are to be governed by reason, emotion must be under more effective control.

Does being informed mean being informed on the issue from my prejudiced party standard? Or does it mean being informed on all sides and all grounds of the argument? A primary child who writes to the newspapers on matters of public debate has been trained not to think, but to come to a decision, a far easier and harmful process probably expressing ideas inculcated by a teacher who has merely come to a conclusion. To come to a decision is by no means the same thing as coming to a wise decision.

Some years ago an experiment was tried to introduce a new type of debate. Instead as is normal where each party by lot is selected to take up the case for or against a proposition regardless of any personal conviction, each person was required to debate with himself. Some minutes were allowed to present the affirmative side, followed by an equal time to present the negative, followed by a summing up, as in the case of a judge in court. The results were often amazing. Regrettably it must be said that those trained in the trade-union atmosphere failed dismally. The positive was presented vigorously and with confidence. The opposite case was presented in a stumbling, unconvincing manner, the summing up being merely a repetition of the affimative more strongly and confidently presented than ever. The idea that summing up meant the balancing of arguments for and against each other was not understood. To add to the implications, some of those later became members of Parliament. Needless to say, the idea did not receive general acceptance. In passing it can be added that those who proved most capable were businessmen. Some who thought on this unexpected result came up with the obvious answer. The businessman who allows his judgment to be overruled by emotion would not long remain in business.

From this follows another problem, that of equality. Nothing is more obvious than that men and women are unequal. No one is absurd enough to question this physically. But we do not apply this obvious evidence in other situations. We strive to obtain our most competent scientists, engineers, doctors, and so forth. These, as students and practitioners, are judged by results. Do results suggest we are using our best brains socially? Can we not get better men and women? Or is it that our institutions either prevent our best men and women from entering the areas of social service or that these institutions restrict the application of our best intellects? The answer is probably "yes" to both questions. From the nature of the circumstances we tend to get ambitious people able to express themselves convincingly. A quiet reasoned argument has much less electoral appeal than fiery oratory, when the skilled speaker plays on the emotions and self-interests of his hearers as skillfully as a good violinist plays his instrument.

As discussed elsewhere, the popular association of liberty with equality is unsound. Liberty of access to the means of development will never produce equality of results; though it certainly could and doubtlessly would produce surprising results and much reversion of status. How then can democracy establish itself as the most effective means of government? This is not just an academic question but a very practical and urgent one. In some countries voting has been made compulsory to ensure that all citizens take part in the election process. Here is another problem of democracy. Apart from capacity, how far is the average citizen interested? It is quite obvious that many are not interested in political affairs at all. Is it because they realize that in a vote of thousands or even millions, one vote either way would have little value? This is doubtlessly true in part, but the main cause could be sheer lack of interest.

If all these arguments are valid, democracy has serious defects. Can they be remedied; can our system be so modified that it will minimize the worst and maximize the best features? If the people cannot do so, the system will yield to another force. This is already poised to take over. People all over the world will again be subject to oligarchy or dictatorship.

A few ideas which could prove of benefit are suggested below. First, all legislators could be required to have a certificate of qualification. The old argument as to who is going to educate the educators appeals only to those who do not understand what education really is. Education in the sense indicated here does not mean acceptance of a certain stipulated idea. An educated person here is one who is fully conversant with the arguments on both sides of a question. Thus to be admitted as being educated on any topic is it impossible that the candidate be required to state the case to the satisfaction of the advocates of both sides? To be sure, this would not have the inevitable result of unbiased understanding and judgment, but at least it could ensure that both aspects were understood; surely better than the legislator having knowledge of only one side of the argument. As a prime condition, as international relationships bulk so largely in legislative decision, it would be merely the barest of logical needs that a knowledge of world history be part of the qualification, not just history according to each national version but according to the historians on both or even of several versions. Further consideration of these matters is to be made later.

As has been said, democracy is on trial. In spite of all the talk of sacrifices made by politicians there is never a shortage of candidates. Indeed one of the problems associated with elections for parliament is the number of names on the ballot paper. To overcome this it is suggested that instead of requiring candidates to deposit a fixed sum of money to be forfeited if sufficient votes are not obtained during the election, that they be required to have the support of a significant percentage of the voters on the electoral roll as a condition of standing for election. This would eliminate those who have no chance of election without having deprived them of their democratic rights

If, as we are affirming, civilization carries the seeds of its own destruction, it would follow that there must be reasons and evidence to support such an argument. What are they? The question of the growth and decay of civilization is not new. It is discussed by Lucretius at the beginning of the Christian era, by Polibius, about a thousand years later by Cyprian, by the Arab historian Ibn Khaldun at the end of the fifteenth century, as well as by modern writers. Certain theories were advanced to explain the phenomena. Civilization was compared to a modern clock, which had run down after an initial winding. It was compared to biological entities which have a cycle of birth, growth, decay, and death, followed by a rebirth. Repetition of evidence can give some support to this idea. Others have seen it as an unexplained phenomenon, a cosmic, cyclic process similar to the universe itself. Here the works of Spengler are well known. Another historian, Arnold Toynbee, who devoted many years and much erudition in an effort to understand the problem, comes up with a less rigid and more optimistic conclusion. For him the evidence of past civilizations argues for a pattern of rise and fall; but there is no inevitable result or inescapable consequence. Man is not the outcome of blind uncontrollable forces. Trends and tendencies obviously exist, but man is endowed with the faculty of reason aided by historical experience. Just as the individual, and in some degree the animal, profits from experience, is it not impossible for man in society to do so?

It should be obvious that any civilization, and also many nations, have internally deteriorated, resulting in an inability to resist a challenge which in a period of vigorous growth would have been defeated. Examples are so well known in history that it would be superfluous to repeat them. The relevant question is then in what way has the decay taken place and why. They may be seen as individual or organizational, spiritual or psychological, or political.

A fundamental defect perhaps inescapably inherent in civilization is that it promises or appears to promise what it cannot perform. Man himself is the limiting factor. His imagination exceeds his capacity to perform. The visionaries see what may be a society of peace and plenty, where men are free from inequality and injustice, where life is full of interest and excitement and without drudgery. While the realist may agree with much of what the visionary sees he is fully aware of the pitfalls ahead; while the visionary sees only the allure and the absence of the irksome.

Wealth today has in great degree freed the masses from the yoke of daily toil and given the means of indulging the emotions. Honest labor earns less respect than freedom from labor. To live well without work is to be envied, and at times is the main objective of life. A few generations ago, a pensioner other than a military pensioner was considered a failure in life. Today, one who does not acquire a pension, *i.e.*, not being supported by those still working, is considered not to have planned wisely. It is a common occurrence for people on the point of retirement to dispose of their assets, go for a prolonged world tour or other indulgence, and live for the rest of their lives on other people's earnings through taxation. The argument that they have paid taxes to the government all their working lives and are thereby entitled to be kept by the government is surely no more than specialized, self-justified pleading.

First, the government does not pay the pension. It merely distributes pensions from taxes paid by those still working and earning incomes, less bureaucratic costs of administration. In addition, it has to be realized that taxes formerly paid by pensioners were to maintain the instruments of government at the time of payment. The difficulty is for society to separate the deserving from those who exploit a situation.

At best, a system of welfare payments removes the worst of poverty, unemployment, misfortune, illness, and old age. At worst, it produces a population dependent, dissatisfied, and making no provision for the future. Freedom from the need to make provision for the future does nothing to develop a sense of personal responsibility. The person who produces something from his own effort is much more satisfied than he who has been given the same: "Tis a poor thing truly but mine own."

Again, if wealth and ease can be obtained as much or more easily by exploiting a situation than by personal exertion, why not take the easier path? At its extreme, this develops into a disregard for the rules of social coherence. The wealth of the affluent is seen as having been gained by some means other than by service to society. The inclination is to judge others by one's self. By easy transition, this rouses a sense of injustice among what can be well meaning reformers, more particularly as it is not without some valid basis. Among others, the resentment takes the form of violent appropriation of another's wealth. This is especially appealing when it is supported by a dogma animated by those who are calculated to benefit by the result. Some, whose sense of responsibility to the rest of society has been released from the bonds of reason and consideration of the rights of others, just rob regardless of their victim. No one can doubt, despite some evidence temporarily, that crimes of all sorts are on the increase everywhere. In a new age we have new crimes, or at least an increase in the incidence and variation of old ones. Governments are put to considerable trouble to prevent the highjacking of planes and the taking of entirely innocent hostages. In many cases a wealthy man, his family, and employees have to be protected by armed guards; frequently quite unsuccessfully. Clearly civilization has not produced a world of peace, of plenty, or of quiet reason. On further consideration, however, it is not the fault of civilization, but of those not fit for a civilized society. The fault is not in our stars but in ourselves. Are we to conclude that man freed from the need for regular toil turns to antisocial action? Is man not yet fit for a life of leisure? Nature at least did not design him for such a life.

In the pursuit of freedom from toil and in the pursuit of heightened experience, a growing evil is the use of drugs. Consumption of alcohol is considerably greater than formerly. Without going into all the causes and possible cures, it is beyond question that access to more purchasing power makes more purchases possible. Whereas there was a judged association between poverty and alcoholism, now it is judged to be due to wealth. Both arguments are doubtlessly false. Clearly not all poor or all rich people are guilty of alcoholism. The main conditioning factor is absence of self-restraint, a psychological factor, though money and social tolerance are strong associations. The success of such an organization as Alcoholics Anonymous proves that the matter is not beyond the control of the individual.

While alcohol is the most widely used of the drugs of addiction, it is not generally as personally harmful as heroin and so forth. A fast, new increase in these drugs has developed.

Confiscations amounting to thousands of dollars are becoming common. While absolutely condemning drug peddlers, it must be admitted they are supplying a market, *i.e.,* people are willing if not eager to buy the product. And beyond question, the beginner is aware—or if he is not it is beyond understanding—of the likely results of his or her pursuits. In spite of it all, worldwide traffic and organizations exist, increasing and supplying the market. Are we to assume that an increasing number of people, particularly among the young, are incapable of looking after themselves? Is part of the cause the growing practice in and out of schools of setting up guidance counselors, creating a people who have not learned to control their own problems?

Two recent judicial decisions illustrate another growing phenomenon. One judge announced in the case of a boy of fifteen having continued sexual relations with a mature woman that this was a normal and natural experience, such extramarital experience being fundamental to a subsequent happy marriage. Apart from the fact that in the past such premarital action was far less common and acceptable, and happy marriage was not a condition unknown, evidence does not support our judge. Evidence of increased divorce rate and delinquent children would surely support the case that happy marriages have not resulted from such social acceptance or reduced condemnation. Other factors are of course involved.

Another judge, when dealing with a case of rape by a schoolboy of a fellow student, stated that in view of the provocative dress of modern women this was but a normal response. While agreeing that much of female attire could be termed sexually provocative, does this yet excuse anyone from such action? Had our learned judge left his car or other property unprotected in the street or elsewhere, it may be quite natural for someone to take it. Now while the owner may be guilty of negligence the person who takes it knows quite well he has no right to take it. Being normal in such a case would be a poor defense against the charge of theft before the same judge. Provocation is no excuse for such acts or else the law has no justification for imposing penalty. All acts of theft, and so forth, are due to provocation.

The prevalence of such acts of judicial tolerance is a direct result of the weakening of moral values. A common expression is that morality is a personal matter. If it were possible for morality to operate with a person in complete isolation this could be valid. But in such a case, morality, in the sense of a human association, could not exist. Morality can be defined as an accepted code of behavior having survival value within a society. But "no man is an island, entirely of itself." A moral decision can be a private affair, but its consequences are definitely social. Any person's "private" morals must affect his family, his friends, and his society. Morals do not operate in a vacuum but in a social context.

FAMILY

Following closely from the easy condonation of morality formerly condemned is the case of those children loosely referred to as belonging to one-parent families. Clearly the child has had two parents as nature had "intended." And every child has a right to contact with two parents, if for no other reason should one parent die there is still one left who by obligation and affection is interested in the child's welfare. Anyone who has had the experience of trying to care for children single-handedly knows the difficulty involved. The best interests of the child must often be sacrificed to the necessity of earning a living. Now no doubt, everyone has a natural sympathy for the parent, man or woman, who by death or desertion is left to care for the child. This is very different from the mother who deliberately decides to have a child outside marriage. In many cases she is entitled to a widow's pension. Put plainly, this means she has decided to have the child and insists on others paying her to maintain it. Certainly the child is entitled to assistance due to the deprivation, but to treat the mother on the same basis as a widow is surely a misplaced sympathy. Nowhere in history is there a record of a people without some form of family relationship. It is at the basis of all social coherence, a strong support of morality, and the training of children, to adjust to a social environment. Is it without significance that after the revolution in Russia in 1917 when marriage was downgraded as a bourgeoise institution that the streets of Moscow had numerous, begging, homeless children? Today the Russian authorities do all they can to raise the status of marriage, having learned by the errors which are now condoned in our society. Is it too much to hope that people could be made aware of the enormous consequences of parenthood? Parents have the power to bring into being a life which may be repeated as long as the earth lasts. Cannot mankind look to the possible future rather than revert to the animal past?

In the history of civilizations, of nations, or of social movements, there is always a strong sense of unity, with some sense of a common objective. In the period of decay this unity is missing and division has taken over. That authoritarian regimes are well aware of this is evident from the pains to enthuse the people with the ruler's ideas. In much of our Western world dissension is part of social life. Placard-carrying protestors are a common sight in the streets of our cities. It is not too much to say that the U.S. and its allies lost the war in Vietnam largely because of the fierce, open opposition at home. This is not here to justify or to condemn participation in the war but merely to demonstrate the division within society which disrupted government policy. Nor is any analysis being advanced on the various motives of the protestors. As a final explanation of the collapse of societies from the failure of its citizens, difficulties must arise when a society has been stabilized.

In previous centuries when a person was dissatisfied, whether from the restriction of his liberty or from ambition, he could migrate to another country; to America, to Australia, to Africa, or elsewhere. There, he could carve out for himself his own little empire, little hindered by the restrictions of government or of society. He could attack the jungle and its inhabitants, both human and animal, with an appeal to impulses of pugnacity and of creativity. He succeeded in creating his own kingdom or died trying. Today, this outlet is denied the person of energy. Society is much more stabilized. The great achievements of mankind are open only to those of more than normal capacity, as leaders within society, in the space activities, and so forth. There is not too much room at the top. The young dissident, from reason or resentment, sees himself as reduced to violent protest, to withdrawal, or to apathy. There is of course a place for protest as an essential for progress, but the dissident who disrupts merely aids decline. Opportunity for creativity is needed to reduce dissent. Any young person needs to feel a sense of attainment.

Aristotle has divided mankind into two classes: the ruler and the slave; the leader and the led. But between these are other groups. First is the civilized man or woman whose life reflects the understanding of, and the moral and intelligent commitment to, fellow man; the person who realizes that if society grants rights it also requires obligations to maintain those rights, and conducts himself accordingly. He is keenly aware of the necessity to maintain the benefits so far gained. "Eternal vigilance is the price of freedom." As thinker or actor he is in the forefront of efforts at reforming and maintaining social good. He desires neither to dictate nor to be dictated to.

Regrettably, there appears to be an increasing percentage of the population who by any means, legal or illegal, see society only as the means of acquiring wealth and power for themselves. These, by violence or corruption, destory the fabric of society and pave the way for the ambitious dictator. They are the "internal worms in the wood" which make the state an "easy prey" for dictatorship.

VIOLENCE, DISHONESTY, AND CORRUPTION

It is unquestioned that the scientific and technological discoveries available today are neither good nor bad in themselves: "Fire is a good servant but a bad master." A car can transport its owner quickly and easily where he wishes to go; it can also just as easily be the instrument of his death. Beyond doubt, modern inventions have increased prosperity as well as being the facilities for criminality and thought control. Facilities, however, are but the instruments of the mind. An active mind utilizes any power available to it, to attain its ends. Men make institutions; institutions make men. Wise men may devise laws and regulations to control society in its best interests. Fools and rogues can also devise plans and by care and planning turn good into bad. The effect of modern financial devices, as has been said elsewhere, has landed governments and people into a morass of debt, inflation, and endemic unemployment, with national collapse coming terrifyingly closer. The powers of the financial world are, judging by results, either fools or rogues. Financial institutions have brought certain men to positions of power, men with the desire, if not the ability, unwilling or incapable to operate them successfully.

Throughout the world, reports of corruption in high places are almost continuous. Repetition of examples is unnecessary. They are all too well known. But corruption and privilege are two of the emotive causes which contribute to the strength of the "leftist" case, an urge which once in the saddle drives its dupes and victims as never before.

But behind all this is the mentality of the age. In some measure, men and women endeavor to live up to their reputations. Approbation by one's fellow is a strong incentive to action, whether for courage, wisdom, skill, or violence. In an endeavor to understand himself, man has made various approaches. Predictions of behavior and of demographic situations are based on statistics. So many will die each year; so many people of both sexes will be born each year or will marry. But while these calculations may yield some benefit for future expectations, they tell nothing of the individual and add nothing to an understanding of the causes of the changing circumstances. Man may be viewed as merely a combination of chemical elements. Certainly the physical body could be reduced to its various chemical constituents. But this again adds nothing to our understanding of why one acts in a certain manner. Chemical elements do not love or hate, do not plan for the future, have no pride or ambition.

One influential school of psychology regards man as merely a special type of animal. So, if as has been indicated, man is regarded as an animal, the natural tendency is to act as an animal. A danger of this concept of man lies in the fact that it has more than an element of truth. This concept requires of the person no effort at understanding, no effort for attainment; nature will fulfill its own unaided course. It needs no self-restraint. Take what you can. Tomorrow never comes.

If one accepts the theory that man has evolved in an evolutionary process, one of the features that distinguishes or should distinguish man from his ancestral fellows is sexual restraint. To regard him as an animal is to revert him to his primitive heritage.

The theories of existentialism are little understood by people in general. To be so would require a deal of effort. In short it is a philosophical expression of the spirit of the age. Is this the Age of Despair as Spengler defined it? Or is it a reaction from the failures of the optimism of the Age of Englightenment? It is atheistic, or at least has no concept of a God who helps man in his upward climb. It is pessimistic; life and all existence is uncertain, lacking in fixed points of reference, and purposeless. The best that can be done is to take advantage of what is offered. We exist but without any objective.

In his theories Freud has given considerable impetus to these impulses of taking what today offers. Those parts of his theories, which see the instincts in common with all the animal kingdom as being the fundamental nature of man, hold man down to the past. According to these ideas, man is subject to the driving force of the impulse of sex. To restrain sex impulse is to generate frustration which will break out in violence somewhere. Doubtlessly, here is a major cause of the increasing incidence of the crime of rape. The moral code of earlier years has been greatly weakened. Crimes against the person, especially among the young, are increasing. The tolerance for them, deadened by repetition, is increasing. Penalties, both social and legal, are reduced.

14

DEMOCRACY IN INDUSTRY?

CHANGES IN INDUSTRIAL RELATIONS

In accordance with current sociopolitical thinking, a deal of change is projected and practiced in the sphere of industrial relations. The roles of shareholders, of management, and of manpower are all changing. In part, at least, this is a reaction also against the earlier industrial and cultural relationships. The old systems of ownership and management arose from the needs and movements of the eighteenth and nineteenth centuries when the earlier cottage system gave place to the large-scale factory system. This was soon condemned because of the apalling conditions it created, aggravated by concentration and the unpredicted effect of machinery on the lives of the operatives.

It is no part of the discussion here to recapitulate the condemnation of those conditions, but it is not irrelevant to state, without condoning them, what those conditions gave to the world. It is affirmed as a preliminary that the luxuries of modern life, which are now seen as necessities, would not be possible without the wealth of scientific knowledge, technical skill, and energy at our disposal today. If one considers the social conditions of a country at the beginning of the nineteenth century and those at the end of that century, the progress is most impressive, perhaps greater than at any other time in history. From a peasant society, the new age ushered in an era of better living standards, increased life span, and improvement of education, health, hours of labour, factory legislation, political democracy, and so forth. One important historical event, of which the significance is not fully appreciated, was that associated with the Tolpuddle Martyrs, out of which came the legal right of trade unions to take up the cause of their members. To argue that these changes need not have occurred with the evils that accompanied them does not remove the fact that this was how the wealth was produced. With the advent of the Scientific Age arises a new set of problems and opportunities which are currently dislocating the smooth implementation of the life-style of the future.

Together with much justifiable criticism of economic and cultural patterns imposed by modern industry, there is in some quarters a rejection of the inevitability and restrictions of work, this particularly among the young. Work is seen as a penalty, brutalizing and destroying initiative, satisfaction, creativity, and health, and merely a prop to the Capitalist system. In support of this position two illustrations may be quoted as symbolical. One young man on his appointment to a committee announced that his objective was to abolish work; it destroyed one both physically and mentally. A youthful writer to the newspaper claimed that it was a lesser evil that society should keep him in idleness than that he should be compelled to work for money. That these are extreme examples may be true; but at least they indicate some feeling of justification, one expects, to some degree shared by associates. That *Pravda* has at times condemned the lack of desirable spirit towards work on the part of Soviet youth would argue that this is not a phenomenon confined to Capitalist society. To overcome both the real and imaginary evils of modern industry, efforts at amelioration have been made in modern industrialized countries; briefly expressed as "democracy in industry." As expected, variation in these efforts has resulted. As illustrated in a few cases, it is proposed to examine how improvement is to be achieved.

In Israel, the system of Kibbutzim has received worldwide attention, first established in the area of primary production. As ideals, the system saw work as a joy, a fulfillment in cooperation with all others in the kibbutz, of man's natural impulses, "each for all and all for each." As a further inspiration the scheme was seen as supporting the state, in turn seen as a fulfillment of Jewish destiny. Briefly, its organizational characteristics are: full and free discussion on all matters affecting the group, with no superior and no inferior status; the various tasks are rotated as far as possible and adjusted to physical capacity, age, and so forth; children are trained and educated in groups; and all profits from the group go to a common fund and are disbursed as the group decides, each receiving only a regular supply of "pocket money." Life is thus closely regulated. Results as seen in high productivity show a degree of efficiency. The needs of the state led to some expansion into industry with some outside, paid labor. This is often regretted and has reduced the success and enthusiasm in the original organization. Strictly speaking, this is not a criticism of the kibbutz concept. However, that the growth rate of the system has slowed down and that recruitment comes very largely from outside sources, suggest two limitations. First it appears that it works best in smaller groups and that it has an appeal for a limited number of people, being too rigid for wide appeal. It is obvious, nevertheless, that it is an interesting development of modern society which could have lessons for future change. It is better seen as commune life than as democracy in industry.

Yugoslavia

Another interesting development can be seen in Yugoslavia. Yugoslavia is not the most suitable area for new social change. The country had been devastated by war, the cultural and economic standards were low, and the people divided by ethnic and linguistic problems. According to the ideas of Tito, the method was to steer a middle course between the fluctuations and inequalities of capitalism and the rigidity and repression of communism. Policy and practice appear not to have fully stabilized yet. This may be regarded as indicating the unsatisfactory nature of the system or perhaps more accurately as a readiness to adapt to needs as they arise.

Ownership of the means of production is vested in the local community, but management is performed by those working in a particular industry. Management is by a council directly elected by all eligible voters with direct participation in small factories; but by representation when on a larger scale. The necessity of a free-market system is accepted perhaps as a temporary arrangement. The factory must operate at a profit and payment made accordingly, thus giving some incentive to effort and efficiency. Rates of reward vary according to the degrees of skill and responsibility as decided by the employees, variation from lowest to highest being about four or five to one. Gross profit is divided between the state, necessary reserves, and needy areas within the country, the remainder going as decided to wages or for other projects. There has been in the past some tendency to give a rather larger share to wages. A definite government policy has been to check the encroachment of the Communist party as operating in Russia, as well as the centralization of government power and bureaucracy. Direct negotiation with banks is encouraged. While the absence of any clear means of comparison makes assessment of success difficult, progress is being made as seen by improved living standards. The people appear to be satisfied and there is little indication if any of the probability of reversing the system. As a criticism, not unexpectedly, employees often show a lack of interest and understanding of the problems of investment and management, generally devoting a disproportionate time to consideration of unimportant matters. The informed manager therefore, though subject to veto if necessary, tends to exercise more power than others.

West Germany

With the German tendency towards thoroughness and organization, economic and industrial change in Germany is legalistic. Where employee power is exercised in industry, by law it is required that management must be equally representative of shareholders and employees elected by all eligible voters. In addition, one neutral, acceptable to both parties, is elected. As a further check is the "labor director," who has the difficult task of attending to current problems in the industry affecting work conditions and so forth. Trade unionism is not strong, employees apparently adopting a policy of cooperative decision rather than union opposition to owner-management. As one prominent union leader was reported to say, "If we want to have the benefit of good homes, good cars, et cetera, we must first produce them." In consequence, real-wage gains in recent years have been significant, up to 100 percent. German industrial output has improved considerably, much of this being directly attributable to employee satisfaction. Also as part of the peace settlement, Germany was not permitted to rearm, so capital was put into industrial investment and reconstruction. This has played a not inconsiderable part in the improved productivity.

United States of America

As the United States has for some years been regarded as the great example of large scale industry and its consequent wealth, it is natural to expect that considerable analysis has been made of industrial processes with a view to greater efficiency. Prominent among earlier advocates was Frederick W. Taylor, who drew up a carefully planned system. An illustration of such a system was that of the "science of shovelling," the result of careful examination to discover the optimum size of a shovel to obtain the maximum amount of material shovelled with minimum weariness, and so maximize effectiveness by the shoveller. The man was adapted to the approved shovel. This faulty analysis is readily seen.

A great achievement was Henry Ford's assembly line, where each operative performed a single type of action as the machine to be built moved past on a conveyor belt. Time and motion studies became part of accepted thinking and planning. Against this, a number of theorists arose, some with practical industrial experience, in an effort to improve conditions. The results are perhaps more noted for their theoretical explanations than for their practical applications. Improvement in conditions of work are very great but perhaps more as the result of enlightened management and Government concern than as a result of "democracy in industry." Contracts, as a result of union and management, are normally the basis of wage and employment conditions. These terms both parties are expected to observe. In explanation of the continuation of management control, it must be accepted that large scale processes in industry must inevitably be subjected to a set of rules enunciated from a center. Individual or small group initiative failing to keep up the regular flow can dislocate the entire flow. However, the slogan "what can be must be" is not without some benefit on individual initative and responsibility with beneficial results where applied.

It is not to be assumed from the foregoing that no acceptance of change exists in the U.S. system. Individual variations exist, often very successfully. Among other examples, an instance of this is seen in the firm of Nunn-Bush Shoe Co. The principle involved is a realization that the three factors in manufacturing—capital or shareholders, labor, and management—are partners in a joint venture, each with responsibilities and rights. The practical innovation is that labor is credited with a fixed percentage of the added value to the raw material purchased, commensurate with their contribution and agreed to by all parties concerned. Reward is a fixed weekly amount based on production plus a monthly amount as measured by the profit resulting. In addition, labor has a direct influence at all levels of production and sale. The welfare of the company is seen as the welfare of the employees as well. Apart from the improvement in productivity and morale, this arrangement goes a long way to overcome the problem of the fixed wage when profits fall. In lean periods, the fixed wage, where operating, can create unemployment with or without bankruptcy to the firm whose profits have declined. The plan is, in effect, a triumph for reasonableness, cooperation, and effort over mutual antagonism.

Scandinavia

These countries, particularly Sweden, have been referred to as the "pattern of the future." Here, "democracy in industry" has progressed farther than elsewhere. The basis of the change was that democracy in politics did not give that equality that vision had seen as desirable. As advantages to new ideas were the existence of strong trade unions and generally homogeneous societies admitting of less internal stress. Theories from England and some men familiar with these ideas were imported. Studies were made of practice in Yugoslavia, Germany, and elsewhere.

Development councils in Sweden were established, being representative of management and blue- and white- collar employees. As a result, not only shop-floor decision was possible, but also participation at all levels up to the top operated. Behind the ideas was the opinion that effort should be directed not only to improvement within the industry itself, but to life outside industry, generally to leisure and culture. A significant feature of the new system is the existence of grouping whereby a number of men operate as a team which is, as a unit, responsible for the success of the operation. Payment is made on a fixed-wage rate plus a percentage according to the profit. Results as seen in the successful competition of Swedish industry against production elsewhere strongly support the development. To what degree this benefit has been extended into life generally can be a matter of some dispute. Nevertheless, wage rates have been increased to a great extent and Sweden has one of the highest per capita living standards in the world. Results in Norway closely parallel those in Sweden and as such, much of what applies there applies here also.

France and Australia

Is it a coincidence that in countries where Communist parties and theories are legal and strong there is less change to democracy in industry than in those countries previously discussed? It is perhaps arguable as to which is cause and which is effect. It is beyond question, however, that Communist dogma is committed to the inevitable collapse and overthrow of the existing economic structure; a result its advocates use their best endeavors to bring about. Industrial change in France has been hampered by several factors, though the standard of living is high. The disturbing effects of the "student-worker" riots of May 1968 are still felt, at times in an unwillingness on the part of management to loosen what they see as their right to control and for fear of giving ground to unwanted pressures. On the other hand, unionism is numerically weak and divided, partly due to the strong Communist influence which is most unwilling to cooperate with management in improving conditions under capitalism. Moreover, government interest and bureaucracy are both influences retarding change. In consequence, in spite of efforts by some sociologists and others, French industry shows little prospects of change for the future.

In Australia, when the system of conciliation and arbitration under court jurisdiction was first established, it was considered to be a progressive step in reducing the conflict between capital and labor. Improved productivity, as a by-product, was also expected. What was not foreseen was the development of a litigious attitude on both sides. Since wages and conditions of employment are by court decision, each side seeks to bend or stretch the court provisions as far as possible in what each claims is its best and just interests. This results in frequent, prolonged, and expensive litigation which does nothing to reduce the mutual antagonism.

In addition, "over-award" pay rates have in many cases become an established part of wages in consequence. These have arisen from the strong position of union leaders with the ever present threat of strikes. A further effort is made by the unions for what is known as "open ended" conditions, whereby the unions are not bound by the original court decision if they consider that conditions, later developing, justify abrogation. This in effect means no binding agreement at all. All this has had the effect that the court no longer fixes wages but merely minimum wages, the court decision being merely in effect a restriction on management who may not pay less than the stipulated wage; but the union can and does claim more for its members.

In all this, the consumer, who is really the final employer of both parties and pays all costs through price, is ultimately the victim of the system. In arbitration and bargaining he has no representation at all.

It is most noticeable that those industries where Communist policies and guidance are strongest are those chiefly involved in industrial dissent and strikes. It is here also that trade-union leadership is most dictatorial towards its members. Opposition to its centralized control is equivalent to asking for dismissal and ostracism. Election to a top executive position in a union has been known to be the result of a vote of less than 2 percent of total eligible voters. The slogans "all out" and "solidarity," and the tabu of the picket line, are so strong that unions can and do defy government legislation that does not suit the leaders. Pressure on management to pay increased wages in depression periods has even, according to some top ACTU executives, resulted in pay scales depriving the business of sufficient profit to replace obsolete machinery or to put aside reserves for future growth.

Yet in spite of this bleak picture, consultation between management and labor does occur at the shop-floor level. But in the realm of policy the unionist is not consulted to any worthwhile degree. A notable exception and an outstanding success to this exists in the clothing firm of Fletcher Jones.

This firm makes no use whatever of the emotive catch cries of "worker participation" or "democracy in industry." But they do have a situation where almost three quarters of the issued capital is owned by the staff, with the expectancy of this percentage increasing. All shares carry equal voting rights. The policy is one of management by consultation, which encourages the fullest possible participation of people involved in any area of activity in the making of decisions which directly affect them. This is regarded as involvement rather than participatory management because the range of subject matter is limited by the fact that the process is very time consuming and, more so, by the fact that there are very few circumstances in which important decisions can be taken in isolation. Basic to the policy is the belief that it is good that the people involved in production and distribution should share in the ownership. It is of course clear that income must be dependent on the profit of the industry. A further consequence is that industrial disputes are nonexistent and trade-union power is absent.

Why is it that industry in general, trade unionism, and governments, make no effort to extend what is most clearly a satisfactory solution to industrial strife and efficient production? It is more than probable that owners do not want to see control passing from their hands. An expansion of this policy would also restrict the power of trade-union leaders, who in the present state of antagonism in industry cannot be expected to be wise enough to see this solution to problems in industry. Why the governments do nothing about it is that, doubtlessly, in the present climate of opinion, it carries no voting power.

Japan

Perhaps the most rapid industrial development anywhere has been in Japan; without any significant changes in management-labor relationships as in most industrialized organizations. There are, no doubt, several rather obvious reason for this. As a result of the peace treaties after World War II, Japan was forbidden to rearm. This left what capital that was available, and it was not small, to be invested in new equipment and techniques. Executives in numbers went abroad to learn the latest ideas which were then incorporated into Japanese industry. Expansion was rapid.

As a further explanation, the traditions of rather a feudal attitude of loyalty to the firm and responsibility to employees by the owners still operated. The laborer is viewed not only as a machine attendant, but as part of the enterprise for whom leisure time is included as part of the system. Thus social, after work cooperation, is included. This mutual consideration is reflected in a high degree of productivity.

Consensus is, for both management and labor, usually accepted as more important than written contract. Government prestige, investigation, and advice are widely accepted. Unionism is not strong and, instead of a basis in craft or occupation, is linked rather to the enterprise. This makes for a degree of union autonomy. Conferences are frequent and conditions for a quorum are set at about two-thirds of eligible membership.

Though Communist influence is strong and at times disruptive, union rules are designed to restrict this. Union officials are elected from among the operatives. In consequence there are no professional leaders as is usual elsewhere. Unionism, though not strong, is increasing. Wages are also rising. In spite of the strong traditional practice, dissent is not absent, especially among the young who in part, due to their higher-educational training, are resentful of the system of seniority and all that goes with it.

In the past, the industrial expansion and the increased profits allowed a good deal of wage gains and improved conditions of labor. Under such circumstances there has been little incentive for employees to disrupt a system which has produced such benefits for them. Should industry fall on less prosperous times it is to be expected that laborers will, as in other countries, claim a greater share in the control of industry.

Accompanying this upward movement, living costs have increased, reflecting how much of the price of goods is due to increased costs both of labor and other factors. In the meantime, Japan is an example of how progress can result by means other than by "democracy in industry."

Conclusion: Democracy in Industry

In the whirlpool of change today, economic, social, cultural, moral, and so forth, it is reasonable to assume that the system or systems to survive will be what best reflect human nature, its potentialities and its limitations. While everyone will agree that human impulses are malleable to some degree, yet all we know of genetics teaches us that there are certain deep-seated, probably ineradicable, impulses which can nullify, modify, or support a society. The brief foregoing account of economic trends in various countries makes possible an analysis of gains and limitations so far operating.

The kibbutz system in Israel, successful insofar as it operates, seems to be so only when operating in small organizations, where direct contact among all is readily possible and easy alteration of occupation within the group is applicable. It relies heavily also on the gregarious side of human nature, in some degree at the expense of personal initiative and pride of possession, and on loyalty to the cause of Jewish destiny. These factors would then limit the scope of its application.

The Jugoslavian system relies fundamentally on the abolition of private property joined to forced compliance. In the absence of competing organizations it is difficult to assess the degree of success. While some success is apparent, it is doubtful if the system could have wide application throughout society.

In operations in other countries it is possible to assess the gains or defects more clearly. Change in human relationships depends perhaps more on social and economic pressures than on planned change. The rationalization of the change is usually developed after the pressure is manifest and the defects of the existing system are apparent. Change to this extent is more often a reaction against the status quo than of a clear insight as to the benefits expected. Pressures inducing adjustment are varied. The old system based on the authority of the owner, wisely or foolishly applied, over man power is best adapted to carrying out tasks without too much question. The rise in education standards has shown that the laborer not only desires, but is capable of greater useful participation in the processes of industry. The concept that a man's labor is a commodity—a concept stressed with almost universal support not only by management but by labor also—which can be bought and sold as can any other commodity—is showing signs of being replaced by the idea that industry is an operation involving three partners, labor, management, and capital or shareholders, each with integral parts to play. Instead of labor being little more than a sentient cog in a mechanical process, the idea of partnership is growing. The older system was responsible for unnecessary boredom and lack of interest, conducive to a quarrelsome, litigous opposition, and plagued by strikes, inefficiency, and dissatisfaction.

As shown in operation of those that were reviewed: What are the results of the new ideas? They are twofold, productively and psychologically. The improved productivity needs little or no discussion. It is clearly obvious and measurable. Psychologically, the change is clear also. The employee has acquired some dignity as a partner in the process at a responsible level. With the knowledge possible only from firsthand experience of the work, he or she has been able to apply intelligence, energy, and initiative. Understanding has replaced acceptance of a task to be performed, both with regard to the immediate task and to the society at large. Job security has improved. Change is more readily accepted when the purpose and need are seen. Briefly, the employee has gained overall satisfaction in his task.

Yet no human relationship is perfect, and certain limitations to the success of "democracy in industry" are apparent. Democracy ideally is a relationship between equals, and complete equality is neither possible nor desirable anywhere. Some authority in all walks of life is inevitable, though direction from an elected official is more acceptable than what is imposed from above. Again, what is given is much less likely to be appreciated than what is gained by one's own efforts. On this assumption it would be advisable for employees to invest their own money in the business. This means, however, that the employee is committed to some possible losses from falling markets or gains, from progress. It can further be argued that insofar as labor has a say in management, it is making decisions concerning other people's money. This, however, is a two-way argument if shareholders can influence the fate of employees. If employees are also shareholders this aspect would not arise.

On the case of investment and policy it is reasonable to assume, and operating in practice, that laborers are less qualified to take either an interest or to make informed decision. Both scientific and managerial knowledge is something acquired only by prolonged, intellectual study and experience. As such, after even the best explanation, the laborer must accept the assurance of others.

Regrettably also, "worker participation" is at times used only as a step to socialism. It is not irrelevant to say that much of the Socialist argument is based on the theories, unsupported by experience, of men such as Rousseau, Comte, and later, Marx. Subsequent events have shown that the ideals of their visions have not produced the predicted results. The procrustian bed of such far-reaching theories is something society must avoid. In conclusion it can be said that a strong case can be made for a variety of systems based on particular circumstances and experiment, no one overall system being demonstrably best. Nonetheless, an inevitable change seems to be toward greater participation in industry by labor.

A century and a half ago the common man was claiming and receiving a degree of political democracy. Now universal franchise is generally accepted, though the results are something less than perfect. Parties, at least claiming to be representatives of the employees and their objectives, have at times attained government. It is not here proposed to discuss how far power has passed or failed to pass into their hands. In the matter of industrial democracy, the position is about where political democracy was about a century ago. It exists more in the realm of industrial theory than in practice. No one can deny that trade-union leaders exercise considerable power in industry. The widespread control over members exercised by leadership through the union system and the ever present threat and fact of strikes has gone far to transfer power from the employer to the employee representative.

It is probable, that while the two parties in industry are separate, there will always be disputes, the balance of advantage going to whichever party is at the time in the stronger bargaining position. With all the wealth available to the unions, the technological skill which the employee group possesses and the widespread belief among unionists that the laborer is exploited, why is it that the unions do not bypass the problem and set up their own industries? If they are sincere Socialists this should be a simple method of replacing privately owned capital by collectively owned capital. The practice at first on small scale could gradually spread with success. Why is this not done? That "political democracy" has been found to have certain apparently inherent problems may be the reason why unions have not adopted this simple and rather obvious solution to remove their disadvantages. It may be also that the Unionists do not want the difficulties inevitably asscociated with management.

However, for the benefit of a society which can realize the conflict between freedom and control, examples have been quoted of systems which bring labor into the management-production process with benefit to both parties. Surely the most satisfactory have been based on reward geared to the productivity of the labor. If operatives invested in their own industry the dispute between capital and labor could not exist.

15

HOPE FOR THE FUTURE

Ah love couldst thou and I with fate conspire
To grasp this sorry scheme of things entire
Would not we shatter it to bits—and then
Remold it nearer to the heart's desire.

We can join with Omar Khayyam and with Fate about the shattering to bits part, but having done so, can we be sure that Fate will further cooperate with us in rebuilding? Fate may have other ideas, including the shattering of us. It is easy to criticize and destroy as has been done in earlier pages. If I wish to destroy a house, anyone can knock it down. If I would build a house I must use skill and effort. So then, how are we to rebuild the structure of society which we see as being in dire need of rebuilding? Since society cannot run on improvisations, as need is encountered, man must have rules to guide. Such rules must be a combination adapted to man's needs, potentialities, and limitations. Where are we to look for these rules? Who are to be our teachers?

Karl Marx and his followers tell us theirs is the way, the truth, and the life. Join us they say: "Destroy our enemy, our fellow man." "Hate ... is the beginning of all wisdom." We have experienced the disaster of attempts to apply this system. Peace and freedom lie not that way.

Freud, obsessed with his own neurotic emotions, would tell us to release the urges of the instincts. He would hold us to the heritage we share with the animals. Not unexpectedly, he himself ends as a pessimist. He doubts if civilization is worth saving.

If we try to formulate rules for ourselves, on what should we base them? Surely we must realize that man is part of something greater than himself. And surely the best interests of all are advanced by respecting the dignity and rights of our fellow man. But again, surely this is the basis of all religious teaching, whether I read the Bible or the Bhagavad Gita. Indeed in the Bible, St. Matthew 23, verses 35-40, Christ summarized all in answer to a lawyer's question as to which was the greatest commandment. "Thou shalt love the Lord thy God with all thy heart and with all thy soul and with all thy mind," and "Thou shall love thy neighbour as thyself." Thus it would seem that we must spell out again in modern terms and for modern conditions a clear explicit statement of what this involves. Mankind, reject the Divine inspiration if you will, but mankind, reject the wisdom at your peril.

A man is not to be judged by how he earns his living but by how he spends his leisure. The carpenter who shapes a piece of wood with hammer and chisel and views with pride and satisfaction the result of his efforts is no less an artist than he who shapes a piece of stone with hammer and chisel and calls himself a sculptor. The farmer who ploughs his land and looks with approving eye at the straight furrow and the smooth soil is an artist as well as he who puts paint to canvas. He who can share thought with Beethoven or Verdi, with Shakespeare, Dante, and Homer, is sharing culture and civilization; though he may have nothing to his name other than what his parents gave him. Can he stand at his door and gaze at the stars so distant in time and space that it is beyond his comprehension, and in the light of day see with wonder a blade of grass and know that he too is part of some vast sequence he cannot fully grasp, and ponder the mystery of existence? Can he in the light of knowledge and experience of mankind say: "Hither we came, here we stand, thither we may go?" Ours is the freedom to fail, to fall, and to rise again. We are still shackled by our feet to the jungle of our instincts. Man is the product of some millions of years of racial experience, during which impulses necessary for primitive survival became ingrained into unreasoned reactions. The development of the enlarged brain, our unique organ, is only some hundreds of thousands of years old. Is is this that carries the capacity for self-awareness, for conceptual thought, and the ability to reason. It has not yet had time to come to terms with the results of millions of years of previous experience. Our minds, though still bemused by our past, may yet have the vision of the future, "some far off Divine event to which the whole creation moves."

Mankind is still engaged in an endless, restless search for the meaning of existence, for self-realization and harmony within society. The word self, implies selfish, and here in yielding to his desires man fails himself; or rather, he does, in yielding to his selfish desires, those urges which drive him to acts with little or no regard for the consequences on others. It is easy to drift down the slope of self-indulgence. Man then becomes the victim of his impulses. Can it be said that the greatest possible freedom lies in self-restraint, in the control of those urges which derive from a lack of concern for others? The need is for spiritual awareness and self-restraint. Whether one does this through the teachings of Buddhism, Hinduism, Christianity, Islam, or any other religion, or through plain common sense, the need is clear. This is not of course synonymous with asceticism. Life can be enjoyed without becoming an ascetic.

For the regulation of social relationships mankind has surely gained sufficient experience to have learned in which direction lies confusion and disaster and in which direction lies peace and progress. Whether we read the theories of Spengler, Toynbee, Ikeda, or Ibn Khaldun, or study the history of nations and civilizations for ourselves, a clear pattern discloses itself. Beginning as simple industrious groups bound by a sense of reciprocal need, finally wealth accompanies decay. No nation has so far resisted affluence as the road to decay. Science has "liberated" greed, ambition, and a desire for power greater than in any previous age. Are we in spite of the experience of other ages to allow ourselves to follow their example to an age of confusion and destruction of both life and property? Unless definite guiding principles can be restated and applied, the future looks bleak.

At present, we are saved by the inertia of the mass of the status quo. But ominous signs are increasing. Below are listed some of the principles which have been tried and tested. Certain clearly observable forces are converging on civilization and which threaten to destroy it. These are:

1. An exponential population-growth rate which unless checked will erupt, in the not too distant future, in a fierce struggle for survival, to gain access to depleted world resources. Some of these may be renewable but others, such as minerals, show alarming indications of depletion. However, there are good indications that the population problem is being successfully restricted.

2. Concurrent with this is the increased pollution to land, air, and water, from increased technology which affects the air we breathe and the sources of our food supply.

3. The spreading menace of communism, as seen by its effect wherever it has assumed control, will drive civilization back to the old dichotomy of controlled and controllers. Initiative, creativity, and individuality would have to be fought for again. In similar manner, the trend to centrally planned systems, whether through loan-debt system of finance or legislation, could similarly restrict through remote control.

4. A very real and close possibility is the threat of a global holocaust of war which could create worldwide ruin.

5. Indications are of a dislocation to world trade and industry resulting from the current loan-debt system of finance.

6. There is disregard for law among certain powerful groups. One sinister aspect of modern society is the decline of and respect for authority. No government in "advanced" countries can be sure that its laws will be obeyed. Laws are frequently opposed by strikes, mass disobedience, and assistance to those opposing established governments. Two paths and only two are possible: the authority of reason or the control of tyranny.

7. The growing polarization between the forces of capital and organized labor. The cure must lie in cooperation and not opposition.

8. The growing use and condonation of the use of force to attain desired ends.

9. Perhaps as a by-product of civilization itself is the de-

velopment of a degenerative morality, where greed, dishonesty, violence, hate, and uninhibited sex could reduce society to a state where civilized values could collapse—as has happened before in history.

A growing need is felt that no system can function unless it rests on sound moral principles. The need is felt for a spiritual revival.

And what has man with which to withstand these onslaughts? He has a marvelous intellect which has brought him from primitive life to a position where peace, justice and plenty are possibilities. Intellect must set itself the task of supporting moral codes based on the dignity of man and justice for all.

16

THE RINGWOOD PEACE PLAN

A PLAN FOR INTERNATIONAL DISARMAMENT AND PEACE

In spite of earnest efforts in the cause of peace, the danger of war is greater than ever. Why have we failed? Probably the failure is basically due to the absence of any concrete plan for turning idealism into complete reality. Mass meetings denouncing atomic warfare do not end our responsibility. A positive lead cannot be expected from politicians trained and experienced in a world of intrigue and suspicion.

But before any plans for the abolition of war can be considered it is necessary to ask ourselves a few questions.

1. Would all-out war as is threatened be disastrous for the people and production of the world and quite possibly destructive of civilization itself? The universal answer would probably be "Yes."
2. Is such a war likely? The answer would again be "Yes."
3. Is it possible to abolish war as an instrument of international policy? Here opinions may vary but the hope is that people in significant numbers would say "Yes."
4. Does the average man and woman in the street, on the farm, in the factory, the office, and in all countries want war,

to kill or be killed? Surely the answer is "No." Yet though men of their own free will do not want to go to war, they can readily be roused by appeals of patriotism and antagonism for other countries, and will go to war. Still, it is hoped that those referred to above would welcome any scheme that would make war obsolete. The remaining question then is: "Who then does want war?" The answer is that there are national leaders who are prepared to advance their own ambitions to the extent that they are willing to see millions of people and billions in wealth destroyed to that end.

Political leaders talk loudly about the need to limit the production of atomic weaponry and the means of delivery. We must conclude that those who stockpile these weapons are not engaged in a gigantic game of make-believe but are prepared to use them. But more terrible and also readily available for use are biological and chemical means of warfare which get scarcely a mention. Yet everyone knows that some production of these has been made. Moreover, the world knows from terrible experience what havoc can be made with "conventional" weapons. Why do these matters not receive the attention they deserve? Partial disarmament has never prevented war. There is no reason to believe it ever will.

To meet the threat then the following scheme has been formulated based on three assumptions:

1. The people of the world do not want war.
2. They would welcome disarmament if practical proposals to that end could be found.
3. An international force could give security that national armies cannot give.

More by force of circumstances than by foresight the United Nations has almost found the way. Particularly in the Middle East, the UN forces have been used to take up positions between the contestants. This then indicates a solution as shown in a three-point plan.

1. Any nation fearing attack could require UN protection, such forces to take up positions inside the complainant country

to remain in position as long as the fear lasts without any right of attack or punishment. If each accuses the other as aggressor it would be desirable that they both should have protection in that they might be more effectively separated

2. The dispatch of UN forces should not be the subject of discussion, thus preventing accusations and delay. It is essential that the troops be sent immediately on request in numbers and types of sufficient superiority over any likely opposition.

3. This involves full national disarmament with all rights of inspection by UN observers. The existence of domestic police forces for the maintenance of internal order and adequately armed could be based on area and population.

Such international cooperation as outlined would solve the three great difficulties which have so far destroyed all efforts to prevent war.

1. There would be no question of naming and denouncing the aggressor. Forces would be asked for and sent without question. No great abuse of this would be likely as the presence of foreign troops is not an unmixed blessing and no great propaganda value would be gained. That some fear would exist would be natural. This may not be a bad thing as it could permit a demonstration by the UN of sincerity.

2. Fear of attack, after disarming, would be eliminated. It is essential to stress that under no circumstances would the UN forces be an attacking or punitive body. No government can be expected to disarm while the possibility exists of invasion by a force, no matter well-intentioned or justified.

3. Action by the UN would not wait for the outbreak of war but would take place as soon as a threat to peace was feared.

While an international force is postulated it should be realized that its authority would rest not on arms but on the prestige of the United Nations and world opinion. It is in fact unlikely that it would be called on except perhaps to police borders in remote areas of the world. It would be an army not of conscripts but of volunteers dedicated to the preservation of peace throughout the world. In a disarmed world, the UN forces would not have to contend with intercontinental missile, atomic, or push button warfare, as no nation would be manufacturing these. While the plan would prevent international warfare it would indirectly solve the problem of national aggression. Without the use of an army, no government lacking the consent and support of a large part of the population could last for any length of time. A domestic police force could not resist the will of the people. On the other hand no external government could assume control unless wanted.

As so far outlined, it could be that the UN force could itself be an instrument of aggression. To prevent this the following simple steps could be taken.

1. The three arms—land, sea, and air—would be under separate commands, subject to the UN, and stationed in widely separated localities.

2. Arms would be produced only under license, only in smaller countries in areas removed from the forces. Ships or planes could be produced in one area, arms in another, and ammunition in another, with any degree of dispersal thought desirable.

3. The membership of the forces would be somewhat proportional to each country's population. No forces would be used in any dispute in which their particular country was interested.

There is much the plan would not do. It is not a method of solving national boundaries or other disputes. It is designed to prevent warfare over the dispute. For any success, change must be based on a change of the ambitious leaders who now see the people as the instruments of their ambitions. Surely the goodwill is there. Must we wait for the next holocaust to overwhelm us? The problem is not one of organization but one of a change of mind. To eliminate war would require a change greater than that required to accept the abolition of slavery. Are we prepared to accept the alternative?

N.B.: It is not a fool-proof method to instantaneous peace, but a plan whereby it may be attained.

17

PRINCIPLES OF ASSOCIATIVE LIVING

INTRODUCTION

If one wishes to have a complete mental picture of a city it would be impossible to do so after a survey of one suburb only. Similarly, in obtaining an adequate survey of the processes of history and the broad sweep of movements and ideas, it is necessary to see these in outline rather than by concentrating on the daily routine and events which are, in the aggregate, what history is made of. Seen in the context of such movements taking centuries to complete their cycles, history is revealed as an endless succession of movements, loosely or closely associated, originating like a seed in the soil, from small groups or from individuals usually unnoticed or unappreciated at the time, with consequences beyond the imagination's ability to grasp.

With the benefit of hindsight it can be said that the nineteenth century was an age of expansion. When compared with conditions of life at the beginning of that era those at the end show great progress. Adult franchise and some participation by the masses in the process of government had been well if not fully established in advanced countries. The benefits of science and technology had greatly improved the lives and living standards of people. This process with its accompanying evils had extended almost to the ends of the earth. Travel and transport had increased many times over, health and welfare services had begun. Education and access to information with steady expansion was available to much of the world.

This progress was rapidly accelerated in the early years of the twentieth century. It was realized that poverty, disease, and crime were not visitations from which there was no escape; but that the good things of the earth could and should be available to all. But a world survey of conditions in the latter part of this century makes it more than probable that it will go down in history as a century of decline and disintegration. What is the evidence? Totalitarian regimes have taken over in much of the world; movement in and from these areas is increasingly restricted. Censorship of news and information is more common. Freedom of access to information is frequently impossible; propaganda has replaced education and the free search for knowledge. While these are the deliberate consequences of government policies, results perhaps more harmful are from the overcrowding of population on diminishing resources, and the accompanying pollution. The old moral values on which civilization has grown are under attack and too often rejected as outmoded. Violence is endemic and even proclaimed as a virtue. In short, democracy is sound in conception; but the implementation requires a standard man has not yet attained.

How is it that this promise, so enthusiastically made in the beginning, has not come to fruition? The increase in technology resulting from scientific knowledge with all its benefits to mankind has also carried with it the seeds of the destruction of civilization. The promises of civilization are impossible to fulfill. Man himself is the limiting factor. Power has passed into the hands of the masses or rather into the voices of those who can control the mass. It is to be regretted that the word "masses" has been wrongly identified with wage earners. As used here it is applied to all those who take little interest in their public affairs, or react to emotion instead of reason and gradual progress as the best means of social improvement. Modern technology has put a previously unimagined power in the hands of the demogogue. From the days of Julius Caesar until recently, one voice could at best reach only hundreds, and the written word reached only an educated and affluent few. Today television has brought the face, the personality, and the voice into millions of homes simultaneously. Mass emotion and mass enthusiasm, twin enemies of reason, are available to the rabble-rouser with the skill to use them.

The picture then presented is that of two classes of mankind; the few who are powerful, greedy, tenacious of their privileges, oppressive, and impervious to reason, justice, and humanity—in short evil. Confronting these are the many who are honest, hard working and dispossessed, inspired with ideas of justice and humanity, and who when in repossession of their just rights would by establishing a classless society abolish the old evils of the past. Society would pass into a new age of peace and brotherhood with the glorious opportunities of the future available to all. Why has this dream failed to materialize? Fundamentally it is due to the fact that the concept of democracy was evolved in the minds of men who from inexperience, idealism, or optimism failed to realize the potentialities and limitations of mankind. They endowed citizens with those attributes needed for the implementation of their theories, attributes which they all too often lacked themselves. Their concept of man in the mass was childishly imaginative. Thus Comte could say that the proletariat had the largest share of good sense and feeling, that philosophers must "mix sufficiently with the nobler members of the working class to raise their own character." Regrettably this ideal, unsupported by any evidence available to Comte, has failed. All that the working class previously lacked was opportunity. When power passed from the grasp of the employers to that of the many, the employees proved to be in no way morally or socially superior. They have proved to be just as ruthless and selfish, just as good and as bad as those they have partially supplanted. Due to this they are the ready victims of the mob orator and the propagandist. Readily they accept the illusory promises of a glorious future by following the lure of those whose voices they listen to. Power has fallen not into the grasp of the masses but into that of their manipulators.

I

Society exists to promote the maximum benefit and to facilitate the maximum development of all, subject to other principles.

It is affirmed as a beginning that society consisting of a community of individuals living in some close association predates civilization. Various species of animals live together in groups, it is assumed, for mutual advantage. This supports the contention that Homo sapiens, or his predecessors had some similar association. If one imagines—doubtlessly inaccurate—an individual living in complete isolation, it is clear that such an individual would be under the natural compulsion of doing for himself all that was needed for his own comfort and indeed for his life. In a group situation there must be an exchange of one set of values for another. Man is partly gregarious, and to obtain the benefits and satisfactions of association he must exchange some of the freedoms of choice for the benefits of association with others. What he loses in one area he more than gains by the aid of others. The compulsions of nature are reduced; but replaced by those of other members of the group, less compulsive, less exacting, and outweighed by the benefits of group protection, assistance in obtaining food, and the benefits of other's experience and mental contact. It has been said that society confers security, stimulation, and identity. These values are there for the good of all members who abide by the rules and assist in their implementation.

It is to be recognized that law is desired as a restriction on would-be law breakers. Thus laws against theft are no restriction on the honest man.

However, it is clear that many laws can be a restriction on the freedom of the unoffending person, but in a multiple society these are necessary to restrict the offender. It is the price all must pay for the benefits of living in an ordered society. Finally, there is no law which can prevent all wrongdoing. But one aspect commonly overlooked is the force of enlightened public opinion when applied to the mind of the offender. In this position, all are guardians of the law, an attitude much too rare in free societies. There is one thing worse than a bad law and that is to have it broken. For an ordered society it is necessary for all to accept the law until it is altered by legal means. The evidence that more and more groups are by violence and power refusing to obey the law on the grounds that it is unwise indicates a deterioration within society.

The question then remains, is deterioration of truly liberal values to continue? There are no inevitable trends or inescapable consequences. To believe otherwise would imply that reason has no part in human affairs. It has been said that for evil to triumph all that is needed is for good men to do nothing. What is needed therefore is for all people of goodwill and understanding, with an appreciation of the values of liberal sociology, to unite not only to resist the encroachment of antisocial force but to reverse the trend. To this end, there are outlined those principles on which any democratic society must be based if we are not to see a continuation of the decline the present generation is witnessing.

II

The quality of life of a society depends on the moral quality of its members.

In modern thinking, morality has been almost identified with chastity. But this aspect, important though it is, is only one of several moral attributes. One has only to think for a moment what would morality or ethics (the words are not synonymous) be for one who lived in isolation. It would have little relevance. Morality for our consideration exists only in a social context. Thus honesty, justice, forebearance, and so forth operate only insofar as they affect our relationship with others. Morality then can be defined as an accepted code of behavior having survival value for a society. It is designed to improve relationships within the group. If society were to attempt to operate on the theory that honesty is of no value, no one could enter into any worthwhile relationship with others. It must be clearly obvious that morality is of the very essence of social cohesion. Without the rules of conduct no society could continue.

It must be clear then that when one says, as is common today, that morality is a personal matter, this attitude, to the extent that it operates, can destroy society. Certainly, whether one speaks the truth or tells a lie is in normal circumstances a matter of personal decision; but the result is very clearly a social one. Indeed if one thinks, it is plain that very little of what one does has no social consequences. I may choose to drink alcohol to excess; but the result is far-reaching in hospital and medical cost to society, accident toll on the road, and so forth. It must be said that man in society is not too far removed from a system where malfunction by one cog in a machine affects the functioning of all other parts. Man cannot act in isolation. Since the lives of all members are affected by the actions of others, all must recognize the rights of the rest. All are in some measure entitled to equal treatment.

Considerable emphasis is given today to one's rights. Unless this implies the acceptance of reciprocal responsibility it is little better, if at all, than an expression of selfishness. The extent and significance of equality, freedom, dissent, and so forth, will be considered more fully later. It is sufficient at present to say that these are part of personal and social morality. In spite of redundancy it might be said that morality is social morality. Co-operation, honesty, forebearance, and other such virtues are then the cement which binds society and determines the quality of life.

It would be an incomplete consideration of morality without some assessment of the role of religion. It must first be said that it is possible to have religion without morality and morality without religion. It is without question that one may be an atheist and at the same time a worthy member of society and an individual. On the other hand, there may be people claiming a religious conviction who, it must be said, are poor individuals and citizens. But having said this, it must also be said that the major religions as we have them today strongly reinforce morality and good citizenship. The teachings of Christianity, of Islam, of Buddhism, and others, all enjoin the need to conduct one's life having regard to the welfare of others. The Ten Commandments are in summary form the requirements of much of the principles consistent with this objective. Further, if one turns to Buddhism, even though it is concerned with the individual rather than with society at large, the same attitude is obvious. Somewhat loosely, the eightfold path reads: right belief; right resolve; right speech; right behavior; right occupation; right effort; right contemplation; and right concentration. It is certain that anyone who endeavored to guide his life in accord with these precepts would be a worthy member of any society.

Finally when it is affirmed that while enjoining the necessity for a good life, religion adds the authority of the objective sanction for the behavior and gives the very strong incentive that in doing so the individual is furthering the ends of a comprehensive design. Without religion in society, morality is deprived of a very great support. The world today has little need for new inventions, but for a better use of the knowledge on which we have based our moral laws of justice, honesty, and dignity of man.

III

The concept of equality implies accessibility by all to the benefits of society, limited only by the ability to profit thereby.

Before elaborating on this principle, it must first be said that nature confers no rights; but merely endows the individual with the capacity to fight for its existence. Any rights then are at best the enunciations in society which have a social and individual survival value and must be justified on that basis.

Much of the changes in sociological concepts and practices are no more than a reaction from an existing evil in society. These opposites of themselves may be either beneficial or harmful. The concept that if a belief or practice is bad then its opposite must be good is an error widely applied today. This belief is very largely the basis of Communist theory. The regrettable effects of this attitude are all too obvious.

This reaction is very much in evidence in the wording of the Constitution of the United States of America. As a natural reaction from the effects of the mercantile theory (and supported by other worthy motives), according to which the colonies existed for the benefit of the mother country, the Founding Fathers emphasized the value of liberty to all, equal rights to "life, liberty, and the pursuit of happiness." As so frequently quoted, this concept is of inestimable value, but cannot be accepted as an ethical or social ultimate. To examine one part only, the right conferred by society to the pursuit of happiness, would depend entirely on how one acquires one's happiness. If this is at the expense of someone else's happiness, then the right is immediately rejected. It is clear then that beyond one's own actions is the effect it has on other members of society. Thus all these values are to be assessed only in a social context.

It would be absurd to reject the Constitution on the basis that mankind are all too clearly unequal, mentally or physically. What is the justification therefore for the claim to equality? Beginning from the principle that society exists for the benefit of all its members, it must be postulated that at birth each member has an equal right to opportunity for self-fulfillment, and the good available to each as a member of the group. In particular, this implies that all should have access to the benefits of education, to health, to security of employment, to choice of occupation, consistent with capacity, and to promotion within one's sphere of activity, again, consistent with some achievement. A complete list of the rights of equality is not here necessary but the foregoing gives some examples of the more obvious ones, where equality is desirable but not yet been adequately attained. But as previously indicated, equality is not without its limits. Thus it cannot be too strongly emphasized that equality is directed to the means and not the ends. Definitely what is not intended is that there should exist in society a dead level of uniformity, either of capacity, of reward, or of status.

As previously stated, society exists to assist the maximum development of all. Fortunately mankind differs in interest, in purpose, and in capacity; in short there are limitless variations in the attributes and endowments of individuals. Thus, if society is to perform its function it will ensure that as the result of social contacts and such, these initial variations will, as a response to stimulus, produce greater divergence than initially existed. A major purpose of any satisfactory society is to seek out these variations and potentialities and to see that they are realized to the maximum. It must be clear, however, that this development is not achieved at the expense of the less gifted. There should be equality of opportunity for the less gifted as well, so far as they are able to profit by it. But society, always, and perhaps more so today when national and international problems are so involved and so urgently in need of solution, should expend all effort to seek out and develop the best members of society. Society needs better doctors, better scientists, better tradesmen, and more particularly, better legislators and administrators. The concept that "every cook should learn to rule the state" is no better than biased nonsense. Put briefly and contrary to popular slogans, society must do all possible to produce its elite; elite in the best sense of the word. How to achieve this objective is indeed the problem of sociology. It is the purpose of these principles to reiterate and to clarify some guidelines for this purpose.

IV

The concept of freedom implies the right to act in accordance with one's wishes, to the degree that this right does not infringe on that of others.

Freedom, so desirable for the individual—freedom to and freedom from—is not an absolute in the sense that one may argue for complete absence from any restraint. Primarily, there are the inescapable restraints of nature, of which those imposed by membership in society are but an extension. Further, there is the question of free will; but this is a question of philosophy and not of sociology, and as such not under consideration here. Freedom here is concerned as existing within a social system.

It is the function of law to specify the extent and limits of the individual freedom. As stated, freedom extends only so far as it does not encroach on the equal rights of others. In its relevant context freedom is closely related to equality. Insofar as it is socially practicable, freedom should include some freedom of choice: thus freedom to choose an occupation limited only by the capacity to perform the duties satisfactorily; freedom to work more industriously or to choose leisure subject to certain social responsibilities; and so forth. All these and allied freedoms should be limited only by the impact on the rest of society.

Much emphasis is rightly placed on freedom of movement, freedom of association, and freedom of expression. These are often considered as basic rights in any worthwhile society, but again they can be assessed only in the light of their effect on the rest of society. This can be illustrated most clearly in consideration of freedom of the press and of public speech. The laws of slander and of libel are essential to protect the character of all. Is there a right where public affairs are concerned to misrepresent, to distort, to deceive, and to generate hatred and violence? There is much of this in society today. Freedom is claimed all too frequently by those who could use freedom of the press to destroy freedom. The issue finally resolves itself into a problem of censorship versus the abuse of freedom. Censorship of public utterance is a very sensitive issue and rightly so. In the final analysis this cannot be clearly specified by laws but must rest on the standards among people themselves. Violent speeches and statements intended to rouse emotions, or misguidedly do so, are the weapons of violent men. In a society where passions are quiet this type of action would not be tolerated.

Throughout the world one vital issue is that of a free press as against a government-controlled one. Of all the freedoms, one not sufficiently emphasized is freedom of access to information. Today it might be said we are living in an age of propaganda. This is due partly to the intensity of social issues; but greatly aggravated by the power conferred by access to radio, television, and newspapers. Information other than that desired by the controllers of news is in many parts of the world eliminated. The truth is hidden, distorted, and falsely criticized. One of the wisest principles ever enunciated is "The truth, the whole truth and nothing but the truth." Unless these three aspects are present in any statement, a correct conclusion is impossible. Control of information is the tool of the tyrant, for without full information the other freedoms are but the efforts of the blind.

Even the truth can be used with harmful consequences in the hands of the agitator. Thus if one uses an injustice with the sinister motive of creating dissension rather than of removing the evil, it could be better than the truth had not been known. The question to be decided is what are the limits allowed to people whose purpose is social disruption. As repeatedly stated the value of any action is to be judged by its effect on society.

Another valuable freedom much in men's minds today is freedom of association. This was dramatically accentuated when laborers first joined together to improve their conditions at work. A small group has gone down in history under the well earned title of the "Tolpuddle Martyrs." This right of laborers and others to associate to gain desired benefits has now degenerated to the extent that one's joining an association is a condition by employee organizations of being permitted to work in a desired occupation. Freedom of refusal to join an organization is an essential part of the overall freedom, otherwise association is no longer a matter of choice but a compulsion. Thus members of many associations have destroyed what their occupational ancestors fought so valiantly to create.

It must be stressed that freedom of expression and of action can and must imply hearing what is not desired to be heard, and seeing done what is not desired to be done. As the law of defamation limits what can be said of an individual, can some similar limitation be set on those desirous of defaming the state? This power, vested in a government, is a terrible instrument of tyranny and thought control. Regrettably also, men and women can be swayed by emotion more than reason as partisan loyalties too clearly illustrate. Summed up, freedom is the right of the individual to absence of restraint, subject to the rights of others to the same conditions. No absolute and clear laws can be laid down in this complex human relationship. Perhaps the best that can be said is "The price of liberty is eternal vigilance." What I wish for myself I must be prepared to concede to others. The rabble-rouser can flourish only in an atmosphere where the right of reply is restricted. For this purpose mob emotion and mob enthusiasm are vital ingredients.

V

Rights are conferred by society and carry a reciprocal obligation to society.

As has been said previously, there are no rights in nature.

These are conferred by society and as such are not inalienable, notwithstanding the United States Constitution. Indeed they can be more easily lost than they were gained, as any examination of the world today can verify. A commonly heard statement is that one good turn deserves another. Within this well-known maxim lies the seeds of the concept that with any social right goes a corresponding obligation. The state of society existing anywhere is the result of long years of effort, of intelligence, and, very often, of injustice and suffering. This state the rising generation inherits just as their predecessors inherited it from a previous age. We did nothing to acquire these social values, and unless we have a lively awareness of their value and fragility, future generations must go through the striving and pain to regain what the present generation loses. Our process of education, our concepts of freedom, justice, and equality, our very language, have all been handed down to us. These we take for granted and use for our own purposes. Do we owe anything, do we have any obligation to maintain and develop these social values?

If the answer is "No," it must be clear that such a concept has no application in a system of social principles and existence. The value of a concept can be assessed by the extent of its application. Anyone who borrows from a neighbor normally accepts the obligation to care for the object borrowed and to return it in as good a state as possible. Surely this simple rule has an application in society. It has been said:

> A point is now coming when the assertion of rights will yield little more, even when backed by power. No society, Socialist or otherwise can live by rights alone. Its very fabric disintegrates if everyone thinks only of what is his due, chases his own satisfactions, stubbornly insists on his pound of flesh. Each right has its corresponding obligation. [*Twentieth Century Socialism*, p. 51]

While this rights-obligation gets general theoretical acceptance, it all too frequently has to be legally enforced. Thus, in industry for a day's work a minimum wage must be paid. The employer is by law required to fulfill his obligation. But an equivalent quota of work is not so readily enforceable, dismissal being the only and unsatisfactory reply. To overcome this position the assembly line has been evolved, a device far from satisfactory in many ways. Legal support for reciprocal action is of a limited value. An unfortunate consequence is the growth of a legalistic, contentious attitude when the adherence to the rules or efforts to evade become part of the relationship between parties. Legal compulsion is no substitute for understanding and realization of the fact that if refusal to accept obligation is extended sufficiently, ordered society would be destroyed. In a recent letter to the press one young writer, so far from admitting his obligation, argued that it was a far lesser evil that society should keep him in idleness than that he should be required to work for money. Another university student complained that his student allowance was so inadequate that he had to spend some of his own money. He apparently assumed that society had a duty to support him even when he, in part at least, could support himself. It must be emphasized that while society should assist everyone to develop to the maximum possible, the student has been given certain privileges and has as yet contributed little if anything in return. While one can hope these examples are extreme and not too common attitudes, yet there is a growing attitude as indicated here that there is a right to the benefits of society but with little or no acceptance of reciprocal obligation. Rights exist only so far as society deems desirable and it cannot be assumed that they are unalienable and require no return.

VI

Centralization of power is inimical to creativity and individuality of citizens.

Associations of primitive man probably had little imposed authority; a chieftain, necessity of circumstances, and custom reinforced by tabu being sufficient. With the growth in numbers in society the need arose for some central authority to bind and control the members. Control became the instrument of the tyrant. Necessarily the law had to apply to all, except the central lawmaker.

As a logical sequence, and more particularly in the complicated world of today, closer and closer control developed. Today the problem is which principle is of greater value; "What liberty consistent with control or what control consistent with liberty?" Modern technology has given considerable impetus and power to the idea of control and planning. The planner being possessed of an orderly mind evolves a plan to implement the ideas he visualizes. Loose ends and individual variations disrupt the neat system he has devised and as such are not to be tolerated. All the techniques and means of mass control of information are at the disposal of the central authority. The decision has been made: "Such liberty as is consistent with planning."

We must all agree that the world is in a state of intellectual and political revolution. As the remedy for these ills, due it is claimed to the uncoordinated assertive individualism, its opposite is necessary. Central planning has therefore become the cultural compulsion of the age, with world currency, world central bank, world taxation, and world central information system. What is not mentioned is a world bureaucracy. As is always the case, the advocates advance that the purpose is for the good of all mankind. What a glorious opportunity for the power hungry. Thus the great reservoir of creativity and individualism is rejected for the mass, and allowed only for a central few; in short a return to the old system of rule.

With modern science and technology it has been possible for the hitherto impossible task of enabling man to walk on the moon, and yet man cannot control his own quarrels. Why is this so? The methods of science and of politics are contrary and mutually exclusive. Science proceeds step by step with a maximum of reason and a minimum of emotion. Each stage in the process is checked, criticized, and evaluated. There are no mobs in the streets carrying placards and generating mass enthusiasm, that enemy of reason. It is forgotten that the struggle for freedom through the ages has been mainly against central control. Today the enemy is pictured as in the influence of wealthy business organizations. This is not without some truth.

But emotion is roused both by rational and irrational appeals. It must not be said that the enemy of my enemy is necessarily my friend. He may be my enemy also. Thus today the world is becoming increasingly controlled by unelected oligarchies, where freedoms gained at great cost by earlier generations are being lost. The appeal to emotion has been man's undoing; his desire to gain at the expense of others has brought loss to all. Too wide a dispersion of authority would produce confusion; but men and women everywhere must be aware of losing what we have, deceived by the allure of a new society free from the old evils. This has so far proved to be little more than a trap baited by those who would control their fellow man. Evidence of the new social systems gives no evidence that this is not so.

Dictatorships of the "Left" and the "Right" must from their nature suppress individuality. Their efforts concentrate increasingly on military rule. Originality is rigidly suppressed by control of information; and freedom of movement, by imprisonment, death, or committal to an institution for the insane. To be effective and enduring, government must rest on the consent of the governed, it must be freely and openly expressed.

VII

Violence to life or property as a means of attaining is destructive of social values.

Among human attributes two mutually exclusive ones are intellect and reason on the one side, with emotion and violence on the other. Whichever is supreme, to the degree that it is so, rules out the other. It is a matter of very great regret that emotion and recourse to violence can be so easily stimulated; but it is scarely a matter of opinion that the exercise of balanced judgment and unemotional discussion is much more difficult than yielding to emotion. Man has not yet fully overcome his primitive nature and has not yet fully assumed the mantle of a civilized being.

Is it too much to say that throughout the latter part of the twentieth century we are witnessing a resurgence on an ever accelerating scale of violence and destruction of property and of life as a means of obtaining one's ends? In its most complete aspect, violence is seen in war. Whereas before the twentieth century wars were largely a matter of competing armies, since then war has become a contest of people against people, of civilians against civilians, and a triumph of the most extended use of violence. However, the problem of war is outside the scope of this discussion and will be taken up elsewhere. With the development of technology and the advent of wide dispersion of mass information and propaganda, violent action has taken on a new dimension. Guerilla warfare is endemic in several areas, lasting for years without apparent finality. Airplanes are highjacked (giving us a new word in common use), hostages are taken and held for ransom, bombs and machine guns are in use in the streets, and rioting is increasingly common; all of which has been elevated to the level of virtue if it is intended to further the causes of it perpetrators. This is carried out by gangs and individuals. Attacks on the person and on women in particular have become so frequent that it is unsafe to walk the streets alone at night. And most tragic of all is the fact that much of this violence is performed by young people.

As in mass movements and attitudes in general, this is no doubt the result of many causes, most significant perhaps being the accessability of the facilities for its performance at the disposal of a new mentality. A full analysis of the causes would entail a thesis of many books at least. So, no full treatment is intended here. But one cause elevating violence to the level of virtue cannot be overlooked. As a young man, Karl Marx had been impressed by the simple dialectic of Hegel and transferred this theory from the world of nature and applied it to human relationships. Fundamental to this theory is the concept that arising from the universal conflict between the status quo and the emerging, the synthesis of the two would create a better state with the inevitability of a natural process. Thus the efforts of the proletariat to assume a new status and power are justified as an inevitable phenomenon from which will arise a new and better world. To attain this, violence is inevitable and an expression of justice; for that which has been misappropriated by power can be regained by power. This concept was extensively elaborated and applied by Lenin, Stalin, Mao Tse Tung, and indeed by innumerable official statements by Communist government officials on all sides. But to refute this theory of inevitability as a necessity for progress, it is merely necessary to examine the progress since Marx wrote.

Living standards have improved enormously, length of life has practically doubled, health has improved with previously unheard of care for the sick and disabled, social welfare programs are now common in all progressive countries, and education is free. A complete statement of progress would be too extensive, but it is so well known as to be unnecessary. And all this has been the result of the application of reason to the solution of man's needs, and of cooperation and not conflict.

Violence is the implement of the dictator, it destroys friendliness, it appeals to the worst in man's nature. The rule of the powerful has been checked over the centuries by men applying reason to the solution of their problems. Violence can only destroy, leaving cooperation to the task of rebuilding. The increase of violent action in the latter part of this century has increased so much that unless held in check it will destroy much that earlier efforts have so painfully and slowly gained. Civilization will have to return to another "forty years in the wilderness," and with pain and effort establish a new age where violence has no part as an instrument for attaining one's objectives.

VIII

Fundamental to civilization are the right to private property and the family.

The family is perhaps the oldest institution known to man, and throughout the history of human endeavor there has always been some form of family relationship. It has remained for the present age to set aside this biological arrangement and display a growing tendency to put children from a very early age in institutions. In support of this change, the advocates assert that in an institution the child is under the care of trained experts who see that the best facilities for moral, physical, and mental well-being are provided. The child grows in a social environment, and is thus trained to fit into adult society. The advocates of this idea often refer to themselves as the architects of human souls.

An examination of those countries which stress the value of institutional life for children will show that these are the countries where freedom of expression and access to information are badly limited and intolerance of its dissidents is most pronounced. Thus considered, the family is an enemy of the state, for under the varied conditions of the family, the attitudes of the parents and the whole family environment afford little scope for the inculcating of the ideas and attitudes the state may desire. The family presents a rival authority to the state and must be controlled to secure the ideas and habits desired by the rulers.

In defense of the family it must be obvious that the family is an arrangement common throughout nature. Nature has decided that every child shall have two parents, both of whom have attributes and emotions needed for the offspring's satisfactory nurture. Contrary to the statement of Karl Marx which says that the only nexus between a man and his son is an economic one, any parent can testify that this is anything but correct. The binding affection of parents for children is the strongest emotion known to normal parents and especially to a normal mother. The caring for their own children is for many the most interesting and fulfilling part of life. The child in his part then grows up in an environment where he can gain those essential experiences for his development. He gains a feeling of security, a feeling that he is valued for himself, that he has a significance in the small world of his understanding. At an early age he learns in the best environment what rights are his and what obligations he owes to the other members of his group where progress is lovingly encouraged and where antisocial acts are reproved. Thus the child learns in a small, simple world the benefits of cooperation, justice, and truth. And in time of trouble in the larger world he knows he can go to the home as a refuge where he will be welcomed even if his action have been disapproved.

It has been said that the training of children is much more the training of parents. Having small children dependent on them, the parents learn if they have not done so earlier, that sacrifices are needed to the benefit of all. Normal parents have pride in their children and their development. As the child regards the parent as the embodiment of what he hopes to be, a natural result is that the parent tends to make some effort to justify this opinion and not let the child be disappointed. Needless to say, not all parents succeed and none succeed perfectly. Perfection is no part of human existence; but with all its limitations, the family is the best and most natural means of enabling the child to acquire those values needed in any society. The family is thus at the basis of morality.

Jointly, with the family, ownership of private property goes in its origin back to an age probably prior to the early stages of rational man. The claim to private property is part of the animal world. One has only to see the action of a dog when a strange dog comes too close to his kennel. Primitive man having not yet evolved to the stage where significant fixed assets were part of his economy, still had private ownership of his spears and his hunting equipment and indeed, of his women. Rousseau has said that man's problems began when one man put a fence round a piece of land and called it his own. It does not escape notice that he is satisfied with the assertion and does not supply adequate supporting evidence. As with the family, it is part of totalitarian regimes to abolish ownership of private property, and this, for the same reasons as exist for the abolishing of the family. Ownership of property gives some independence from authoritarian control. Indeed it can be claimed that it is an essential of freedom. It is a natural extension of man's personality; it fulfills the basic human need for creativity. Man is by nature a creator and in some measure one who takes delight in achievement to the measure of his ability to do so. It is a natural incentive needing no external stimulus.

It is often asserted and with obvious justice that a serious defect of modern production is that the employee has no sense of achievement and pride in his work. This, private ownership provides with unequalled benefit. That ownership of private property has caused great inequality and injustice in the past is beyond question. But just as one would not abolish the motorcar because of some undesirable associations, so what is needed is not the abolition of property rights but the eliminations of the evil aspects. Abolition can benefit only in a system where the controllers of property exercise power over the many. In a totalitarian regime there is only one employer, and freedom to choose one's employer ceases to exist. Ideas have been elaborated as to how this evil may be overcome. The solution is as yet nowhere in sight. Private property under adequate control trains every possessor to respect the rights of others and his duty to society so that his own rights may be respected.

IX

Until altered by legal means obedience to the law is obligatory on all.

It is of the nature of any organization, that rules are needed to give an adequate statement of its purpose. These rules state the extent and nature of its operation and the degree to which it can control its members. Clearly no one who would not accept obedience to the rules would be accepted as a member. Otherwise the organization would degenerate into confusion, chaos, and complete disruption. When this view is applied to society, it can be seen that law is the cement of society without which the parts would disintegrate.

In the stages of man's growth in establishing communities, the law was often the will and whim of the ruler. But at an early stage efforts were made clearly to set out and codify the law. These can be seen as an effort, by trial and error, to progress to a state whereby was accepted the principle of equal rights, justice, and benefits of all members. But as men are not all wise, this desirable objective has not yet been fully achieved. The law is in an endless state of flux, the intention being to improve the situation and to accept the need to do so.

This alteration can be brought about by either of two processes: the first by discussion, by elasticity in application and readiness to make gradual growth; the second by violent overthrow of the existing authority and the establishing of a system more in line with the desires of the new power. Almost universally, all advocates of the violent overthrow technique draw an emotionally inaccurate but similar picture of the situation, and advance the same promises of a better world. Existing authority is seen as operated by the few, who are powerful, evil, oppressive by nature, and tenacious of their control of the many. The many, among whom the most vociferous include themselves, are good, reasonable, and full of the desire to give justice and equality to all in a system where the old powerful elite will be swept away and be replaced by the good as the voice of the many. This is a triumph of emotion and prejudice over reason and evidence. Those regions that have yielded to the violent overthow technique are perhaps the most systematically authoritarian regimes the world has ever seen where dissent of even a mild nature is punishable. The new rulers have proved to be at least no better or wiser than their predecessors. As a means of arousing the mass impulses to overthrow, the use of the world "conscience" is becoming increasingly applied. That man's conscience may demand a greater loyalty than does obedience to the law is accepted. Indeed it has often been the voices and lives of the martyrs, which have been the cause of progress. But it by no means follows that any change must be for the better. There can be martyrs to a bad cause as well as to a good one. These martyrs were men and women who set greater loyalty to their moral convictions than to the law of the land.

But today many of those who claim freedom of conscience adhere to principles which affirm that morality is seen in any act which serves the purpose of revolution, and stratagems and subterfuges are seen as a virtuous means to this end. Surely this makes a mockery of the meaning of the word "conscience." Together with these are two other classes. There are those who from a deep-seated, pervasive belief hold that their values are more important than obedience to the law. These beliefs may be either good or bad, wise or unwise; yet these beliefs must be held in respect even if judged to be in error, which they need not necessarily be. But a third group are those who are persuaded that certain action is required of them. Thus one hears of men who claim that loyalty to their organization directive is greater than loyalty to the law. The logical conclusion to this is that one is entitled to disregard any law with which one disagrees. Conscience then becomes nothing more than a deep-seated conviction which can be more often the result of emotion and prejudice than of reason of universal validity. This type of loyalty sets up a law within the state, obedience to which would destroy any society.

18

CONCLUSION

As has been stated previously, one of the causes contributing to the collapse of the Roman Empire was administration. The burden of legal and administration problems became too great to be carried. To ease this the Empire was split into East and West. It at best merely postponed the evil. Today, society is burdened more and more with the same trouble and is trying in many ways to use the same remedies. More and more, administration is trying to control the relationships between citizens.

Every parliament adds to the existing number of laws. Frequently heads of government point with pride to the fact that they have added so many more laws to the statute books. They have added more controls to the existing mass. To an increasing extent business must set aside some part of staff to understand and comply with the new conditions. That regulation for an increasingly close association is obvious; but experience shows the inherent danger. With regulations come costs. To the normal income earner the cost of taxation, direct and indirect, is often the greatest single item of annual expenditure. As a reaction, evasion of taxation has become a profession.

Briefly, it is costing too much to run the country. Taxpayers now have to work nearly half of their time to provide for taxes, and this only for the obvious, direct taxation. Following this is a complaining populace, complaining of the inability to cope with their problems. As a solution society has set up a series of counsellors, family guidance counsellors, student counsellors, and a host of others, professional, wise men and women, a phenomenon existing nowhere in history. The spirit of independent self-reliance is being replaced by expecting others to solve one's difficulties. The Welfare State is replacing independent effort. More and more it is becoming the responsibility of some authority to satisfy the complaints of the citizens.

Civilization at present is in the position of an army marching under an uncertain leader. It does not know whether to halt or to charge. If it halts, events will go ahead without it and the forces of violence take control, with ensuing disaster and disorder. If it charges it may, lacking clear and proved principles of action, like the Gadarene swine, rush headlong over the cliffs of disaster and be destroyed. Mankind is like a traveller in the desert who has lost his compass. Without this he has lost his sense of direction and wanders aimlessly till he finally collapses. For mankind the compass is those principles of associative living which have stood the tests of time and criticism. Those principles, if sound, can apply to a wide variety of changing circumstances. Their enunciation is dealt with elsewhere.

The mind is an imperfect instrument, in which emotions are in endless conflict among themselves and with reason, the individual against the collective. Our best brains endeavor to set up organizations, customs, and laws, to control the conflict. Some conflict is inescapable and necessary to progress. Yet as soon as the organization is set up, our minds, like termites in the wood, start boring and devising means of evading, diverting, or controlling, whatever the individual sees as to his advantage. Probably Adler was right when he said that the fundamental impulse in man is the will to power expressed in ambition. The only person who could be safely trusted with power is he who would not take it at any price. A well-known statesman once said, "I would trust no man with that power, not even myself." "Power corrupts, absolute power corrupts absolutely."

Can this ambition for power be used without abuse? It is argued that it is easily possible in theory but difficult in practice. In many churches and social organizations the position of president is held only for a stipulated period, usually only for one year. In "democratic" countries the office of governor or president is similarly limited. If this return to the ranks had been in operation, history would not have witnessed the excesses associated with Hitler, Stalin, Mao, or Amin. Also, why must our parliamentary system allow one man to lead the party till rivalry or party failures at election lead to his fall? It is not sound thinking to say his leadership would be lost. His experience would be still available. It must always be borne in mind that what others lack in general is no more than experience. A change of leadership would allow for more experience to be spread over a wider range of men. Ambition would be rewarded without its unfortunate consequences. The professional politician and party leader is not an unmixed blessing. It would doubtlessly be a benefit if parliamentarians also were required to return to normal occupations.

As has often been said the trade-union leader has a vested interest in discontent. The union movement in Japan has endeavored to check this evil by not having professional leaders, representatives being elected from working members. In most Western parliaments, labor-party representatives pay their union dues as the only qualification needed for membership, most not having worked at the relevant occupation for years and some never having done so. Men in such positions must of necessity view matters with some consideration for their own permanence rather than the merits of the case.

At the other end of the ambition scale is the worshipper. Aristotle has described man as belonging to either of two classes, the master and the slave. This is not without some accuracy, a more adequate discussion having been made earlier. The hero worshipper is but the tool of the ambitious leader. Hitler and Stalin had no power in themselves. Those who cheered enthusiastically, or involuntarily, were but the instruments of ambition; tools to be used in advancing the ideas of their leader. They put into effect the ideas and ambitions of the leaders, satisfied with the derived power and the sharing of the reflected glory.

In another situation we have the two extremes: the wealthy powerful head of a far-reaching organization with the poor underprivileged at the foot of the scale. Before discussing this in more detail, two stories may be told to illustrate the points to be made later. A well-known story was circulated a few generations ago among children, with considerable amusement. It was of a man erecting a fence and finding the rail was short at one end. So he cut a piece off the other end and nailed it to the short end, to his dismay finding the rail was shorter than ever. The second one is one that is repeated endlessly, without our legislators realizing they are cutting off one end of the rail to put it on the other. The goverment by enactment had increased building-employees' wages by one pound per week. A prominent builder was asked how it had adversely affected him. Smilingly he informed his enquirer that there were "still a few pickings" and then seriously continued, "It has added about a hundred pounds to the cost of a new house." The position here illustrated is that increased taxation generally is done partly to equalize incomes. This is most widely applied in the welfare legislation to help the unemployed, the aged, the children, and so forth, with, we hope, the best possible intentions. But taxation is a cost on production as every employer knows quite well. Costs are of course recovered in prices. So the cost of the taxation, as do all other costs, falls on the consumer. Thus, not only does the amount of taxation fall on the social-welfare consumer, as on all consumers alike, but the cost of administration and the welfare man power as well. The rail, *i.e.*, the cost of consumption, is worse than before. Our welfare recipient is just a little worse off in a plight divided among all consumers including the taxpayer. Until our legislators realize that to tax industry is almost impossible—merely adding to the price of all goods involved—the vicious spiral of prices and incomes will get worse.

But to return to our wealthy magnate who by his organization takes more from the total of production than he puts in; it is well realized that to take this vast wealth from the owner and distribute it among the poor, would, apart from the harm it would cause, make it so thinly spread as to be worthless to all. But what is significant, is the power it gives the wealthy.

In the United States, the total supply of money available to business and pleasure is determined by the Federal Reserve Board, a body of men who decide when the money supply is to be expanded or diminished, all of whom being involved in the business of money lending stand to profit by the decisions. Policy is decided by the Board of Governors. But why must this enormous power be placed in the hands of twelve unelected men of whom it is safe to say the public does not even know their names?

This places enormous power in society out of government control. Where then is government "of the people, for the people, by the people" operating? Positions such as this are one of the main levers used in Socialist propaganda, in that the government does not have access to a significant part of social and political regulation. Laws against restraint of trade, applied elsewhere, leave this position unchanged.

Many people who claim to be forward thinking and may refer to themselves as liberal intelligentsia support the ideas of more than a century ago that here lies the cause and cure of all our social malaise. In broad terms, they belong to one school or another of socialism and condemn their opponents as conservatives. But a conservative is not so much one who holds certain social or political theories, as one who has a certain state of mind; an adherence to an early state of mind, an adherence to former ideas, and an unwillingness to modify or abandon these in the light of events. The person who proudly asserts that the ideas advanced are those held since adolescence, or perhaps since childhood, is merely asserting his conservativeness.

Experience has shown that the theories of Marx are so full of fallacies, theoretical and in practice, as to be unacceptable to any impartial enquiry. Here the Marxist is the most conservative of men. In similar manner, the liberal does not realize that the untrammelled power that the big industrialist wielded when liberalism was first formulated is no longer unchallenged.

The trade-union leader—with his slogans, "one out, all out" and "solidarity of the working class," the tabu of the picket line, the right to strike, and tyranny of the mob over the dissenting member—has power enough to defy openly the law of the land and to force a will over an impotent population. The confrontation between the two forces of capital and labor is the history of society today. One would intensify and expand its control to stabilize the status quo, with all its inequalities, and the other would destroy the system and establish its own system of control. The employee who would work when the union says "strike" is a victim of ostracism and of violence and a "scab." He must leave the locality if he would work. Association and expression have become compulsory and real freedom of association and expression is denied. In one sense the conflict is between two monopolies, each ruthless and inconsiderate of its victims. In another sense it is between unlimited property rights and the equally disastrous idea of its total abolition. As has been argued elsewhere, the desire for private property is natural, and when under control an expression of man's creative impulse. Its abolition would destroy that essential element in man, the impulse to think and act for himself. Both unionism and capitalism are good or bad according to the use to which they are put.

Experience shows that complete elimination of an evil is impossible. Wisdom would argue for a reduction to tolerable proportions. History has shown in endless repetition that ideas and leaders can always find followers and doubtlessly always will. Political movements react to remedy an existing evil, real or imagined. To remedy this, new institutions are set up. But it is of the nature of man to identify his own ideas with the common good. At best, idealism is steadily eroded by the system.

Thought moves in cycles. Just as the Age of Enlightenment evolved a system of thought and action, an innovation from the past which advocates claimed would solve man's problems, thinkers today are evolving new schemes. They are seeking a new compass and a new map to guide them past the shoals and currents of the twentieth century. That the ideas of the Age of Enlightenment produced great good for mankind is undeniable; that it did not produce the age of peace and plenty its protagonists prophesized is just as obvious. With the benefit of this experience it may be possible to evaluate the new theories and to avoid some of the consequences.

Fundamental to the failure of the theories of the Age of Enlightenment was a too optimistic belief in human nature and its limitations. Recent experiences have demonstrated that man is not wholly the product of his environment as so much of the earlier belief taught. It was expected that given the required environment his virtues would bloom and his vices wither away. In other words, man, having been falsely endowed with those qualities necessary for the triumph of democracy, has fallen short of his hopes. Is man fit for democracy or is democracy fit for man? It is now realized man is a compound of impulses held in varying degrees, both good and bad by all people, both so fundamentally deep-seated that they can be modified only to a certain degree, and that far short of being capable of sustaining an ideal society. The best that can be hoped for is for society to develop those institutions and customs which encourage the one and discourage the other.

It is accepted that the threat of atomic warfare is not a theory but a fact; and some effort has been made to control arms sales, but with marked lack of success. The cost of arms production has actually increased with considerable resources in material, manpower, and knowledge expended in the production. After World War I, disarmament conferences were held but did not prevent the outbreak of World War II. If mankind can learn from experience it is plain that what is necessary is not reduction of arms but abolition. A plan for this purpose is given in other pages. But existing trends give clear indications that the concept of central planning, as expounded by Marxism, sees an alternate route other than atomic warfare to the objective of world communism. The method operating with success is to spread influence and control where possible by propaganda and gradual force of arms and so gradually isolate the "freer" world which is yet outside their control. The technique of gradualism is such that it is difficult to limit this encroachment in small issues. But the cumulative effect is clear. World disarmament to the extent needed merely to maintain internal order without power to wage war is an absolute. The problem is not an organizational one, but the development of a peace mentality among rulers. Such a psychological change would be greater than what was needed to bring about the abolition of slavery. Failure will spell disaster.

The present age is witnessing a great increase in the use of violence, both within nations and for the purpose of national aggression. For this purpose arms are readily available from manufacturing countries; but more sinister perhaps is the condonation by other people and governments of this use of violence. Indeed the World Council of Churches has on more than one occasion given considerable sums of money to people who, to put it in unvarnished terms, say in actions rather than words: "We will continue to kill people; men, women, or children, regardless of their involvement until we get what we want." Is it that the WCC knows of an esoteric clause in the Commandments which reads: "Thou shall not kill unless he is on the other side." The excuse offered by the donors that the money is to be used for humanitarian purposes convinces no one. To their credit, certain churches have refused to take part in such an organization. But the fact must not be overlooked that the money so provided is from individual contributions. Violence as a means to an end is no part either of religion or of civilization.

Whereas in the Age of Enlightenment power resided in the forces of government and the owners of private property; since then the pendulum of power has swung in the direction of those outside these limits. With the aid of factory laws and so forth, (something which was greatly needed), and the wealth resulting from industrialization, trade-union leaders are in a position to confront both employers and governments. The resulting antagonism has gone far to dislocate industry, to restrict employee freedom from mass control and from its own leaders, and to spread the doctrine of violence. Unions are now strong enough to defy the law of the land. Some conflict of interest between capital and labor is natural, but the extent of the common interest is greater. Both are necessary for the society and in their own interest. A scheme has been referred to earlier whereby the conflict could be reduced and by reason and example produce a more satisfied work force and reduced dissension.

A feature of the latest decade has been the dislocation of local and international trade and industry. This is the result mainly of two factors. As has been referred to previously, our financial system which requires the greater the wealth the greater the debt, is an anomaly if ever there was one. The second factor is that man's thinking is still in the mental straitjacket of the ages of scarcity. The idea of expansion is so deep-seated that even when the needs of a society are satisfied, *i.e.*, as in a glut, producers do all in their power to produce more, going to the extent of creating obsolescence in order to condition buyers to continue buying. It is but the clearest common sense that when one has satisfied the needs and desires that effort should cease; just as an animal which has eaten its fill lies down to relax. The urge to expand is depleting the planet of its unrenewable resources. To check this practice is needed a new mentality which does not venerate wealth, and a system which does not link inextricably wealth with debt. The system of loan-debt must be gradually reduced to the extent that expansion is funded from reserves. Man is not wholly conditioned by economic factors as Marx taught. Can the man of today learn that there are better interests to absorb his efforts other than those of material gain and satisfaction? Can man control his urge to power and indulgence? Man is the cause of his own ills. Here is his limiting factor.

Mankind, in its nations, has consisted so far of disparate and conflicting organizations. With the expansion of travel and communication facilities, growth of knowledge and global interdependence, it has become obvious that effort must be directed to producing a more coherent and friendly arrangement. With this end in view, numerous well-intentioned people have devised plans to bring order and system to the confusion. Few indeed would argue for a continuation for "things as they are" so that time and pressures would, like gravity in the water, produce some equilibrium. International planning is the cultural compulsion of the age. The case for the limitation for this has been given. Control is no substitute for cooperation based on understanding.

Beyond all the need for improved institutions and organization of society is the need for a spiritual revival. No institution can be devised and no set of laws enacted which can control all man's actions. The *sine qua non* of any progress is the ethos, the psychological attitude of the populace. To the Greek of the age of Pericles the highest objective was service to Athens. With us today, all our institutions will fail unless supported by the sound philosophy and morality of the people. No people are better than the philosophy and morality by which they live. Can this be more aptly expressed than by the prayer, "Please God reform the world beginning with me."

If social organization is to fulfill these functions, how is it to be done? For identity to be realized the individual must to a significant degree be freed from the compulsion of the collective by custom or by government regulation, yet accepting the responsibility towards members of the group. Each person has an individuality to be developed limited only by the encroachment on that of others. Freedom, though valuable, is not an ultimate. Security implies physical and mental safety so long as the individual is conforming to the rules of association. This further implies a close check on government authority. It should never be forgotten that the struggle for freedom has largely been a resistance to governmental and organizational regulation. For stimulation, society must establish systems and institutions, economic and cultural, devised to develop each individual's potentialities having social values. Care is needed to see that no section of society is sacrificed for another.

For the solving of the increasing problems of the age, society has the need of its best brains, men and women, intelligent, committed, and widely informed on current conflicts and needs. Today too many of our best brains are directed to scientific research and development. These efforts are desirable, but regrettably these men and women are taken from the more urgent task of social progress, from the need for a peaceful ordered society, with a minimum of injustice and a maximum of opportunity for everyone.

Man through the ages does not solve the problems of citizenship, he merely transfers them to a higher and more complicated plane. Today, previously unknown freedoms of choice movement, occupation, access to information, and so forth, have been made available. What is then owed to society by those who have been able to develop beyond the level of the average citizen? A gifted person, with capacity above the average, may direct his energies in various ways. He may waste his talent in pursuit of pleasure and easy satisfaction. He may devote his attention to the acquisition of wealth and power and ignore the needs of his fellow men. He may, from better motives, join a reform group, a party committed to a specific end.

This is commendable but in a party one becomes a partisan. Intellect then is used not to the improvement of society but improvement becomes identified with the party objectives. Better still, the intelligent person, while being vitally aware of social needs, refrains from becoming too closely involved with any party. He must always remain a critic. No reform can be deemed to be perfect, but his task is to remain outside the stream. Mentally he must dwell apart in peace, to observe and to meditate. His entry into the turmoil of the market place is to mix with the throng to observe at close range, to pose his questions, and so to arouse the new ideas, but not to participate in the turmoil himself. This uncommitted stand has perhaps become obsolete. The problem is now immediate and urgent.

People will and must have leaders, good or bad. They will follow; be it a president, a prime minister, a trade-union leader, or any personality able to appeal to and arouse people's desires. The tragedy of society is that power has fallen into the hands of the politicians and party leaders. These have come into prominence in an atmosphere of one set of ideas; opposite to the other party's and loyally adherent to their party's tenets. They are proud of the fact that the ideas they hold are those they acquired in adolescence or earlier. All this demonstrates is that they have not benefited from experience and evidence. For a party leader to abandon his party platform is regarded as the worst form of heresy. To replace these political party leaders, the need is for society's best brains to unite, with a commitment only to basic principles of proved social-survival value, to educate and to lead people away from party dogma and antagonism.

Mankind can and should have a better world. Civilization is swaying on the brink of the precipice of disaster. To save ourselves we need a crusade in which there will be neither victors nor vanquished. The enemy is all too often within the self. Violence can lead only to more violence. There is no final solution. In unity, for a freer more just world, we have everything to lose but our gains.

* * *

As a conclusion to what has been written, perhaps the most concise description of society today that has ever been written is as follows:

> For as rust is the inbred bane of iron, and worms of wood, and these substances even though they should escape external violence, at last fall prey to the evils that are, as it were, congenial to them; in the same manner likewise, every single kind of government breeds within itself some certain vice which is attacked by nature to its very form, and which soon causes its destruction. Thus royalty degenerates into tyranny, aristocracy into oligarchy, and democracy into savage violence.
>
> And thus the frame of democracy was dissolved; and gave place to the rule of force. For when once the people are accustomed to be fed without any cost or labor and to derive all the means of their subsistence from the wealth of other citizens, if at this time, some bold and enterprising leader should arise whose poverty has shut him out from all the honors of the State, then commences the Government

of the Multitude; who run together in tumultuous assemblies and are hurried into every kind of violence, assassinations, banishments, division of lands, till being reduced at last to a state of savage anarchy, they once more find a master and a monarch and submit themselves to arbitrary sway.

Scholars will know the source and name of the writer. Can anyone doubt the accuracy of its description?

FUNDERBURG LIBRARY
MANCHESTER COLLEGE

DATE DUE